"This volume is a must-read for practitioners of community econoꟷ development, or anyone interested in revitalizing their community through social entrepreneurship."
— *Emilie de Rosenroll, Group CEO, South Island Prosperity Partnership*

"The features of a place – its comforts and familiar scenes, its shops and buildings and landscapes, its people and families, its sense of safety and belonging – these are a community's true sources of wealth. When communities are threatened or falter, it is these resources that give a community the strength and will to carry on. By equipping communities to leverage their resources and harness the power of social enterprise, the PLACE Framework provides a vital tool for community development and regeneration. *Revitalizing PLACE Through Social Enterprise* is itself a source of compelling stories and important insights. I highly recommend it."
— *Tom Lumpkin, Professor Emeritus of Entrepreneurship, University of Oklahoma*

"The book presents a framework, a conceptual scaffolding, blending concepts of place, community development principles, and the unique and sometimes puzzling aspects of social enterprises... The author teams' active collaborations and balanced crafting of the chapters are all based on real life and shared experiences in the community contexts about which they write. They have been there. The collaborating chapter authors skillfully integrate their analysis, reflection and presentation. A significant achievement and contribution."
— *David J.A. Douglas, Professor Emeritus, Rural Planning and Development, University of Guelph*

"Having spent a large part of my academic life participating in local community gatherings, I am excited about this volume. It contributes to making visible the incredible ingenuity, efforts, and persistence of local communities in addressing multiple crises and working towards a sustainable future. The cases capture the essence of community-based initiatives, which manifest through an array of diverse labels and tools, including community economic development, community-based enterprises, cooperatives, place-based businesses, local business networks or any other innovative models. What truly matters is the recognition and understanding of the agency that communities possess in tackling their most pressing needs and building a better future. This underscores the collective nature of community solutions, moving away from the individual-centric approach often associated with social entrepreneurship. Embracing the rich knowledge held by practitioners is a fine example of community-university partnerships."
— *Ana Maria Peredo, Canada Research Chair in Social and Inclusive Entrepreneurship, Telfer School of Management, University of Ottawa*

"From re-imagining hotels, hospitals and harbours to creating new entrepreneurship hubs, innovation centres and trans-community networks, every chapter offers gems on how place-based social enterprises support and enhance economic, social, environmental and cultural development, wellness and flourishing."
— *Helen Haugh, Professor in Community Enterprise, Research Director at the Cambridge Centre for Social Innovation*

Revitalizing PLACE through Social Enterprise

Edited by

Natalie Slawinski

Brennan Lowery

Ario Seto

Mark C.J. Stoddart

Kelly Vodden

MEMORIAL
UNIVERSITY
PRESS

Library and Archives Canada Cataloguing in Publication
Title: Revitalizing PLACE through social enterprise / edited by Natalie Slawinski,
  Brennan Lowery, Ario Seto, Mark C.J. Stoddart, Kelly Vodden.
Names: Slawinski, Natalie, editor. | Lowery, Brennan, editor. | Seto, Ario, editor. |
  Stoddart, Mark C. J., 1974- editor. | Vodden, Kelly, 1970- editor.
Series: Social and economic papers ; no. 41.
Description: Series statement: Social and economic papers ; no. 41 | Includes
  bibliographical references and index.
Identifiers: Canadiana (print) 2023054777X | Canadiana (ebook) 20230547788
  | ISBN 9781990445170 (softcover) | ISBN 9781990445187 (EPUB) | ISBN
  9781990445194 (PDF)
Subjects: LCSH: Social responsibility of business—Case studies. | LCSH: Social
  entrepreneurship—Case studies. | LCSH: Sustainable development—Case
  studies. | LCGFT: Case studies.
Classification: LCC HD60 .R53 2023 | DDC 658.4/08—dc23

Copy editing: Richard Tallman and Rebecca Roberts
Index: Morgen Mills
Cover design, page design and layout: Alison Carr
Cover artwork: Svetlana Piatigorskaia/iStock.com

Published by Memorial University Press
Memorial University of Newfoundland and Labrador
P.O. Box 4200
St. John's, NL A1C 5S7
www.memorialuniversitypress.ca

Printed in Canada   Funded by the Government of Canada   Canada
                          Financé par le gouvernement du Canada

CONTENTS

Foreword *by Rob Greenwood*   xiii

Acknowledgements   xvii

Introduction   I
Natalie Slawinski, Brennan Lowery, Ario Seto,
Mark C.J. Stoddart, and Kelly Vodden

PART I: CASE STUDIES FROM NEWFOUNDLAND AND LABRADOR

Chapter 1   The Genesis of the PLACE Framework: 27
             Lessons from Shorefast on Community
             Economic Revitalization
             ¶ *Natalie Slawinski, Jennifer Charles, Alan Cobb,*
             Zita Cobb, Susan Cull, Diane Hodgins, Amy Rowsell,
             Wendy K. Smith, Mark C.J. Stoddart, and Blair Winsor

Chapter 2   Promoting an Inclusive Group of Community   52
             Leaders: A Case Study of the Bonne Bay Cottage
             Hospital Heritage Corporation
             ¶ *Brennan Lowery, Joan Cranston, and Jennifer Charles*

Chapter 3   Linking Divergent Perspectives and   78
             Stakeholders: A Case Study of St. Anthony
             Basin Resources Incorporated
             ¶ *Brennan Lowery, Sam Elliot, Sara Langer,*
             Mark C.J. Stoddart, and Kelly Vodden

Chapter 4   Amplifying Local Capacities and Assets: 109
             Findings from Placentia West and Bonavista
             ¶ *Ario Seto and Elizabeth Murphy*

Chapter 5   Conveying Compelling Stories: 135
             The Revitalization of Battle Harbour
             ¶ *Mark C.J. Stoddart and Gordon Slade*

Chapter 6   Engaging Both/And Thinking: 159
             A Case Study of Fishing for Success
             ¶ *Jennifer Brenton and Kimberly Orren*

PART II: CASE STUDIES BEYOND NEWFOUNDLAND AND LABRADOR

Chapter 7   Place-Based Pursuit of Economic   185
             Self-Determination by the Toquaht
             Nation in Canada
             ¶ *Matthew Murphy, Johnny Mack,*
             Lorenzo Magzul, Astrid Pérez Piñan,
             Cloy-e-iis Judith Sayers, and Hadley Friedland

Chapter 8   Revitalizing an Urban Core: 208
             The Case of TulsaNow
             ¶ *Rebecca J. Franklin and Jamie Jamieson*

Chapter 9   From Welfare to Work: Marsh Farm   232
             Outreach and the "Organization Workshop"
             in Luton, United Kingdom
             ¶ *Michelle Darlington, Glenn Jenkins, and Neil Stott*

Chapter 10   Stories of an Evolving Social Enterprise   258
             Ecosystem: The Experience of Waterford, Ireland
             ¶ *Felicity Kelliher, Senan Cooke, Sinead O'Higgins,*
             Nicola Kent, and Liz Riches

             Epilogue   285
             ¶ *Natalie Slawinski, Ario Seto, Mark C.J. Stoddart,*
             Brennan Lowery, and Kelly Vodden

Contributors   300
Index   314

LIST OF FIGURES

Figure I.1.   An illustration of the five key principles of the PLACE Framework.

Figure 1.1.   The punt chair produced by Fogo Island Workshops.

Figure 1.2.   Surpluses from Shorefast's social enterprises support a holistic set of charitable programs that contribute to community well-being.

Figure 1.3.   An example of Economic Nutrition^{CM} label.

Figure 2.1.   The Old Cottage Hospital is an example of a social enterprise providing tangible services for the community.

Figure 3.1.   Map of communities in which SABRI has worked.

Figure 3.2.   Timeline of SABRI's projects since 1997.

Figure 3.3.   Forms of community capital and related assets.

Figure 3.4.   Two-mode collaboration network of actors and SABRI projects.

Figure 3.5.   St. Anthony Cold Storage, a SABRI initiative.

Figure 4.1.   Livyer's Lot and the Garrick Theatre as public spaces.

Figure 5.1.   The location of Battle Harbour.

Figure 5.2.   Battle Harbour as history in place.

Figure 5.3.   Survey participant perceptions of the impacts of Battle Harbour for the surrounding region.

Figure 6.1.   Fishing for Success's Pride dory.

Figure 7.1.   Indigenous social enterprise's guiding sustainability principles: interconnectedness, respect, and reciprocity.

Figure 8.1.   Example illustrating the revitalizing of downtown Tulsa.

Figure 9.1.   Milestones in the evolution of MFO.

Figure 9.2.   Participation in the Marsh Farm Organization Workshop in 2015.

Figure 10.1.   The social enterprise ecosystem in Ireland.

Figure 10.2.   County Waterford and Copper Coast European Geopark, Ireland.

Figure 10.3   Members of Barefoot Farm with examples of their products.

LIST OF TABLES

Table 3.1.   A sample of SABRI's regional development projects, partnerships, and community capital impacts.

Table 4.1.   A shortlist of historical structures in Bonavista.

Table 7.1.   Research team composition.

Table 7.2.   Illustrative examples of indicators of well-being.

Table 10.1.   Authors' roles in Waterford social enterprise ecosystem.

Table 10.2.   The main actors in the Waterford social enterprise ecosystem.

LIST OF ABBREVIATIONS

ABCD   Asset-Based Community Development

ABCE   Asset-Based Community Engagement

ACOA   Atlantic Canada Opportunities Agency

AHP   Analytic Hierarchy Process

BBCHHC   Bonne Bay Cottage Hospital Heritage Corporation

BHTF   Bonavista Historic Townscape Foundation

BHHT   Battle Harbour Historic Trust

BHS   Bonavista Historic Society

CONTENTS

BUD	Bottom-up Development
CBDC	Community Business Development Corporation
CEO	chief executive officer
CIC	Community Interest Company
CIHR	Canadian Institutes of Health Research
CLG	Company Limited by Guarantee
COSAF	Cabinet Office Social Action Fund
COVID-19	coronavirus disease of 2019
DFBA	Dunhill, Fenor, Boatstrand & Annestown Community Enterprises Ltd.
DFO	Department of Fisheries and Oceans, Newfoundland and Labrador
ENCM	Economic Nutrition Certification Mark
ESER	European social enterprise regions
EU	European Union
FARNET	European Commission's Fisheries Areas Network
GAA	Gaelic Athletic Association
GNP	Great Northern Peninsula
GNPDC	Great Northern Peninsula Development Corporation
IET	Department of Industry, Energy, and Technology, Newfoundland and Labrador
IGA	International Grenfell Association
ISER	Institute of Social and Economic Research, Memorial University
IT	information technology
LEO	Local Enterprise Offices
LTE	long-term evolution
MFO	Marsh Farm Outreach
MMDMF	Mauri Model Decision Making Framework
MUN	Memorial University
NDC	Government's New Deal for Communities
NGO	non-governmental organizations
NL	Newfoundland and Labrador

NPR   National Public Radio, USA
NSERC   Natural Sciences and Engineering Research Council of
             Canada
OCH   Old Cottage Hospital
OW   Organization Workshop
PAC   Performing Arts Center
PAR   Participatory Action Research
PBSE   place-based social enterprise
PWDA   Placentia West Development Association
RCMP   Royal Canadian Mounted Police
SABRI   St. Anthony Basin Resources Inc.
SDG   Sustainable Development Goals
SERI   Social Enterprise Republic of Ireland
SETU   South East Technological University, Ireland
SICAP   Social Inclusion and Community Activation Program
SNA   social network analysis
SSHRC   Social Sciences and Humanities Research Council
TPAS   Toquaht Project Assessment System
TRICORP   Tribal Resource Investment Corporation
UK   United Kingdom
UN   United Nations
UNESCO   United Nations Educational, Scientific and Cultural
             Organization
UVic   University of Victoria
VOBB   Voice of Bonne Bay
WAP   Waterford Area Partnership
WCC   Waterford City and County Council
WiSH   Women Sharing Heritage
WSEN   Waterford Social Enterprise Network
YPTulsa   Young Professionals of Tulsa

FOREWORD

Norwegian anthropologist and politician Ottar Brox said that it was only by coming to Newfoundland in the 1960s and studying the fishery here that he became able to understand the fishery in Norway. This book carries on a tradition of looking to other communities, in Newfoundland and Labrador but also in British Columbia, the US, the UK, and Ireland, for lessons about one's own community and pathways for social and economic revitalization.

Brox carried out his work in conjunction with the Institute of Social and Economic Research (ISER) at Memorial University. ISER was one of several key vehicles at Memorial University that worked to connect the university with the needs of the province. The Memorial University Extension Service was another. Many Memorial University scholars from numerous disciplines have explored the society, economy, culture, and environment of this place. After the Extension Service was closed in the early 1990s, Memorial University needed a new vehicle to connect faculty, students, and staff with the province's needs. This need led to the creation of the Harris Centre in 2004, and in 2017 the Harris Centre collaborated with the Faculty of Business Administration to develop the Centre for Social Enterprise, which supports social entrepreneurs and social ventures in Newfoundland and Labrador. Memorial University has long been an incubator for community-engaged research that is both locally grounded and applicable beyond the provincial setting. This book extends these efforts by developing and elaborating on the PLACE Framework.

When Natalie Slawinski saw Zita Cobb present her vision of community revitalization at a conference in 2011, she committed to collaborating with Cobb to learn about the exciting social enterprise that Cobb and her brothers were developing on Fogo Island. Part of Cobb's inspiration came from Memorial University's Extension Service and the "Fogo Process," a participatory media initiative that brought together locals and outsiders from Memorial University and the National Film Board to help the communities of Fogo Island resist resettlement and develop the Fogo Island Co-op as a new economic foundation for the island. Publicly engaged research with academic and community partners, inspired by and committed to place — this place — has generated a unique capacity in Newfoundland and Labrador that this book reflects and extends.

Arising from a focus on place and the role of social enterprises in contributing to sustainable community development comes the latest contribution of Memorial University researchers and their community and international partners: the PLACE Framework. The studies in this book emphasize that the Framework does not pretend to be all-encompassing but can serve as a heuristic device or a set of general principles to inform theory and practice. The book also emphasizes that such an application of the Framework is best achieved through dialogue among scholars, practitioners, and community residents.

Much of the PLACE Framework is a restatement of well-established lessons in community development theory and practice: building on a broad range of leaders, identifying and leveraging local assets, and building local capacity. Social enterprise sharpens the focus on these valuable elements of community development practice. However, the PLACE Framework also highlights aspects that have only been embedded in broader concepts and introduces new elements that deserve distinct recognition in theory and practice. The emphases on linking divergent perspectives and engaging in both/and thinking provide refreshing and powerful insights for social enterprise and community development scholars and practitioners.

The unique realities of particular geographic places demand holistic approaches. The silos of academic disciplines, government departments, and sectoral organizations cannot reflect the interconnectedness of social, economic, cultural, and environmental factors in particular places at particular times. In community development studies, questions often have no clear answers; rather, there are competing interests and perspectives. Ambiguity is the norm, not the exception. The PLACE Framework, the diverse cases in this book, and the emphasis on dialogue all recognize the importance of embracing ambiguity to move forward with community development, whether urban or rural. The Framework also calls for taking a paradoxical approach, that is, one that links seemingly disparate perspectives and approaches. For many in the physical and social sciences, this represents a challenge to the constant demand to isolate factors and specialize, and for government agencies under the constant pressure of accountability and performance measures this ambiguity represents the uncomfortable reality that community development work is difficult to measure or control. And yet, increasingly, impactful research and good practice call for interdisciplinary and holistic approaches. The PLACE Framework helps to answer this call and provides insights for further research and application.

The emphasis on conveying compelling stories is another aspect of the PLACE Framework that builds on previous work and productively applies it to community development. Marketers have known the importance of conveying compelling stories, and critical social scientists, going back to Antonio Gramsci (1891–1937), have highlighted the importance of language in shaping our thinking and exercising power. All perception is conceptually mediated, and the emphasis on narrative in the social sciences in recent years needs to catch up to community development theory and practice. This book provides excellent case studies demonstrating the efficacy of narrative approaches and the need for community development practitioners to be deliberate in communicating their visions, approaches, and successes to local and external audiences.

Further work is needed in the ongoing effort to discern generalizable lessons from case studies. When Brox studied the Newfoundland fishery, he did not expect the result to be a better understanding of the fishery back home. But, such are the insights of comparative research that considers meaningfully similar cases. What factors are local, unique, or contingent? Which are transferrable? How will transferrable factors interact with the local, unique, and contingent factors of another particular place and time? This work certainly requires a high tolerance for ambiguity. Through dialogue and practice, and over time (often a lot of time, as some of the cases in this book highlight), progress can be made in the theory and its practical applications. This is the essence of the scholarship of engagement.

Finally, some well-established generalizable lessons in community economic development and the broader field of political economy need to be flagged as fundamental to the context within which social enterprises and community leaders operate. Many of the chapters in this book, including the Introduction and Chapter 1, note that the elements of the PLACE Framework do not account for the fundamental role of governments and the types of supports and services on which social (and private) enterprises depend, and which are beyond the control of leaders in non-governmental organizations. Indeed, the power of the state and the power of capital (large corporations, markets, and the national and international systems of global capitalism) must be taken into account by all scholars and practitioners who seek to understand the prospects for social enterprise and community development.

The PLACE Framework, with its embrace of dialogue, ambiguity, and paradox, and its emphasis on community action, provides a tonic for those weary from the long slog of community development. The cases in this book offer rich lessons and, more importantly, inspiration for how community development theory and practice can move forward, particularly through the integrative principles from the PLACE Framework.

ACKNOWLEDGEMENTS

We are deeply grateful to all the individuals and organizations who have contributed to making this book volume possible. First and foremost, we extend our sincere appreciation to Fiona Polack, Academic Editor at Memorial University Press, and Alison Carr, Managing Editor at Memorial University Press, whose exceptional guidance and commitment to academic excellence have been invaluable throughout the publication process. We are also grateful to Morgen Mills, Rebecca Roberts, and Richard Tallman for their copy editing. We also wish to express our gratitude to the two anonymous reviewers whose constructive feedback significantly improved the manuscript.

We gratefully acknowledge funding from the Future Ocean and Coastal Infrastructures project of the Ocean Frontier Institute, which is supported by the Canada First Research Excellence Fund, the Atlantic Canada Opportunities Agency, the Government of Newfoundland and Labrador's Department of Industry, Energy and Technology, and the Canadian Federation for the Humanities and Social Sciences, which made this publication possible. We are grateful to Memorial University's Centre for Social Enterprise, Harris Centre, and Office of Public Engagement, the Judge Business School's Centre for Social Innovation at Cambridge University, and the Centre for Social and Sustainable Innovation at the University of Victoria's Gustavson School of Business for partnering with us on disseminating this research.

We extend our thanks to Marie Louise Aastrup, Bruna Brito, and Pedram Pourasgari for their invaluable research assistance and to

MacKenzie Young for her exceptional project management of the New-foundland-based research.

Finally, we would like to thank the research participants for generously providing us with their time and insights. In particular, we are deeply grateful to the social entrepreneurs, community champions, research partners, and organizations mentioned in this volume for being such integral partners in this endeavour. Your collaborative spirit and commitment to revitalizing communities have left an indelible mark on our work, and we are immensely grateful for the opportunity to learn from and share your experiences.

With heartfelt thanks,

Natalie Slawinski, Brennan Lowery, Ario Seto, Mark C.J. Stoddart, and Kelly Vodden

INTRODUCTION

Natalie Slawinski, Brennan Lowery, Ario Seto,
Mark C.J. Stoddart, and Kelly Vodden

A community is a physical geographic place where people live
in some kind of tangle. They have a shared fate. And if a community
is going to survive at all, it needs to have an economy.
— Zita Cobb, founder and CEO, Shorefast

C ommunities bind people together, provide important sources of meaning and identity, and contribute to human well-being. They are places where human and natural elements come together and where the everyday practices and politics of sustainability play out around issues like land-use planning, food security, climate adaptation, energy use, and transportation. In an increasingly fragmented world, they offer a sense of belonging and connection. Yet communities around the world, both rural and urban, continue to face multiple intersecting challenges to their social, economic, and environmental sustainability, including trends towards globalization, deindustrialization, growing inequality, natural resource depletion, and climate change.

Confronted with such mounting threats, community leaders are increasingly turning to place-based social enterprises (PBSEs) to reimagine and reshape their community's future. In this volume, we define PBSEs as organizations that rely on market-based activities to advance a social mission focused on building and anchoring community wealth, including its economic, physical, natural, cultural, and social dimensions (Lumpkin and Bacq 2019; Shrivastava and Kennelly 2013; Tracey, Phillips, and Haugh 2005). Unlike profit-driven businesses, PBSEs use their business activities to contribute to the social, economic, and environmental well-being of their communities (Bacq and Janssen 2011), thereby acting as important agents of community transformation. They provide bottom-up solutions that are rooted in place by drawing on and enhancing local resources and capacities. PBSEs also empower community members to participate in the difficult work of sustaining and revitalizing their places, engaging local stakeholders directly in decision-making about the enterprises and their outcomes (Lumpkin and Bacq 2019; Peredo and Chrisman 2006). Nonetheless, we still have a limited understanding of how PBSEs contribute to overcoming the many challenges facing communities around the world and to strengthening their assets and opportunities.

This volume offers a collection of empirical studies that deepen our understanding of the role of PBSEs in strengthening communities, while providing examples to guide practice. It is organized around the PLACE Framework, a heuristic device developed through a decades-long study of Shorefast, a PBSE in the Canadian province of Newfoundland and Labrador (NL) (Slawinski et al. 2021), and refined over subsequent workshops with community leaders and social entrepreneurs from communities across the province (see Chapter 1 in this volume). In addition to highlighting examples from rural coastal communities in NL, this volume includes cases from British Columbia, the United States, the United Kingdom, and Ireland that deepen the PLACE Framework by demonstrating how social enterprises advance community resilience in various contexts, including rural, urban, and Indigenous communities. Importantly, chapters are collaboratively written by researchers and community leaders, thus integrating academic insight with practitioner expertise.

Given the co-created nature of this volume, we opted to allow for a variety of writing styles and to elevate the voices of our community partners. For example, in Chapter 9 the practitioner-authors' opinions are expressed in italicized sentences, and in Chapter 10 they are presented in entire paragraphs. Both chapters incorporate the informal tone of a popular writing style. Chapters 2, 4, and 6 directly incorporate the practitioner-authors' voices by listing their names while acknowledging that their voices and tones may differ from those of academic researchers. In doing so, we intend to honour our community partners, while advancing the field of researcher–practitioner collaborative writing (Bartunek and Rynes 2014; Van de Ven 2007).

Place-Based Social Enterprises as a Vehicle to Sustainable Communities

In 2015, the United Nations launched the Sustainable Development Goals (SDGs) in which 193 member countries made commitments to address 17 goals with 169 targets by 2030. Recognizing the essential role communities play in fostering sustainable development, SDG 11, "Sustainable Cities and Communities," revolves around the mission to "make cities and human settlements inclusive, safe, resilient, and sustainable" (UN 2015a). Whether in urban or rural settings, local communities are essential to human well-being as they provide their members with a sense of place and belonging (Lumpkin and Bacq 2019; Peredo and Chrisman 2006; Stoddart, Cruddas, and Ramos 2021). While various types of communities exist, including communities of interest, communities of identity, and intentional communities (Lumpkin, Bacq, and Pidduck 2018), in this volume we focus on geographical communities, in which members generally share elements of a collective culture and a sense of identity that emerge from social ties and a shared history in a particular geographic context (Lumpkin and Bacq 2019; Peredo and Chrisman 2006). Technological innovations have allowed for the development of online communities, which are made up of identity- or affinity-based groups (Best et al. 2017; Jørring, Valentim, and Porten-Cheé 2018). While online communities provide a variety of benefits, they do not replace geographical communities, which remain meaningful for residents and for community development (Markey et al. 2015, 108; Ramsey, Annis, and Everitt 2002; Seto 2020).

Community development is challenged by multiple forces that threaten to erode place and create obstacles to building more sustainable communities. For example, urbanization continues to increase; by 2018, over half (55 per cent) of the world's population lived in cities and this rate was expected to increase to two-thirds by 2050 (UN 2015b). Growing urbanization puts pressure on cities and neighbourhoods to grapple with issues such as increased pollution, congestion, and noise levels, loss of green space, and housing accessibility and affordability (Kuddus, Tynan, and McBryde 2020). Climate change has also posed threats to community well-being by causing an increase in natural disasters — including flooding, droughts, forest fires, hurricanes, and other extreme weather events — that lead to loss of life and infrastructure, along with displacement and decline (Williams and Sheppard 2016). Connected to both of these forces is the increasing globalization of production, in which a single product may travel through multiple countries to minimize the costs associated with raw material harvesting, processing, packaging, distribution, and retailing; this process has separated from both profits and employment countless communities that have historically depended on primary industries like forestry, agriculture, fisheries, and mining (Cohen et al. 2019; Gerritsen 2014; MacKendrick and Parkins 2004; Winkler et al. 2016). These global forces coalesce to exacerbate the depopulation of rural regions, the loss of people's ways of life, place-based livelihoods, and identities, and interruptions in long-established relationships and senses of belonging. These disruptions in turn often lead to experiences of social isolation and decreased physical and mental well-being for individuals (Holt-Lunstad et al. 2015). The communities left behind may experience a downward spiral of social, economic, and cultural decline that challenges their viability (Emery and Flora 2006).

In this context, place-based development is an important avenue to revitalize local economies. Researchers from diverse fields such as human geography and social and environmental psychology have demonstrated the importance of place in crafting sustainable solutions for community development (Cresswell 2015; Daniels, Vodden, and Baldacchino

2015; Proshansky and Fabian 1987; Relph 1976; Tuan 1977). A growing literature on place-based development is shaped by diverse scholarship ranging from economic geography (Horlings and Marsden 2014) and rural community development (Vodden, Baldacchino, and Gibson 2015) to public administration (Krawchenko 2014), management (Shrivastava and Kennelly 2013), and entrepreneurship (Korsgaard, Ferguson, and Gaddefors 2015). Place-based development can be described as a holistic approach to interventions that seeks "to reveal, utilize and enhance the unique natural, physical and/or human capacity endowments present within a particular location for the development of the *in situ* community and/or its biophysical environment" (Markey et al. 2015, 5). This approach acknowledges that every community or region offers opportunities to enhance well-being by advocating for development that addresses the specific needs of each place, in contrast to spatially blind policies that tend to leave many places behind (Beer at al. 2020; Rodríguez-Pose 2018), particularly rural constituencies that are often overlooked in favour of urban centres with larger electoral bases. Through a place-based lens, such opportunities are evaluated in the context of existing local assets and values (Murphy et al. 2020; Rennie and Billing 2015) and approached in a balanced manner so that enhancements to economic or social welfare do not come at the expense of other valued forms of community capital, such as ecological integrity or cultural identity (Emery and Flora 2006; Fernando and Goreham 2018).

Increasingly, researchers and policy-makers view social enterprises as an important means to address sustainable development challenges (Lumpkin, Bacq, and Pidduck 2018; UN 2020). Broadly speaking, social enterprises refer to organizations that pursue "business-led solutions to achieve social aims" (Haugh 2006, 183), having emerged to fill market and public-sector gaps in addressing societal challenges (Dees 1998). Social enterprises are sometimes referred to as hybrid organizations because they combine multiple organizational goals, such as social and commercial value creation (Battilana and Lee 2014). While social enterprises can be global in scope, many exist to address "locally situated social needs" (Seelos et al. 2011, 337), and as such they play a crucial role in community development by prioritizing economic and social value creation for communities (McKeever, Jack, and Anderson 2015; Murphy et al. 2020). Place-based social enterprises are distinct in that they exist to serve a particular geographical community. While they can vary widely in size, governance, ownership structure, mission, and economic sector, PBSEs share a number of similarities. For example, they reinvest profits and centre key decision-making in the community (e.g., Murphy et al. 2020; Stott, Fava, and Slawinski 2019). PBSEs also offer solutions and strategies rooted in place, meaning that they recognize, draw on, and ideally enhance the local assets of a place, including its natural, historical, social, and cultural endowments, to revitalize the community (Shrivastava and Kennelly 2013). These enterprises draw on local resources that others may view as offering little value, or worse, as liabilities. For instance, rather than viewing an abandoned building as a symbol of economic decline or a source of shame, social entrepreneurs (i.e., those who launch and/or lead place-based social enterprises) may see its historical and economic values and opt to repurpose it, thereby re-energizing and unleashing new possibilities into the community that originate from existing community assets.

While the term social enterprise emerged as recently as the 1990s (Dees 1998), organizations involved in community economic development can be considered forerunners of place-based social enterprise (Stott, Fava, and Slawinski 2019). These enterprises have existed historically in different forms, including the first retail cooperatives in England in the nineteenth century, as well as a number of fishers' co-operatives established in communities in NL starting in the late 1800s (Rompkey 2009). Modern PBSEs offer complementary approaches to other community development strategies, including those led by governments and non-governmental organizations (NGOs). Given that social enterprises often blend the practices and logics of private-sector and non-profit organizational models (Haugh and Brady 2019), they can integrate strategies through a multi-sectoral approach and even act as boundary spanners to bridge divides between different sectors (Selsky and Smith 1994).

PBSEs offer some unique advantages. First, PBSEs look for market-based opportunities to advance community development, including enhancing the community's economy. While local, provincial, or federal governmental agencies may provide valuable contributions to communities, they face difficulties creating revenue-generating activities that can spark local economic activities. As such, PBSEs complement such sectors by offering an entrepreneurial, bottom-up approach to community revitalization (Bhatt and Qureshi 2023). Second, because PBSEs are embedded in the community, they can more quickly identify problems and create solutions that outside actors may miss or be slow to respond to (Berrone et al. 2016; Lumpkin and Bacq 2019). Community actors are often best positioned to understand and effectively address the challenges they face rather than relying mainly on outside actors (Berrone et al. 2016; Lumpkin and Bacq 2019). Finally, PBSEs can join in cross-sectoral initiatives that reach across various levels of government, NGOs, businesses, and other organizations and, as noted above, are often well positioned to do so. At the same time, with fiscal austerity and a lack of resources and capacity being felt in many jurisdictions, it is vital to understand not only the possibilities, but also the limitations related to the roles that non-state actors, including PBSEs, might play in bridging community development gaps (Bhatt et al. 2023).

A growing body of research has been examining how place-based social enterprises contribute to revitalizing community well-being (Hertel, Bacq, and Belz 2019; Tracey, Phillips, and Haugh 2005). This volume contributes to this expanding literature by demonstrating with empirically grounded cases how social entrepreneurs rely on both local and external resources and partnerships to create value in their communities (Korsgaard, Ferguson, and Gaddefors 2015). In this volume, the researcher–practitioner author teams advance knowledge through community-engaged research and share lessons relating to community revitalization practices. Furthermore, this volume draws on research from multiple disciplines and domains, including organization studies, social entrepreneurship, sociology, geography, and community development studies.

This multidisciplinary approach promises holistic solutions to the increasingly complex problems faced by communities. Finally, we join and advance research conversations on community development that underscore the importance of empowerment (Lumpkin and Bacq 2019), self-determination (Murphy et al. 2020), micro-solutions (Tàbara et al. 2020), and positive tipping points (Tàbara et al. 2018), while further elaborating a diverse and evolving understanding of place-based development (Vodden, Baldacchino, and Gibson 2015).

A Place Framework of Community Resilience

Newfoundland and Labrador: Exemplifying the Power of Place

It is fitting that this volume starts with examples of PBSEs from the Canadian province of Newfoundland and Labrador, whose residents feel the strongest sense of belonging of any province in Canada (Statistics Canada 2013). This love of place has been guiding social innovation activity in NL for generations, as examples such as the Fogo Process and the creation of the Fogo Island Cooperative Society (see Chapter 1) illustrate. Building on this history of social innovations, the province has continued to witness a growth in the number of social enterprises dedicated to revitalizing coastal communities since the collapse of the cod fishery. When the groundfish moratorium was announced in 1992, around 30,000 people in NL suddenly lost their livelihoods, and soon the province witnessed a massive wave of out-migration (Higgins 2009). Many of those who decided to remain in coastal communities faced significant economic and social challenges. Vacant and abandoned houses and buildings became reminders of this troubled time, including the loss of a way of life and rich culture that had grown out of the fishery over hundreds of years. Several of the PBSEs discussed in this volume have sought to protect and build upon this culture and way of life beyond the moratorium.

Introducing the PLACE Framework

We offer the PLACE Framework to capture revitalization efforts to tackle the widespread sustainability threats facing communities around the world. As we describe in Chapter 1, the PLACE Framework emerged from a longitudinal study of Shorefast, a non-profit charitable organization founded in 2006 with a mission to revitalize Fogo Island (Slawinski et al. 2021). Like many other NL communities, the community of Fogo Island suffered from significant economic and population decline after the collapse of the cod fishery in 1992. Among its many initiatives, Shorefast launched the Fogo Island Inn, a social enterprise that has created hundreds of jobs for the island's population and whose profits are reinvested into funding community initiatives. The award-winning Inn features locally made furniture and textiles that blend contemporary design with local culture and traditions and has attracted visitors from around the globe. Shorefast also launched an artist residency program on the island and started the Fogo Island Workshops, a social enterprise that repurposes traditional skills like quilting and woodworking to produce unique high-end products to sell in the global market. Shorefast's cultural and economic revitalization is attracting new residents and bringing former residents back to Fogo Island (see Chapter 1).

This volume is organized around the five principles of the PLACE Framework: *Promote community leaders, Link divergent perspectives, Amplify local capacities and assests, Convey compelling stories, and Engage both/and thinking.* The acronym PLACE was intentionally chosen to honour NL community leaders' historical and cultural attachment to the place that motivated them to launch new initiatives, such as social enterprises that serve their communities, and to persevere despite the many barriers they have encountered. Our focus on place also acknowledges this volume's contribution to the growing scholarship and experiences of place-based development outlined above. The five key principles are illustrated in Figure 1 below.

The chapters in this volume are organized into two sections. The first section offers six chapters based on studies conducted in NL. Chapter 1 begins by providing a detailed overview of the genesis of the PLACE Framework through a study of Shorefast's impact on the community of Fogo Island, while the next five chapters each elaborate one pillar (key principle) of the Framework. The second section consists of four chapters that offer cases from outside NL to explore the generalizability of the Framework by studying how PBSEs offer bottom-up solutions for community resilience in other contexts. We provide a brief introduction to each chapter below.

Figure I.1. An illustration of the five key principles of the PLACE Framework. (Designed by Michelle Darlington, 2022)

Promote Community Leaders

Community leaders play a critical role in mobilizing others to drive community-based initiatives through social enterprise activities. As greater numbers of community members join in revitalization efforts, energy and momentum grow, fuelling more initiatives and events, and fostering a sense of collective pride. On Fogo Island, for example (see Chapter 1), Shorefast encouraged Fogo Islanders who had moved away to move back to their community while also attracting people from other parts of the province and from outside NL to make Fogo Island their new home. These new and returning residents, in turn, joined efforts to advance other initiatives and opportunities, thereby further revitalizing Fogo Island (Slawinski et al. 2021). This first principle of the PLACE Framework reflects the importance of local residents as the strongest assets in a community (Kretzmann and McKnight 1993) despite often being overlooked in mainstream economic development models (Arias Schreiber, Windgren, and Linke 2020). It also implies the need for an equitable approach to community leadership that centres on local residents and their needs. External actors and new residents can support this effort, but their needs cannot be placed above the needs of long-time community members (a theme explored further in Chapter 2).

The case of the Bonne Bay Cottage Hospital Heritage Corporation in Norris Point (Chapter 2) demonstrates the importance of leadership in community renewal and expands our understanding of leadership beyond an individualized leadership approach that is common in the management literature. Instead, we see more diffuse, inclusive, and community-based forms of leadership. Leadership is a quality that different people take on in different contexts. The cases of TulsaNow (Chapter 8) and Marsh Farm Outreach (Chapter 9) also pay particular attention to collective and distributed forms of leadership, recognizing that entrepreneurs often depend on wide networks of enablers and supporters (see also Thompson 2010) and that community revitalization depends on the work of many (Lumpkin and Bacq 2019). Indeed, in their work, social entrepreneurs and community leaders pay particular attention to building entrepreneurial ecosystems to create sustainable economic development. Chapter 10 describes the formation of a social enterprise ecosystem in Waterford, Ireland, as another powerful example. In so doing, the chapter discusses the complexity of different kinds of operating models (e.g., social entrepreneurship, social enterprise, and community enterprise) that can respond differently to the ecosystem's network of stakeholders.

Link Divergent Perspectives

Community development work requires inviting different perspectives into decisions and finding ways to bring them together to foster creative solutions. Given their hybrid nature, social enterprises can play bridging roles between different stakeholder groups, acting as "boundary spanners" by working across diverse perspectives and logics (Powell et al. 2018; Steiner, Farmer, and Bosworth 2020). One of the strengths that social entrepreneurs and community leaders show in this volume's case studies is their ability to quickly incorporate new knowledge by linking divergent perspectives from other leaders on local, regional, international, and other scales.

Chapter 1 depicts, for example, how Shorefast became a broker, building linkages between local and outside knowledge and between new and traditional skills to create new capacities. Using social network analysis, Chapter 3 explains how St. Anthony Basin Resources Inc. (SABRI) formed a variety of linkages between local and external actors and partners from multiple sectors to leverage resources from different sources and enhance local community development by feeding and improving multiple, interconnected forms of community capital (economic, human, cultural, natural, built, and social). The chapter demonstrates the important connecting role that PBSEs can provide while also highlighting challenges in network-building, particularly in rural and remote contexts, that contribute to persistent collaboration gaps. Meanwhile, Chapter 10 illustrates how social enterprises in Waterford, Ireland, created employment opportunities for marginalized groups by linking knowledge from NGOs, academics, and the private sector to provide a variety of supports to clients, including advocacy and professional service referrals.

Amplify Local Capacities and Assets

By being embedded in the community, PBSEs are well-positioned to recognize the value of local assets even when others do not, and to leverage them to create opportunities for economic development. Relying on local assets allows communities to tap into the nearest resources available and provides them with more control over their pathways to economic development. Shorefast, for example (Chapter 1), was informed by frameworks like Appreciative Inquiry (Cooperrider and Srivastva 1987) and Asset-Based Community Development (ABCD) (Kretzmann and McKnight 1993), approaches to organizational and community development that are designed to engage community members in dialogue by asking questions that help them uncover their unique strengths and the opportunities in their communities. Shorefast asks community members questions such as "What do we have? What do we love? What do we miss?" to uncover Fogo Island's potential.

The Placentia West Development Association and the Bonavista Historic Townscape Foundation (Chapter 4) and Marsh Farm Outreach (Chapter 9) invest in their communities' local assets, whether by restoring historic properties or enhancing local skills and capacities, recognizing such investments as more sustainable paths to development that retain investment within the communities themselves. These PBSEs emerged and evolved to guide their community's revitalization based on investment in heritage protection, arts, and culture to enhance the town's livability and attract new residents. These chapters demonstrate how such an economic development strategy that amplifies local place-based assets can rebuild community identity and collective pride.

The example of TulsaNow (Chapter 8), an urban-based civic organization in Tulsa, Oklahoma, also illustrates how amplifying local capacities and assets can become a population retention strategy. Both the Bonavista (see Chapter 4) and Tulsa (see Chapter 8) cases show how PBSEs helped revitalize the downtown core and resulted in visible development of new investments and new residents. Echoing the efforts of local community leaders and entrepreneurs profiled throughout the volume, TulsaNow demonstrates that economic development can and should go hand in hand with other processes in enhancing the place's livability. The group mobilized Tulsa's citizens to revitalize the city's downtown as an initial step, showing how place-based activists and entrepreneurs have capitalized on their ability to "link divergent perspectives" and "amplify local capacities and assests" to face obstacles from established bureaucratic interests, path dependencies and old-boy networks. Other chapters, such as Chapter 5 on Battle Harbour Trust, Chapter 6 on Fishing for Success in Petty Harbour, and Chapter 7 on the Toquaht Nation's economic self-determination, also illustrate how amplifying local capacities and assets brings a sense of pride to communities while enhancing economic development.

Convey Compelling Stories

Positive stories about a community can provide hope about the future to local residents and counter negative, self-defeating narratives in places facing social and economic challenges (Lowery et al. 2020). In addition to recognizing the importance of narratives for changing mindsets and providing hope within communities, PBSEs also recognize their importance for audiences outside the community. For example, media attention can help draw tourists, and over time, positive narratives can bring new economic opportunities and even new residents (Chapters 1 and 4).

Chapter 5 shows how compelling stories about Battle Harbour's historic significance as the unofficial capital of the Labrador cod fishery have attracted tourists, investments, and public recognition, which in turn have driven social and economic growth for nearby communities in the region. These compelling stories have been constructed through collaboration between local social entrepreneurs and academics to build public recognition of the community's identity. The authors illustrate three pillars of creating a compelling community story, while also highlighting the competing forces that social entrepreneurs must constantly navigate, such as the desire to preserve a historical site's authenticity and "tourism first" orientations.

The community leaders of Marsh Farm Outreach described in Chapter 9 created a compelling new narrative of community potential when they empowered Marsh Farm's citizens in the UK using the internationally-recognized Morais-Freireian Organization Workshop method of community development (Carmen and Sobrado 2013). In doing so, they encouraged their community to amplify local assets by reimagining the role of locally-owned enterprises in capturing and recirculating money locally to enhance self-reliance and provide citizens with greater agency to revitalize their community.

Engage Both/And Thinking

Social enterprises must simultaneously pursue financial and social goals; thus, they must navigate tensions between competing forces, such as between the competing logics of heritage preservation and tourism development or between local needs and global pressures. These tensions are a recurring theme in studies that examine history and heritage as foundations for tourism and economic development (e.g., Antonova and Rieser 2019; George, Mair, and Reid 2009; Horikawa 2021; Kimmel et al. 2015; Overton 2007; Rothman 1998; Stoddart, Catano, and Ramos 2018; Sullivan and Mitchell 2012). Other tensions include those that emerge between competing stakeholder demands (Siegner, Pinkse, and Panwar 2018), as social enterprises straddle the worlds of business, civil society, and local government (Tracey, Phillips, and Haugh 2005). Therefore, studying social enterprises requires delving into the nature and management of these tensions (Smith, Gonin, and Besharov 2013, 408), while these organizations' responses to the tensions often shape their social and financial outcomes (Smith and Besharov 2019).

Approaching oppositional forces as both/and possibilities instead of either/or forced choices can help communities imagine new innovations. For example, Chapter 6 tells the story of an eco-education program, Girls Who Fish, which was both a strategy for revenue generation and an educational program on fishing activities for youth, focusing on teaching heritage skills, promoting awareness about ocean conservation, and encouraging the sharing of culture. Viewing fishing as not only a source of income but also as an educational tool to help marginalized groups connect to nature and culture helps Fishing for Success, a PBSE in Petty Harbour, NL, create social and economic value simultaneously. Chapter 6 uses the case study of Fishing for Success to examine the PLACE Framework idea of engaging both/and thinking as a way to address paradoxical tensions (Lewis and Smith 2022; Smith and Lewis 2022), such as local and global concerns, insider and outsider knowledge, and social goals and financial sustainability.

Chapter 7 on the Toquaht Project Assessment System (TPAS) provides another salient example of both/and thinking by depicting how modern economic activities can go hand in hand with an Indigenous world view of well-being. Like many Indigenous Peoples globally, the Toquaht People are working to become self-sufficient through economic development activities that preserve and strengthen Toquaht values, culture, traditions, and the natural environment. Working with and for the community, TPAS combines methods of a contemporary socio-culturally sensitive evaluation and monitoring system with place-based Indigenous knowledge and underscores the Toquaht understanding of economic principles through "interconnectedness and balance, personal and communal security, freedom, and happiness" as a model of engagement with integrated thinking.

Conclusion

As communities everywhere face increasing challenges from social, economic, and environmental disruptions, including urbanization, deindustrialization, inequality, and climate change, people are turning to PBSEs to reimagine and reshape their futures. This volume advances PBSE research while offering examples of leaders and organizations leveraging the power of place to strengthen their communities, which we discuss in more depth in the Epilogue. It highlights the triumphs and setbacks that the social entrepreneurs featured in this volume have witnessed and endured in their decades of experience in organizing place-based social enterprises and working with their fellow community members. Our hope is that this collection of case studies can offer insights into, and lessons towards, building more resilient communities.

References

Antonova, Anna S., and Alison Rieser. 2019. "Curating Collapse: Performing Maritime Cultural Heritage in Iceland's Museums and Tours." *Maritime Studies* 18: 103–14.

Arias Schreiber, Milena, Ida Wingren, and Sebastian Linke. 2020. "Swimming Upstream: Community Economies for a Different Coastal Rural Development in Sweden." *Sustainability Science* 15, no. 1: 63–73. https://doi.org/10.1007/s11625-019-00770-0

Bacq, Sophie, and Frank Janssen. 2011. "The Multiple Faces of Social Entrepreneurship: A Review of Definitional Issues Based on Geographical and Thematic Criteria." *Entrepreneurship and Regional Development* 23, nos. 5–6: 373–403.

Bhatt, Babita, and Israr Qureshi. 2023. "Navigating Power Relations in Community-Driven Development: An Exploration of Constructive Work." In *Social Entrepreneurship and Gandhian Thoughts in the Post-COVID World*, edited by Babita Bhatt, Israr Qureshi, Dhirendra M. Shukla, and Vinay Pillai, 49–65. Singapore: Springer. https://doi.org/10.1007/978-981-99-4008-0_3

Bhatt, Babita, Israr Qureshi, Dhirendra M. Shukla, and Pradeep K. Hota. 2023. "Prefiguring alternative organizing: Confronting marginalization through projective cultural adjustment and tempered autonomy." *Organization Studies*. https://doi.org/10.1177/01708406231203295

Bammer, Gabriele. 2019. "Key Issues in Co-creation with Stakeholders when Research Problems Are Complex." *Evidence & Policy* 15, no. 3: 423–35. https://doi.org/10.1332/174426419X15532579188099

Bartunek, Jean M., and Sara L. Rynes. 2014. "Academics and Practitioners Are Alike and Unlike: The Paradoxes of Academic–Practitioner Relationships." *Journal of Management* 40, no. 5: 1181–1201.

Battilana, Julie, and Matthew Lee. 2014. "Advancing Research on Hybrid

Organizing: Insights from the Study of Social Enterprises." *Academy of Management Annals* 8, no. 1: 397–441.

Beer, Andrew, Fiona McKenzie, Jiří Blažek, Markku Sotarauta, and Sarah Ayres. 2020. *Every Place Matters: Towards Effective Place-based Policy.* Abingdon, Oxon, UK: Regional Studies Association.

Berrone, Pascual, Liliana Gelabert, Federica Massa-Saluzzo, and Horacio E. Rousseau. 2016. "Understanding Community Dynamics in the Study of Grand Challenges: How Nonprofits, Institutional Actors, and the Community Fabric Interact to Influence Income Inequality." *Academy of Management Journal* 59, no. 6: 1940–64.

Best, David, Ana-Maria Bliuc, Muhammad Iqbal, Katie Upton, and Steve Hodgkins. 2017. "Mapping Social Identity Change in Online Networks of Addiction Recovery." *Addiction Research & Theory* 26, no. 3: 163–73. https://doi.org/10.1080/16066359.2017.1347258

Carmen, Raff, and Miguel Sobrado, eds. 2013. *A Future for the Excluded: Job Creation and Income Generation by the Poor: Clodomir Santos de Morais and the Organization Workshop.* London: Zed Books.

Centre for Social Enterprise, Memorial University. "PLACE Framework." https://www.mun.ca/social-enterprise/about-us/what-is-social-enterprise/place-framework/

Cohen, Philippa, Edward H. Allison, Neil L. Andrew, Joshua Cinner, Louisa S. Evans, Michael Fabinyi, Len R. Garces, Stephen J. Hall, Christina C. Hicks, Terry P. Hughes, Svein Jentoft, David J. Mills, Rosalie Masu, Emmanuel K. Mbaru, and Blake D. Ratner. 2019. "Securing a Just Space for Small-Scale Fisheries in the Blue Economy." *Frontiers in Marine Science* 6: 1-8. https://doi.org/10.3389/fmars.2019.00171.

Cooperrider, David L., and Suresh Srivastva. 1987. "Appreciative Inquiry in Organizational Life." *Research in Organizational Change and Development* 1, no. 1: 129–69.

Cresswell, Tim. 2015. *Place: An Introduction,* 2nd ed. New York: Wiley.

Daniels, Jennifer, Kelly Vodden, and Godfrey Baldacchino. 2015. "Matters of Place: The Making of Place and Identity." In *Place Peripheral: The Promise and Challenge of Place-Based Development in Rural and Remote Regions,* edited by Kelly Vodden, Godfrey Baldacchino, and Ryan Gibson, 23–40. St. John's: ISER Books.

Dees, J. Gregory. 1998. *The Meaning of "Social Entrepreneurship."* Kansas City, MO: Kauffman Center for Entrepreneurial Leadership.

de Sousa Santos, Boaventura. 2018. *The End of Cognitive Empire: The Coming of Age of Epistemologies of the South.* Durham, NC: Duke University Press.

Emery, Mary, and Cornelia Flora. 2006. "Spiraling-Up: Mapping Community Transformation with Community Capitals Framework." *Community Development* 37, no. 1: 19–35.

Fernando, Felix N., and Gary A. Goreham. 2018. "A Tale of Two Rural Cities: Dynamics of Community Capitals during a North Dakota Oil Boom." *Community Development* 49, no. 3: 274–91.

Galeano, Eduardo. 1997 [1973]. *Open Veins of Latin America*, translated by C. Belfrage. New York: Monthly Review Press.

George, E. Wanda, Heather Mair, and Donald G. Reid. 2009. *Rural Tourism Development: Localism and Cultural Change.* Bristol, UK: Channel View Publications.

Gerritsen, Peter R.W. 2014. "Working with Indigenous Women on Multifunctionality and Sustainable Rural Tourism in Western Mexico." *Journal of Rural and Community Development* 9, no. 3: 243–57.

Gudynas, Eduardo. 2011. "Buen Vivir: Today's Tomorrow." *Development* 54, no. 4: 441–47.

Hall, Peter A., and David Soskice, eds. 2001. *Varieties of Capitalism: The Institutional Foundations of Comparative Advantage.* Oxford: Oxford University Press.

Haugh, Helen. 2006. "Social Enterprise: Beyond Economic Outcomes and Individual Returns." In *Social Entrepreneurship*, edited by Johanna Mair, Jeffrey Robinson, and Kai Hockerts, 180–205. New York: Palgrave Macmillan.

Haugh, Helen, and Andrew Brady. 2019. "Community Perspectives on Social Entrepreneurship." In *A Research Agenda for Social Entrepreneurship*, edited by Anne de Bruin and Simon Teasdale, 67–81. Cheltenham, UK: Edward Elgar.

Hertel, Christina, Sophie Bacq, and Frank-Martin Belz. 2019. "It Takes a Village to Sustain a Village: A Social Identity Perspective on Successful Community-Based Enterprise Creation." *Academy of Management Discoveries* 5, no. 4: 438–64.

Higgins, Jenny. 2009. "Cod Moratorium." Heritage Newfoundland and Labrador. https://www.heritage.nf.ca/articles/economy/moratorium.php

Holt-Lunstad, Julianne, Timothy B. Smith, Mark Baker, Tyler Harris, and David Stephenson. 2015. "Loneliness and Social Isolation as Risk Factors for Mortality: A Meta-Analytic Review." *Perspectives on Psychological Science* 10, no. 2: 227–37.

Horikawa, Saburo. 2021. *Why Place Matters: A Sociological Study of the Historic Preservation Movement in Otaru, Japan, 1965–2017.* Cham, Switzerland: Springer.

Horlings, Lummina Geertruida, and Terry K. Marsden. 2014. "Exploring the 'New Rural Paradigm' in Europe: Eco-economic Strategies as a Counterforce to the Global Competitiveness Agenda." *European Urban and Regional Studies* 21, no. 1: 4–20.

Jørring, Louise, António Valentim, and Pablo Porten-Cheé. 2018. "Mapping a Changing Field: A Literature Review on Digital Citizenship." *Digital Culture & Society* 4, no. 2: 11–38. https://doi.org/10.14361/dcs-2018-0203

Kimmel, Courtney, Andrew Perlstein, Michael Mortimer, Dequn Zhou, and David Robertson. 2015. "Sustainability of Tourism as Development Strategy for Cultural-Landscapes in China: Case Study of Ping'an Village." *Journal of Rural and Community Development* 10, no. 2: 121–35.

Korsgaard, Steffen, Richard Ferguson, and Johan Gaddefors. 2015. "The Best of Both Worlds: How Rural Entrepreneurs Use Placial Embeddedness and Strategic Networks to Create Opportunities." *Entrepreneurship and Regional Development* 27, nos. 9–10: 574–98.

Krawchenko, Tamara. 2014. "Bringing Municipalities into Rural Community and Economic Development: Cases from Atlantic Canada." *Journal of Rural and Community Development* 9, no. 3: 78–96.

Kretzmann, John P., and John L. McKnight. 1993. *Building Communities from the Inside Out: A Path toward Finding and Mobilizing a Community's Assets.* Evanston, IL: Center for Urban Affairs and Policy Research.

Kuddus, Md Abdul, Elizabeth Tynan, and Emma McBryde. 2020. "Urbanization: A Problem for the Rich and the Poor?" *Public Health Reviews* 41, no. 1.

Lewis, Marianne W. and Wendy K. Smith. 2022. "Reflections on the 2021 decade award: navigating paradox is paradoxical." *Academy of Management Review* 47, no. 4: 528-548.

Lijphart, Arend. 2012. *Patterns of Democracy: Government Forms and Performance in Thirty-Six Countries,* 2nd ed. New Haven, CT: Yale University Press.

Lowery, Brennan, John Dagevos, Ratana Chuenpagdee, and Kelly Vodden. 2020. "Storytelling for Sustainable Development in Rural Communities: An Alternative Approach." *Sustainable Development* 28: 1813–26. https://doi.org/10.1002/sd.2124

Lumpkin, G.T., and Sophie Bacq. 2019. "Civic Wealth Creation: A New View of Stakeholder Engagement and Societal Impact." *Academy of Management Perspectives* 33, no. 4: 383–404.

Lumpkin, G.T., Sophie Bacq, and Robert J. Pidduck. 2018. "Where Change Happens: Community-Level Phenomena in Social Entrepreneurship Research." *Journal of Small Business Management* 56, no. 1: 24–50.

MacKendrick, N.A, and J.R. Parkins. 2004. *Frameworks for Assessing Community Sustainability: A Synthesis of Current Research in British Columbia.* Edmonton: Canadian Forest Service.

Markey, Sean, Sarah-Patricia Breen, Kelly Vodden, and Jen Daniels. 2015. "Evidence of Place: Becoming a Region in Rural Canada." *International Journal of Urban and Regional Research* 39, no. 5: 874–91.

Marti, Ignasi, David Courpasson, and Saulo Dubard Barbosa. 2013. "'Living in the Fishbowl': Generating an Entrepreneurial Culture in a Local Community in Argentina." *Journal of Business Venturing* 28, no. 1: 10–29. https://doi.org/10.1016/j.jbusvent.2011.09.001

McKeever, Edward, Sarah Jack, and Alistair Anderson. 2015. "Embedded Entrepreneurship in the Creative Re-Construction of Place." *Journal of Business Venturing* 30, no. 1: 50–65.

Murphy, Matthew, Wade M. Danis, Johnny Mack, and (Kekinusuqs) Judith Sayers. 2020. "From Principles to Action: Community-based Entrepreneurship in the Toquaht Nation." *Journal of Business Venturing* 35, no. 6: 106051.

Overton, James. 2007. "A Future in the Past? Tourism Development, Outport Archaeology, and the Politics of Deindustrialization in Newfoundland and Labrador in the 1990s." *Urban History Review* 35, no. 2: 60–74. https://doi.org/10.7202/1015922ar

Peredo, Ana María, and James J. Chrisman. 2006. "Toward a Theory of Community-Based Enterprise." *Academy of Management Review* 31: 309–28.

Proshansky, Harold M., and Abbe K. Fabian. 1987. "The Development of Place Identity in the Child." In *The Built Environment and Child Development,* edited by Thomas G. David and Carol Simon Weinstein, 21–40. New York: Plenum.

Powell, E. Erin, Ralph Hamann, Verena Bitzer, and Ted Baker. 2018. "Bringing the Elephant into the Room? Enacting Conflict in Collective Prosocial Organizing." *Journal of Business Venturing* 33, no. 5: 623–42.

Ramsey, Doug, Robert C. Annis, and John C. Everitt. 2002. "Definitions and Boundaries of Community: The Case of Rural Health Focus Group Analysis in Southwestern Manitoba." *Prairie Perspectives: Geographical Essays* 5: 187–201.

Relph, Edward. 1976. *Place and Placelessness*. London: Pion.

Rennie, Frank, and Suzannah-Lynn Billing. 2015. "Changing Community Perceptions of Sustainable Rural Development in Scotland." *Journal of Rural and Community Development* 10, no. 2: 35–46.

Rodríguez-Pose, Andrés. 2018. "The Revenge of the Places That Don't Matter (and What to Do About It). *Cambridge Journal of Regions, Economy and Society* 11, no. 1: 189–209.

Rompkey, Ronald. 2009. *Grenfell of Labrador: A Biography*. Montreal and Kingston: McGill-Queen's University Press.

Rothman, Hal K. 1998. *Devil's Bargains: Tourism in the Twentieth-Century American West*. Lawrence: University Press of Kansas.

Seelos, Christian, Johanna Mair, Julie Battilana, and Tina Dacin. 2011. "The Embeddedness of Social Entrepreneurship: Understanding Variation across Local Communities." In *Communities and Organizations*, edited by Chris Marquis, Royston Greenwood, and Michael Lounsbury, 333–63. Bingley, UK: Emerald Group.

Selsky, John W., and Anthony E. Smith. 1994. "Community Entrepreneurship: A Framework for Social Change Leadership." *Leadership Quarterly* 5: 277–96.

Seto, Ario. 2020. "After Community: Upscaling and the Flux of Online Civic Engagement in Indonesia." *Asiascape: Digital Asia* 7, nos. 1–2: 42–68. https://doi.org/10.1163/22142312-bja10003

Shrivastava, Paul, and James J. Kennelly. 2013. "Sustainability and Place-Based Enterprise." *Organization and Environment* 26: 83–101.

Siegner, Meike, Jonatan Pinkse, and Rajat Panwar. 2018. "Managing Tensions in a Social Enterprise: The Complex Balancing Act to Deliver a Multi-Faceted but Coherent Social Mission." *Journal of Cleaner Production* 174: 1314–24.

Slawinski, Natalie, Blair Winsor, Daina Mazutis, John W. Schouten, and Wendy K. Smith. 2021. "Managing the Paradoxes of Place to Foster Regeneration." *Organization and Environment* 34, no. 4: 595–618.

Smith, Wendy K., and Marya L. Besharov. 2019. "Bowing before Dual Gods: How Structured Flexibility Sustains Organizational Hybridity." *Administrative Science Quarterly* 64, no. 1: 1–44.

Smith, Wendy K., Michael Gonin, and Marya L. Besharov. 2013. "Managing Social-Business Tensions: A Review and Research Agenda for Social Enterprise." *Business Ethics Quarterly* 23, no. 3: 407–42.

Smith, Wendy K. and Marianne W. Lewis. 2022. *Both/and thinking: Embracing creative tensions to solve your toughest problems.* Boston, MA: Harvard Business School Press.

Statistics Canada. 2013. "Sense of Belonging to Canada, the Province of Residence and the Local Community." *Spotlight on Canadians: Results from the General Social Survey.* 89-652-X. https://www150.statcan.gc.ca/n1/pub/89-652-x/89-652-x2015004-eng.htm

Steiner, Artur, Jane Farmer, and Gary Bosworth. 2020. "Rural Social Enterprise: Evidence to Date, and a Research Agenda." *Journal of Rural Studies* 70: 139–43.

Stoddart, Mark C.J., Gary Catano, and Howard Ramos. 2018. "Navigating Tourism Development in Emerging Destinations in Atlantic Canada: Local Benefits, Extra-local Challenges." *Journal of Rural and Community Development* 13, no. 2: 57–75.

Stoddart, Mark C.J., Emma Cruddas, and Howard Ramos. 2021. "Do Neighbourhood Environmental Perceptions Affect Practices?" *Canadian Journal of Urban Research* 30, no. 1: 67–83.

Stott, Neil, Michelle Fava, and Natalie Slawinski. 2019. "Community Social Innovation: Taking a Long View on Community Enterprise." In *Handbook of Inclusive Innovation: The Role of Organizations, Markets and Communities in Social Innovation,* edited by Gerard George, Ted Baker, Paul Tracey, and Havovi Joshi, 145–66. London: Edward Elgar.

Sullivan, Claire, and Clare Mitchell. 2012. "From Fish to Folk Art: Creating a Heritage-Based Place Identity in Ferryland, Newfoundland and Labrador." *Journal of Rural and Community Development* 7, no. 2: 37–56.

Tàbara, J. David, Niki Frantzeskaki, Katharina Hölscher, Simona Pedde, Kasper Kok, Francesco Lamperti, Jens H. Christensen, Jill Jäger, and Pam Berry. 2018. "Positive Tipping Points in a Rapidly Warming World." *Current Opinion in Environmental Sustainability* 31: 120–29.

Tàbara, J. David, Takeshi Takama, Manisha Mishra, Lauren Hermanus, Sean Khaya Andrew, Pacia Diaz, Gina Ziervogel, and Lois Lemkow. 2020.

"Micro-Solutions to Global Problems: Understanding Social Processes to Eradicate Energy Poverty and Build Climate-Resilient Livelihoods." *Climatic Change* 160, no. 4: 711–25.

Thompson, John. 2010. "'Entrepreneurship Enablers' — Their Unsung and Unquantified Role in Competitiveness and Regeneration." *Local Economy* 25, no. 1: 58–73. https://doi.org/10.1080/02690940903545406

Tracey, Paul, Nelson Phillips, and Helen Haugh. 2005. "Beyond Philanthropy: Community Enterprise as a Basis for Corporate Citizenship." *Journal of Business Ethics* 58, no. 4: 327–44.

Tuan, Yi-Fu. 1977. *Space and Place: The Perspective of Experience*. Minneapolis: University of Minnesota Press.

United Nations. 2015a. "Goals: 11." Sustainable Development Goals. https://sdgs.un.org/goals/goal11

United Nations. 2015b. "Topics: Sustainable Cities and Human Settlements." Sustainable Development Goals. https://sdgs.un.org/topics/sustainable-cities-and-human-settlements

United Nations. 2020. "Chapter 1: Social Entrepreneurship." *World Youth Report: Youth Social Entrepreneurship and the 2030 Agenda*. https://www.un.org/development/desa/youth/wp-content/uploads/sites/21/2020/10/WYR2020-Chapter1.pdf

Van de Ven, Andrew. 2007. *Engaged Scholarship: A Guide for Organizational and Social Research*. Oxford: Oxford University Press.

Vodden, Kelly, Godfrey Baldacchino, and Ryan Gibson. 2015. *Place Peripheral: The Promise and Challenge of Place-Based Development in Rural and Remote Regions*. St. John's: ISER Books.

Williams, Trenton A., and Dean A. Shepherd. 2016. "Building Resilience or Providing Sustenance: Different Paths of Emergent Ventures in the Aftermath of the Haiti Earthquake." *Academy of Management Journal* 59, no. 6: 2069–2102.

Winkler, Richelle, Lorri Oikarinen, Heather Simpson, Melissa Michaelson, and Mayra Sanchez Gonzalez. 2016. "Boom, Bust and Beyond: Arts and Sustainability in Calumet, Michigan." *Sustainability* 8, no. 3: 284.

PART I

Case Studies from Newfoundland and Labrador

CHAPTER 1

The Genesis of the PLACE Framework: Lessons from Shorefast on Community Economic Revitalization

Natalie Slawinski, Jennifer Charles, Alan Cobb,
Zita Cobb, Susan Cull, Diane Hodgins, Amy Rowsell,
Wendy K. Smith, Mark C.J. Stoddart, and Blair Winsor

S horefast is a charitable organization launched in 2006 with a mission to build cultural and economic resilience on Fogo Island. Situated off the northeast coast of the island portion of the province of Newfoundland and Labrador (NL), Canada, this settler island community depended for hundreds of years on fishing cod. At its peak in the 1950s, Fogo Island's population was over 4,500. Fifty years later, declining fish stocks and dwindling economic opportunities resulted in the population declining by more than half. Fogo Islanders left their home and way of life in search of employment, and the former vibrancy of the place diminished along with hope for the future. Yet despite economic and demographic decline, many cultural and natural assets remained. Recognizing the inherent value of Fogo Island, Shorefast leveraged the power of place and social enterprise to expand the existing economy (see Introduction to this volume for a definition and overview of social enterprise). The organization harnessed Fogo Island's many assets, including the island's rugged subarctic landscape, its rich cultural traditions, and the population's resourcefulness and hospitality, to build the award-winning Fogo Island Inn, among its many initiatives. As a social enterprise, the Inn has employed hundreds of Fogo Islanders and reinvested its profits into the community through Shorefast's charitable programs (Slawinski et al. 2021).

Like Fogo Island, many local communities around the world, both urban and rural, have been affected by uneven development and socio-ecological decline that often strips their local resources and capacities (Di Domenico, Haugh, and Tracey 2010; Johannisson and Nilsson 1989). Locally-owned businesses are being replaced by multinationals, moving profits and decision-making farther away from communities. As business decisions continue to be made in distant corporate headquarters, financial capital becomes increasingly placeless, resulting in significant repercussions to communities (Shrivastava and Kennelly 2013). For example, with the global mobility of investment capital, decisions about factory closures and relocations are often made at a distance, abstracted from the local economies impacted by those decisions. These communities are then left to grapple with unemployment and other social problems (Johnstone and Lionais 2004; McKeever, Jack, and Anderson 2015). Meanwhile, there is growing recognition that impacted communities are best positioned to understand and effectively address the challenges they face rather than relying solely on outside actors such as remotely located governmental agencies that are less attuned to local contexts (Berrone et al. 2016; Lumpkin and Bacq 2019). Researchers increasingly point to place-based social entrepreneurship as an important source of local solutions that can foster resilience in communities facing socio-economic challenges (Kim and Kim 2021; Lumpkin, Bacq, and Pidduck 2018).

Recognizing the importance of community-based action and social enterprise for rebuilding community well-being, scholars have called for further research into how place-based social enterprises can revitalize communities (Hertel, Bacq, and Belz 2019; Tracey, Phillips, and Haugh 2005) and for more in-depth understandings through community-engaged research (Murphy et al. 2020). This chapter answers this call by describing Shorefast's novel approach to social entrepreneurship and community development. Our team of researchers, led out of Memorial University, spent almost a decade partnering with Shorefast to study its approach and mobilize the results from this research. In 2018, we convened a workshop on Fogo Island for community leaders from across the province to derive generalizable principles for revitalizing communities. The PLACE Framework was born out of our community-engaged research approach and through dialogue with community leaders from across NL, a province whose people hold a deep sense of place.

This chapter begins with an examination of Shorefast's place-based work on Fogo Island and beyond to address and reverse the negative effects of our placeless economic system. We then examine the opportunities and challenges the research team faced in doing community-engaged research on Fogo Island. Finally, we detail the emergence of the PLACE Framework's five core principles, which outline how social enterprise can be leveraged for building community resilience. The name of the PLACE Framework recognizes the critical importance of place in a globalized world experiencing cultural flattening and unprecedented ecological, social, and economic crises. We end with a discussion of future research directions.

Shorefast's Place-Centric Approach to Strengthening Community Resilience on Fogo Island and Beyond

Like many communities across Newfoundland and Labrador, Fogo Island was settled by Europeans — mostly from Ireland and England — because of its proximity to the rich North Atlantic fishing grounds. For 400 years, these settlers supported their families by fishing cod close to shore. By the 1950s, large factory trawlers from various countries, including Canada, appeared off the shores of NL. They dragged the ocean floor, destroying ecosystems and diminishing the inshore stocks that had sustained families for generations, including settlers and Indigenous Peoples.

In 1992, the Canadian government imposed a moratorium on fishing the rapidly diminishing cod stocks. Industrial overfishing, combined with insufficient resource management practices, had led cod to the point of near-extinction (Bavington 2010; Higgins 2009). The moratorium left more than 30,000 Newfoundlanders out of work, forcing many to move from their outport and coastal communities to larger centres within or outside the province in search of employment. A number of federal government programs, including the $1.9 billion Atlantic Groundfish Strategy, were launched to financially support job training or skill development for those left unemployed by the moratorium (Hamilton and Butler 2001). Yet despite these efforts, many NL communities continued to suffer population decline and out-migration, including Fogo Island (Gibson 2013).

In 2006, recognizing that this population decline was threatening Fogo Island's future, Zita Cobb and two of her brothers, Alan Cobb and Anthony Cobb, founded Shorefast, a Canadian registered charity, to help Fogo Island develop a more robust economy and a viable future. Zita Cobb moved back to Fogo Island from Ottawa, where she had built a successful career as a senior executive in the high-tech sector, retiring as a multi-millionaire at age 42. Shorefast began its work on Fogo Island by building four artist studios. Guided by Cobb's belief that art engages our senses and our reason and contributes to the critical thinking needed to resist being culturally flattened, Shorefast launched Fogo Island Arts, a residency-based contemporary art and ideas organization that has hosted artists from around the globe.

Shorefast drew inspiration for its engagement with art from the Fogo Process, a model of community development that used film to spur social change on Fogo Island in 1968. This model of community development helped Fogo Island navigate the pressures of resettlement and has also since been used by various other communities around the world (Newhook 2009). Developed through a partnership between Memorial University's Extension Service, the National Film Board of Canada, filmmaker Colin Low, and local residents, the Fogo Process created films that sparked and captured dialogues between residents of various communities on Fogo Island. While these community members had been previously isolated from each other, the films helped them realize that they shared many similar concerns about the prospect of resettlement. Between 1954 and 1975, tens of thousands of NL residents were relocated to larger centres as part of a provincial government-sponsored resettlement program designed to reduce the costs of providing essential services to remote communities (Loo 2020). Through the creation and local screening of the films, residents of Fogo Island found a shared voice to oppose resettlement (Martin 2007). Joining forces, they created the Fogo Island Co-operative Society (Co-op) to create employment on Fogo Island and secure its future. The Co-op built modern fishing boats and fish processing plants, took over seafood processing plants abandoned by private industry, and sought out new markets for their product. The employment created by the Fogo Island Co-op helped slow out-migration and sustain the island's communities until the cod moratorium in 1992 (Fogo Island Co-operative Society 2010).

Inspired by the Fogo Process, Shorefast used art to promote dialogue and foster social change. Shorefast brought artists and designers to the island to help forge a path forward (Brinklow 2013). Designers worked alongside local artisans to co-create unique handmade modern furniture and textiles for the Fogo Island Inn, a 29-room luxury inn that Shorefast opened in 2013. The Inn was designed by Newfoundland-born architect Todd Saunders to pay homage to the place, including its natural and cultural features. Over time, such dialogue and collaboration between insiders and outsiders led to a new appreciation and a reimagining of Fogo Island's unique assets. Finding new ways with old things, one of Shorefast's core principles, guided Shorefast's approach to honouring place while reaching out to the rest of the world. Shorefast leveraged cultural traditions and local knowledge, while connecting with the world of contemporary design. For example, Shorefast connected local makers with an international textile designer, who together co-created quilts to sell to discerning tourists for what Shorefast called the "right price," a price that ensured the makers received a fair price for their work. Quilts that had once been made from scraps of material and signified a subsistence way of life began to sell for thousands of dollars to visitors who appreciated them as beautiful handmade pieces born of the specific culture of Fogo Island and created from hundreds of hours of detailed and painstaking work.

Shorefast's approach involved collaboration with global experts, as well as engaging with local residents and their traditional knowledge. Shorefast's initiatives depended on leveraging local knowledge. Drawing on Asset-Based Community Development (often referred to as ABCD) approaches (Kretzmann and McKnight 1993), Shorefast started by creating what they called a bubble map to list Fogo Island's many assets (Mazutis, Slawinski, and Hookey 2013a). Such learning and collaboration took time, as did engaging with local residents. As Shorefast members often repeated, they needed to move "at the speed of trust" (Trelstad, Smith, and Slawinski 2020, 6). Some community members were anxious about the uncertainties that came with any significant development, especially the bold ideas that were being proposed by Shorefast. For example, prior research on Fogo Island found that while most of the community were broadly supportive of tourism development, there were concerns about increased traffic, including additional strain to the local ferry system (Rockett and Ramsey 2017). While community consensus was often not possible, Shorefast held town hall meetings in every community on Fogo Island and looked for ways to work with the community and to explain their novel approaches to fulfilling their mission.

Shorefast sourced the building materials for the Fogo Island Inn as locally as possible, and when local suppliers were not available, the organization selected suppliers with high sustainability standards from countries with strong environmental and labour laws. Every aspect of the Inn, including its finishings and furniture, drew from local knowledge and traditions. For example, the wooden "punt chair" (Figure 1.1) adorning each guest room was inspired by the island's traditional inshore fishing boat — called a punt — and co-created by a local woodworker and an international designer. The punt chair and other handmade pieces designed for the Inn were soon offered for sale through Fogo Island Workshops, another of Shorefast's social businesses that created jobs and stimulated the local economy by selling locally inspired contemporary furniture and textiles made on Fogo Island.

The Inn served as more than just an economic engine for Shorefast's mission. Its very design served to symbolize Shorefast's philosophy of both recognizing the value of place and honouring holism, in which opposite elements were viewed as interconnected. The Inn was shaped as an "X," with one wing containing the gathering spaces of the lobby, dining room, library, cinema, and art gallery, and the other wing containing the private guest rooms. The "X" symbolized the intersection "between the old and the new, and between people from Fogo Island and people from away" (Trelstad, Smith, and Slawinski 2020, 5). The Inn's community host program employed local residents to take global guests around the island and offered guests a personalized connection to the site. By creating linkages among people from very different worlds, Shorefast leaders aimed to show that place-based business could offer human connection and enrichment, rather than the anonymous, isolating exchanges that had become so pervasive in a globalized economy. To show the community that the Inn was not only inspired by Fogo Island, but also built to benefit Fogo Island, Shorefast offered every resident of Fogo Island and neighbouring Change Islands a free night's stay at the Inn in 2013, when it opened, and again in 2023 on the occasion of its 10th anniversary.

Figure 1.1. The punt chair produced by Fogo Island Workshops. (Photo credit: Shorefast, 2022)

Zita Cobb invested close to $30 million of her own capital to build the Inn and the Fogo Island artist studios. The federal and provincial governments subsequently contributed $5 million each in grant funding to support the long-term economic development opportunities provided by these projects. Fogo Island Inn operates as a social business with no private gain; all profits are reinvested into Shorefast programs to strengthen the island's economy and culture (Figure 1.2).

By 2017 the Inn started to generate surpluses, and by 2018 Shorefast accounted for 20 per cent of Fogo Island's non-governmental GDP, with its various enterprises employing close to 200 staff, mostly Fogo Islanders. In 2020, during the COVID-19 pandemic, the NL government closed the province's borders to non-residents. With the loss of its primary tourist market, Shorefast was forced to lay off the majority of the Fogo Island Inn's staff, reopening 16 months later in July 2021 when the province's borders reopened to vaccinated visitors from within Canada. During the lengthy closure, Shorefast struggled financially, while also planning for and shaping

Figure 1.2. Surpluses from Shorefast's social enterprises support a holistic set of charitable programs that contribute to community well-being, including initiatives focused around youth and environmental stewardship. Here, students visit Shorefast's Punt Premises on World Oceans Day. (Photo credit: Shorefast, 2022)

a new normal for tourism businesses: one that would be carbon light and characterized by an ongoing deep engagement with place.

Even as Shorefast's work revolved around revitalizing Fogo Island's culture and economy, the organization also pursued a larger ambition of contributing to a growing international movement focused on shifting the global economy to make it more inclusive, just, and sustainable (Trelstad, Smith, and Slawinski 2020). One way of doing this is to bring an added level of transparency to everyday economic transactions and practices to allow people to make more principle-based buying decisions. In this spirit, the Shorefast team developed the Economic Nutrition^{CM} Certification Mark (ENCM, Figure 1.3), modelled after the nutrition labels found on processed foods (Slawinski et al. 2021). It includes information about what percentage of the revenue from each sale goes to creating jobs or to other costs such as materials and marketing.

The ENCM also shows which geographic regions benefit from the purchase. For example, the ENCMs for stays at the Inn and quilts and wood furniture from their online shop show that the majority of the financial benefit stays on Fogo Island. In addition to using the ENCM on the products they sold, Shorefast aimed to develop a strategy to promote widespread adoption of the certification mark globally. By 2020, after 14 years of focusing on its mission "to build cultural and economic resilience on Fogo Island," Shorefast

Economic Nutrition^{CM}

Fogo Island Inn
Community Enterprise

Nightly Stay

What does the money pay for?

Labour	49%
Food, Room Supplies	12%
Commissions, Fees	5%
Operations, Admin	18%
Sales, Marketing	4%
Surplus	12%

Where does the money go?

Local 65%	National 19%
Provincial 13%	Global 3%

* Values are calculated retrospectively and updated when changes are material. Figures shown are for illustrative purposes, reflecting pre-COVID operations.

Economic Nutrition^{CM} is a certification trademark of Shorefast, used under license by Fogo Island Inn.

Figure 1.3. An example of Economic Nutrition^{CM} label. (Photo credit: Shorefast, 2022)

added to its mission the following: "to serve other communities by sharing place-based models of economic development" (Shorefast, n.d.). The Shorefast team was ready to share their place-based and holistic approach with the global community, and described its work as "helping local communities thrive in the global economy."

Partnering with Shorefast: Our Academic Team's Approach to Community-Engaged Research

The research team approached this research project as a tightly woven partnership between academics and community members. The first author, Natalie Slawinski, first met Zita Cobb at the North Atlantic Forum in St. John's in October 2011, where Cobb offered a keynote address. Intrigued by Cobb's vision to transform our unsustainable global economy by starting with bold action on Fogo Island, Slawinski was keen to study Shorefast's novel place-based approach. This first encounter evolved into a long-term partnership involving several members of Shorefast and a multidisciplinary team of scholars from Memorial University and the University of Delaware. The partnership started with several research trips to Fogo Island to study Shorefast's approach to community revitalization and to develop some teaching case studies (Mazutis, Slawinski, and Hookey 2013a, 2013b; Trelstad, Smith, and Slawinski 2020). On her second trip to Fogo Island in January 2012, Slawinski invited several members of Shorefast, including Cobb, to dine at the house she was renting. Trying to impress the Shorefast team, Slawinski and her husband cooked pad thai using locally-sourced shrimp. None of the other ingredients for the dish could be sourced locally. It was while discussing ways of reviving Fogo Island's economy around the dinner table that evening that Slawinski was struck by the realization that her menu choice had not contributed much to the local economy. This revelation subsequently guided the research team's approach, offering key insights into the process of doing community-engaged research, including that researchers can and should think carefully and holistically about the variety of contributions they can make, however small, to their research site and partners.

Before long, members of the Shorefast team were making guest appearances in Slawinski's and other research team members' business courses at Memorial University. From there, the partnership grew into a multi-year, federally funded research project involving dozens of trips to Fogo Island by the team members and months of in-depth data collection. Storms sometimes intervened in the researchers' travel plans. Nevertheless, the research team managed to visit the island a number of times per year, with two members of the team living on Fogo Island for several months at a time. One member of the team who was a graduate student at the time, Jennifer Charles, now lives on Fogo Island full time with her husband Tim and their three children and runs a health and wellness business, Wild Cove Wellness.

Although it can be very rewarding, community-engaged research presents a number of challenges to researchers and community partners. Compared to more traditional forms of research, where the community or organization is the object of the research, community-engaged research involves co-creating the research goals and outputs with community stakeholders acting as equal partners in the research and its dissemination (Murphy et al. 2020). Generally, this process takes more time and requires larger research budgets as researchers spend years developing trust and learning about the needs and interests of their community partners (Hacker 2013). As Halseth and colleagues have noted, "It takes time to build relationships, it takes time in the field to be respectful of the needs and rhythms of places and communities, and it takes time after the research is completed to honour the [community-based research] relationship by staying in contact with communities" (Halseth et al. 2016, 48). Community-engaged research involves going beyond the typical academic work of researching and publishing articles by seeking to create meaningful benefits for community partners (Slawinski et al. 2023).

When the research site is remote, as was the case with Fogo Island, challenges may become amplified. Travel time to remote areas can be lengthy and can also be unpredictable when the weather interferes with already complicated logistics involving coordinating different transportation modes such as cars, planes, and ferries. On one occasion, University of Delaware professor Wendy K. Smith, a member of our research team, was delayed by more than a day getting from her hometown of Philadelphia to Gander, the closest international airport to Fogo Island. On another occasion, after several days of weather-related travel cancellations, Smith was forced to cancel her trip altogether when she realized she would not make it to a knowledge dissemination workshop on Fogo Island that she had helped organize. Finding accommodations in rural communities also presents challenges as some communities may have very limited offerings or none at all. Furthermore, accommodations in communities that rely on tourism may be closed in the off-season when community partners and potential research participants may have more time available for researchers. Conversely, accommodations may be more available during the on-season, but that is when many community partners and potential participants may be too busy with the day-to-day demands of their tourism business to engage with researchers. Finally, the smaller potential sample group found in rural places represents challenges to accessing a wide cross-section of perspectives and to honouring confidentiality as a requirement of research ethics (Halseth et al. 2016).

Community partners face their own challenges when engaging with researchers. Often they have limited time, and they may rely heavily on volunteers for community functions rather than on paid staff. In addition to having less capacity to participate in research, community partners may also have limited time to consider how best to capture the benefits of the research for their organization and/or community. At Shorefast, employees were often very busy working on the charity's many initiatives and associated businesses. Running the award-winning Fogo Island Inn itself was no small feat. Meeting the expectations of discerning guests while also honouring the needs of the community was one thing; dealing with ferry cancellations and supply challenges relating to operating on a remote island in the North Atlantic was a whole other challenge. As such, thinking about the goals of the research project and participating in the research were less urgent and important than day-to-day business operations.

The research team sought to overcome some of these challenges by working closely with Shorefast. For example, the team members who spent months at a time on Fogo Island collecting data did so in the off-season so as not to take limited accommodations away from tourists or staff. Shorefast employees also had more time in the off-season to engage with the research team. Longer stays gave the research team more time to build trust and work around Shorefast employees' busy schedules. In addition, the research team made it a priority to work closely with Shorefast to understand their goals for the research project and took the time to co-create a knowledge dissemination plan that would help Shorefast achieve its goal of distilling and sharing its community development learnings with other communities across the province and beyond.

While challenging and rife with tensions, community-engaged research can offer a number of benefits to both community partners and researchers. When researchers are attuned to the goals of their community partners and are earnest in contributing to them, community partners typically reap greater benefits (Bartunek and Rynes 2014). In addition, collaborating with researchers can help community partners gain wider recognition and legitimacy for their work. Academics often benefit from public trust and have wide reach with their global networks (Hoffman 2021). Increasingly, academics are being called on to disseminate their research findings more broadly, beyond the academy, to have greater impact on society (Chen et al. 2022; Sharma and Bansal 2020). Such dissemination includes writing blogs (Slawinski and Smith 2019; Smith and Slawinski 2020), using social media, creating podcasts, and writing for a wider audience through outlets such as *The Conversation*, which publishes free articles online that are written by academics (Slawinski and Smith 2020). For academics, the benefits of community-engaged research include conducting meaningful work, having broader impact on policy and practice, and gaining access to richer data and more reve-latory research insights (Bartunek 2007).

The partnership between Shorefast and the Memorial University-led research team has yielded a number of benefits including knowledge ex-changes, greater visibility for the research and partners, expanded social networks, and contributions to Fogo Island's economic development. Each research trip resulted in money spent on Fogo Island and therefore support for the local economy. In addition, a number of research articles, blogs, teaching cases, media articles, conference presentations, and in-dustry presentations have resulted from the partnership, which have helped promote Shorefast's goals to a wider audience. Some of the bene-fits have accrued beyond the partnership, including to community lead-ers across the province who have participated in a series of workshops called the PLACE Dialogues, which have guided — and been guided by — the PLACE Framework of Community Resilience. The Dialogues, which we describe in greater detail below, grew out of the research part-nership and have become a yearly gathering of community leaders, which we have defined broadly to encourage participation from those who play informal and formal leadership roles in advancing local initiatives.

The PLACE Dialogues and the PLACE Framework of Community Resilience

Researchers using an engaged approach often seek to mobilize findings to address community-based issues in real time (Bansal, Smith, and Vaara 2018). Both the researchers and Shorefast's leadership team decided that what was learned from the research project could be useful to community leaders across the province. They decided to host a workshop on Fogo Island in 2018 to discuss the challenges of, and opportunities for, rural community development, while also building a cross-sector network of individuals rep-resenting organizations focused on advancing rural development in NL.

While it was important to host the workshop on Fogo Island, a num-ber of challenges arose. On the weekend of the workshop, a powerful storm passed over Newfoundland, creating massive waves and seismic activity off the coast of Fogo Island. The storm not only made driving conditions treacherous, but also caused ferry cancellations for over 36 hours, forcing the organizers to postpone the workshop by a day. In addition, the storm brought power outages across Fogo Island, which interfered with the workshop. At one point during roundtable discussions in the Joe Batt's Arm town hall, the power went out, leaving the room dark and cold. Participants put their coats on, created makeshift lanterns with their cell phones, and continued to work through the storm and power outage.

Despite such challenges, the organizers observed several advantages to hosting the workshop in a rural community. First, it allowed participants to be immersed in the very setting — rural Newfoundland and Labrador — that constituted the theme of the workshop (Brenton and Slawinski 2023). Rather than sitting in a generic hotel in the city, removed from the realities of rural life, participants were fully immersed in the topic they were discussing — how to make rural places more resilient. Second, this immersion allowed the organizers to create experiential activities that connected community leaders to the place and its local customs and heritage. These activities also brought the group of community leaders, who were dedicated to the work of local regeneration, closer together as they realized the similarities between Fogo Island communities and their own, and shared their stories with the others. In other words, a feeling of solidarity was developing (Stott et al. 2021). Finally, hosting the workshop in a rural locale brought to light the many assets of rural places and the challenges of doing community development work there.

Beyond building a network of community leaders, another important outcome of the Fogo Island Workshop was the "PLACE Framework of Community Resilience." Five key principles emerged as central to developing resilient communities from the research on Fogo Island. These principles were reinforced through conversations among the workshop participants, as community leaders from across the province noted similar lessons in their own work. The team then labelled and organized the five principles to form the acronym "PLACE," which is meant to honour the love of community that motivated these leaders to launch new initiatives, such as social enterprises that served their community, and to persevere through the hard work of revitalizing their places. The five PLACE principles are:

- *Promote community leaders.* Community leaders play a critical role in catalyzing others to help drive positive changes and nurture pride in the community. They often do so by launching social enterprises or other initiatives to advance the community's interests by, for example, building leadership capacity in others. Community leaders may occupy formal or informal roles and, importantly, they energize others to join in the work to strengthen their place. On Fogo Island, the research team had observed how Shorefast's initiatives had encouraged several Fogo Islanders to move back to their community while attracting people from outside Newfoundland to make Fogo Island their home. These new and returning residents in turn joined in efforts to advance new initiatives and opportunities, including new small businesses, becoming champions for Fogo Island.

- *Link divergent perspectives.* Community development work requires inviting different perspectives into decisions and then finding ways to bridge them. Social enterprises are well-positioned to do this linking work, as they are often led by pragmatic entrepreneurial individuals who recognize that opportunities lie in unlikely places and that leveraging these opportunities relies on a variety of individuals who may hold very different perspectives. On Fogo Island, Shorefast became a broker, building linkages between insider and outsider knowledge and new and traditional skills, thereby creating new capacities. As one example, Shorefast invited globally recognized designers to work alongside local woodworkers to create new, place-inspired pieces for the Inn that are now sold in the Fogo Island Workshops.

- *Amplify local capacities and assets.* To be successful in both fulfilling their social mission and becoming financially viable, social enterprises recognize the value in the assets of their place and leverage them, even when others do not. Shorefast helped Fogo Island residents to rediscover and repurpose their human, ecological, institutional, and infrastructural assets, and to leverage these strengths. Cobb and other Shorefast members used approaches like Asset-Based Community Development (ABCD) (Kretzmann and McKnight 1993) and Appreciative Inquiry (Cooperrider and Srivastva 1987) by asking the community questions such as, "What do we have? What do we know? What do we love? What do we miss?" to uncover Fogo Island's potential.

- *Convey compelling stories.* Positive stories can provide hope and counter negative, self-defeating discourse in places impacted by economic decline. Shorefast recognized that narratives could be a powerful tool for changing mindsets both within the community and about the community. As such, its leadership team often repeated positive messages about Fogo Island's history and culture in presentations and in interviews with media.

- *Engage both/and thinking.* Approaching opposites as a both/and possibility instead of as an either/or choice can reveal important innovations for community development (Smith and Lewis 2022). For example, Shorefast's approach to finding new ways with old things inspired handmade modern textiles, such as quilts and rugs, and place-based contemporary architecture, such as the Fogo Island Inn and the artist studios, that have drawn global attention, commanded premium prices, and stimulated the local economy.

The community workshop on Fogo Island and the development of the PLACE Framework sparked interest in holding subsequent workshops, called the PLACE Dialogues, to continue to build a network of community leaders that could learn from each other. A second province-wide workshop took place in 2019 in Petty Harbour, a small fishing community on the east coast of Newfoundland that, like Fogo Island, was deeply impacted by the collapse of the cod fishery. The research team co-organized the workshop with Fishing for Success, a social enterprise based in Petty Harbour working to preserve Newfoundland's fishing heritage. Participants once again consisted of individuals working on solutions to help rebuild their communities and coming from a variety of sectors, including all levels of government (municipal, provincial, and federal), the non-profit sector, the for-profit sector, and academia.

Since it was co-created at the Fogo Island PLACE Dialogues in 2018, the PLACE Framework has been presented to local and global audiences, including at the Community Business Development Corporation (CBDC) annual general meeting in Charlottetown, Prince Edward Island in September 2019 and the European Commission's Fisheries Areas Network (FARNET) conference in Brussels, Belgium in December 2019. It has also evolved through subsequent PLACE Dialogues. As a conceptual tool that reflects the co-production of knowledge between academia and community, the PLACE Framework can be thought of as a way of translating back and forth between academic knowledge and locally oriented policy and practice.

In 2019, the research team decided to extend the Framework through a multi-case study of five other place-based social enterprises in other rural NL communities, including Fishing for Success (Petty Harbour), Placentia West Development Association (Burin Peninsula), the Bonavista Historic Townscape Foundation (Bonavista), the Bonne Bay Cottage Hospital Heritage Corporation (BBCHHC) (Norris Point), and St. Anthony Basin Resources Inc. (SABRI) (St. Anthony). The Framework continues to evolve as we study these other research sites and convene our annual PLACE Dialogues with community leaders across the province.

Conclusion

This chapter has presented a community-engaged process of studying Shorefast's approach to place-based social enterprise and its impact on community resilience over a 10-year period. In addition to producing academic articles and conference presentations, our research team has co-constructed and shared insights from our study of social entrepreneurship on Fogo Island through a variety of channels, including op-eds, blogs, and public presentations. In particular, two interrelated outcomes from our research approach have enabled deeper insights and created greater impact for a wider audience. The first is the PLACE Dialogues, which have allowed the research team to seek input and learn from community leaders across NL, thereby deepening our research insights and enhancing the generalizability of the findings. The second outcome was the PLACE Framework, which emerged from both the research and the PLACE Dialogues workshop, and which we have continued to refine and expand through subsequent Dialogues and field research.

The Framework consists of five principles that together form the acronym PLACE. Creating an acronym served an important function: it made the research more accessible and relevant to community leaders who share a love of place. As we have pointed out, academic research can be inaccessible and is therefore most impactful when translated for a broader audience (Gioia 2021; Hoffman 2021). Importantly, the five principles are designed to provide guidance rather than a recipe for other communities to duplicate. In other words, the principles are designed to be broad enough to allow community leaders to use them in their specific community context, but not so broad as to be generic and meaningless. Each principle represents a process that can help community leaders leverage social enterprise as a tool to strengthen their communities. The five principles, while not exhaustive, reinforce each other; as our team extends our in-depth study to other research sites, we will extend the five principles and explore other key elements not currently included in the PLACE Framework.

Through these two outcomes (the PLACE Framework and the PLACE Dialogues) and the research approach that yielded them, we extend scholarship on community-engaged research by exploring approaches to broadening impact (Halseth et al. 2016; Murphy et al. 2020). We also highlight the importance of using language and visual representations that can be interpreted in different ways. Such openness to interpretation invites the audience into complex research ideas by simplifying the ideas in ways that make them approachable, without losing the underlying complexity. We propose that community-engaged research can be an effective way to capitalize on research findings that suggest that communities are best positioned to understand and effectively address the challenges they face (Berrone et al. 2016; Lumpkin and Bacq 2019). Our study also resonates with research that highlights the role of social entrepreneurship in providing local solutions to challenged communities (Kim and Kim 2021; McKeever, Jack, and Anderson 2015), as well as research that emphasizes the need to cultivate a diverse breadth of transformative local "micro-solutions" to global social or environmental issues (Tàbara et al. 2020).

Several avenues for future research emerge from this study. First, given increasing calls for organizational research that is relevant to practice (Gioia 2021; Hoffman 2021) and that addresses grand challenges (Chen et al. 2023), we suggest that the opportunity is ripe for studies that can further our understanding of communities' needs and that contribute positive impacts to those communities. Community-engaged research is especially promising in this regard (Murphy et al. 2020). Second, there is an opportunity for multidisciplinary research to examine how place-based social enterprises can revitalize communities (Hertel, Bacq, and Belz 2019; Tracey, Phillips, and Haugh 2005). The topic of community development invites insights from a wide variety of disciplines including sociology, geography, sustainable community development studies, and organization studies, to name a few. Finally, multi-level research could be a promising avenue in which to study community resilience, given the role of community entrepreneurs (Johannisson and Nilsson 1989; Johnstone and Lionais 2006), organizations (Di Domenico, Haugh, and Tracey 2010; Shrivastava and Kennelly 2013), and community- level factors (Lumpkin, Bacq, and Pidduck 2018) in processes of community development.

Attempts to relocalize economic relationships and practices are among the diverse ways to bring greater transparency and accountability to an increasingly placeless global economic system. As such, expanding community-engaged research on place-based social enterprise is a promising area of future research. Moreover, building resilient communities that can counter placelessness and respond to growing socio-ecological crises is essential to building a more viable future. Community-engaged research offers a promising approach to advance both research and practice in social enterprise and community resilience.

Acknowledgements

This work was supported by the Social Sciences and Humanities Research Council of Canada (Grant No. 890-2015-0099). We are grateful to all who helped advance our research insights, including Oana Branzei, Jennifer Brenton, Tom Cooper, Michelle Darlington, Rob Greenwood, Nicole Helwig, Daina Mazutis, Gillian Morrissey, John Schouten, Garima Sharma, Neil Stott, and Paul Tracey. Finally, we are indebted to the residents of Fogo Island who participated in this research, and to participants of the PLACE Dialogues for sharing with us and each other their deep knowledge of place and social enterprise.

References

Bansal, Pratima, Wendy K. Smith, and Eero Vaara. 2018. "New Ways of Seeing through Qualitative Research." *Academy of Management Journal* 61, no. 4: 1189–95. https://doi.org/10.5465/amj.2018.4004.

Bartunek, Jean M. 2007. "Academic–Practitioner Collaboration Need Not Require Joint or Relevant Research: Toward a Relational Scholarship of Integration." *Academy of Management Journal* 50, no. 6: 1323–33.

Bartunek, Jean M., and Sara L. Rynes. 2014. "Academics and Practitioners Are Alike and Unlike: The Paradoxes of Academic–Practitioner Relationships." *Journal of Management* 40, no. 5: 1181–1201.

Bavington, Dean. 2010. *Managed Annihilation: An Unnatural History of the Newfoundland Cod Collapse.* Vancouver: University of British Columbia Press.

Berrone, Pascual, Liliana Gelabert, Federica Massa-Saluzzo, and Horacio E. Rousseau. 2016. "Understanding Community Dynamics in the Study of Grand Challenges: How Nonprofits, Institutional Actors, and the Community Fabric Interact to Influence Income Inequality." *Academy of Management Journal* 59, no. 6: 1940–64.

Brenton, Jennifer, and Natalie Slawinski. 2023. "Collaborating for Community Regeneration: Facilitating Partnerships in, through, and for Place." *Journal of Business Ethics* 184, 815–34. https://doi.org/10.1007/s10551-023-05365-5.

Brinklow, Laurie. 2013. "Stepping-stones to the Edge: Artistic Expressions of Islandness in an Ocean of Islands." *Island Studies Journal* 8, no. 1: 39–54.

Chen, Suwen, Garima Sharma, and Pablo Muños. 2022. "In Pursuit of Impact: From Research Questions to Problem Formulation in Entrepreneurship Research." *Entrepreneurship Theory and Practice.* https://doi.org/10.1177/10422587221111736.

Cooperrider, David L., and Suresh Srivastva. 1987. "Appreciative Inquiry in Organizational Life." *Research in Organizational Change and Development* 1, no. 1: 129–69.

Di Domenico, MariaLaura, Helen Haugh, and Paul Tracey. 2010. "Social Bricolage: Theorizing Social Value Creation in Social Enterprises." *Entrepreneurship Theory and Practice* 34, no. 4: 681–703.

Fogo Island Co-operative Society. 2010. "Fogo Island Coop." http://www.fogoislandcoop.com/.

Gibson, Ryan. 2013. "Life beyond Zone Boards: Understanding the New Reality of Regional Development in Newfoundland and Labrador." *Newfoundland Quarterly* 105: 39–42.

Gioia, Denny. 2022. "On the Road to Hell: Why Academia Is Viewed as Irrelevant to Practicing Managers." *Academy of Management Discoveries* 8, no. 2: 174–79. https://doi.org/10.5465/amd.2021.0200.

Hacker, Karen. 2013. *Community-based Participatory Research.* Thousand Oaks, CA: Sage Publications. https://dx.doi.org/10.4135/9781452244181.

Halseth, Greg, Sean Markey, Laura Ryser, and Don Manson. 2016. *Doing Community-based Research: Perspectives from the Field.* Montreal and Kingston: McGill-Queen's University Press.

Hamilton, Lawrence C., and Melissa J. Butler. 2001. "Outport Adaptations: Social Indicators through Newfoundland's Cod Crisis." *Human Ecology Review* 8, no. 2: 1–11.

Hertel, Christina, Sophie Bacq, and Frank-Martin Belz. 2019. "It Takes a Village to Sustain a Village: A Social Identity Perspective on Successful Community-based Enterprise Creation." *Academy of Management Discoveries* 5, no. 4: 438–64.

Higgins, Jenny. 2009. "Cod Moratorium." *Newfoundland and Labrador Heritage.* https://www.heritage.nf.ca/articles/economy/moratorium.php.

Hoffman, Andrew J. 2021. *The Engaged Scholar: Expanding the Impact of Academic Research in Today's World.* Stanford, CA: Stanford Briefs.

Johnstone, Harvey, and Doug Lionais. 2004. "Depleted Communities and Community Business Entrepreneurship: Revaluing Space through Place." *Entrepreneurship and Regional Development* 16, no. 3: 217–33.

Johannisson, Bengt, and Anders Nilsson. 1989. "Community Entrepreneurs: Networking for Local Development." *Entrepreneurship & Regional Development* 1, no. 1: 3–19.

Kim, Suntae, and Anna Kim. 2021. "Going Viral or Growing Like an Oak Tree? Towards Sustainable Local Development through Entrepreneurship." *Academy of Management Journal* 65, no. 5. https://doi.org/10.5465/amj.2018.0041.

Kretzmann, John P., and John L. McKnight. 1993. *Building Communities from the Inside Out: A Path toward Finding and Mobilizing a Community's Assets.* Evanston, IL: Center for Urban Affairs and Policy Research.

Loo, Tina. 2020. "Development's Travelling Rationalities: Contextualizing Newfoundland Resettlement." In *Resettlement: Uprooting and Rebuilding Communities in Newfoundland and Labrador and Beyond*, edited by Isabelle Côté and Yolande Pottie-Sherman, 43–78. St. John's: ISER Books.

Lumpkin, G.T., and Sophie Bacq. 2019. "Civic Wealth Creation: A New View of Stakeholder Engagement and Societal Impact." *Academy of Management Perspectives* 33, no. 4: 383–404.

Lumpkin, G.T., Sophie Bacq, and Robert J. Pidduck. 2018. "Where Change Happens: Community-level Phenomena in Social Entrepreneurship Research." *Journal of Small Business Management* 56, no. 1: 24–50.

Martin, Melanie. 2007. "Resettlement." *Newfoundland and Labrador Heritage.* https://www.heritage.nf.ca/articles/politics/resettlement.php.

Mazutis, Daina, Natalie Slawinski, and Brad Hookey. 2013a. *Social Entrepreneurship on Fogo Island: Searching for New Ways in an Old Continuity (A).* Lausanne: Institute for Management Development.

Mazutis, Daina, Natalie Slawinski, and Brad Hookey. 2013b. *Social Entrepreneurship on Fogo Island: Searching for New Ways in an Old Continuity (B).* Lausanne: Institute for Management Development.

McKeever, Edward, Sarah Jack, and Alistair Anderson. 2015. "Embedded Entrepreneurship in the Creative Reconstruction of Place." *Journal of Business Venturing* 30: 50–65.

Murphy, Matthew, Wade M. Danis, Johnny Mack, and (Kekinusuqs) Judith Sayers. 2020. "From Principles to Action: Community-based Entrepreneurship in the Toquaht Nation." *Journal of Business Venturing* 35, no. 6: 106051. https://doi.org/10.1016/j.jbusvent.2020.106051.

Newhook, Susan. 2009. "The Godfathers of Fogo: Donald Snowden, Fred Earle and the Roots of the Fogo Island Films, 1964–1967." *Newfoundland Studies* 24, no. 2: 171–97.

Rockett, Jennifer, and Doug Ramsey. 2017. "Resident Perceptions of Rural Tourism Development: The Case of Fogo Island and Change Islands, Newfoundland, Canada." *Journal of Tourism and Cultural Change* 15, no. 4: 299–318.

Sharma, Garima, and Pratima Bansal. 2020. "Co-creating Rigorous and Relevant Knowledge." *Academy of Management Journal* 63, no. 2: 386–410.

Shrivastava, Paul, and James J. Kennelly. 2013. "Sustainability and Place-based Enterprise." *Organization & Environment* 26: 83–101.

Shorefast. n.d. Shorefast (website). Accessed July 28, 2023. https://shorefast.org

Slawinski, Natalie, Bruna Brito, Jennifer Brenton, and Wendy K. Smith. 2023. "Rapid Problem Formulating for Societal Impact: Lessons From a Decade-Long Research Practice Partnership." *Journal of Business Venturing Insights* 19. https://doi.org/10.1016/j.jbvi.2023.e00390

Slawinski, Natalie, and Wendy K. Smith. 2019. "Rebuilding Community through Social Innovation: A PLACE Model." *Cambridge Social Innovation Blog.* June 2, 2019. https://socialinnovation.blog.jbs.cam.ac.uk/2019/02/06/rebuilding-community-through-social-innovation-a-place-model/.

Slawinski, Natalie, and Wendy K. Smith. 2020. "Fogo Island Shows How Social Enterprises Can Help Rebuild Communities Post-Coronavirus." *The Conversation.* May 26, 2020. http://theconversation.com/fogo-island-shows-how-social-enterprises-can-help-rebuild-communities-post-coronavirus-138182.

Slawinski, Natalie, Blair Winsor, Daina Mazutis, John W. Schouten, and Wendy K. Smith. 2021. "Managing the Paradoxes of Place to Foster Regeneration." *Organization & Environment* 34, no. 4: 595–618.

Smith, Wendy K., and Marianne W. Lewis. 2022. *Both/and thinking: Embracing creative tensions to solve your toughest problems.* Boston, MA: Harvard Business School Press.

Smith, Wendy K., and Natalie Slawinski. 2020. "What Can the COVID-19 Crisis Teach Us about the Importance of Geographical Communities to Enable Human Connection?" *Responsible Research in Business & Management* (blog). April 16, 2020. https://www.rrbm.network/what-can-the-covid-19-crisis-teach-us-about-the-importance-of-geographical-communities-to-enable-human-connectionwendy-smith-natalie-slawinski/.

Stott, Neil, Michelle Darlington, Jennifer Brenton, and Natalie Slawinski. 2021. "Partnerships and Place: The Role of Community Enterprises in Cross Sector Work." In *Handbook on the Business of Sustainability: The Organization, Implementation, and Practice of Sustainable Growth,* edited by Gerard George, Martine R. Haas, Havovi Joshi, Anita M. McGahan, and Paul Tracey, 117–36. Cheltenham, UK: Edward Elgar.

Tàbara, J. David, Takeshi Takama, Manisha Mishra, Lauren Hermanus, Sean Khaya Andrew, Pacia Diaz, Gina Ziervogel, and Louis Lemkow. 2020. "Micro-Solutions to Global Problems: Understanding Social Processes to Eradicate Energy Poverty and Build Climate-Resilient Livelihoods." *Climatic Change* 160: 711–25.

Tracey, Paul, Nelson W. Phillips, and Helen Haugh. 2005. "Beyond Philanthropy: Community Enterprise as a Basis for Corporate Citizenship." *Journal of Business Ethics* 58, no. 4: 327–44.

Trelstad, Brian, Wendy K. Smith, and Natalie Slawinski. 2020. *Shorefast: A Strange and Familiar Way to Reimagine Capitalism.* Cambridge, MA: Harvard Business School.

CHAPTER 2

Promoting an Inclusive Group of Community Leaders: A Case Study of the Bonne Bay Cottage Hospital Heritage Corporation

Brennan Lowery, Joan Cranston, and Jennifer Charles

Introduction

To help build sustainable and vibrant communities, community-based social enterprises promote, engage, and mobilize diverse community leaders across a wide range of abilities and roles. This first principle of the PLACE Framework reflects the principles of Asset-Based Community Development, which begins with individuals as the most important assets in a community (Kretzmann and McKnight 1993), and seeks to show the value of their efforts, which is often overlooked in mainstream economic development models (Arias Schreiber, Wingren, and Linke 2020). This approach also considers more inclusive ideas of leadership (Selsky and Smith 1994) and entrepreneurship (Welter et al. 2017), highlighting the diverse ways that people can act as leaders in their communities and how entrepreneurs often depend on wide networks of enablers and supporters (Thompson 2010). It also acknowledges that, although local residents should lead the charge in revitalizing their communities, outsiders also can play important roles and even slowly become accepted as insiders (see Chapter 7). Through this inclusive and asset-based approach, community-based enterprises can help transform communities facing long-standing structural barriers (Peredo and

Chrisman 2006) or experiencing recent socio-economic downturns (Haugh and Brady 2019).

One such social enterprise is based at the former Bonne Bay Cottage Hospital (which we will refer to as the Old Cottage Hospital), a multi-functional community innovation hub that operates out of a former cottage hospital in the heart of Norris Point, one of several host communities within Gros Morne National Park, on the Great Northern Peninsula of Newfoundland and Labrador. In a 2001 grassroots movement, local residents fought to keep this unique heritage building from being torn down (Charles 2021). Since then, the Old Cottage Hospital and the social enterprise that runs it — the Bonne Bay Cottage Hospital Heritage Corporation (BBCHHC) — have brought together community members from many walks of life and fostered leaders and change-makers around a shared vision of preserving culture and heritage, and promoting health and wellness and rural community development (BBCHHC n.d.).

This chapter tells the story of the BBCHHC as an example of diverse local leaders working together and promoting a shared vision for rural community renewal. We start by exploring how prior academic research on rural development and entrepreneurship has tended to focus on one heroic leader. We then outline the benefits of a more inclusive view on community change-makers, brokers, and all the other characters who contribute to sustainable rural communities. We use the story of the Old Cottage Hospital to highlight how a variety of community leaders, supporters, and partners have worked together over the past 20 years. We also share models that reflect the roles various people play in successful rural development and propose that anyone in these roles can act as a leader, based on the qualities, passion, and vision they bring to the table. Finally, we offer reflections for future research on rural community development and community entrepreneurship, lessons learned for the PLACE Framework, and guidance for rural community leaders and policy-makers seeking to truly promote, support, and sustain the people who build social enterprises.

About the Authors

This chapter represents a process of co-creation between academic researchers and community leaders working in rural Newfoundland. Joan Cranston is a physiotherapist and serves as the coordinator for the Bonne Bay Cottage Hospital Heritage Corporation, as described further below. Brennan Lowery is a community-engaged researcher based at Grenfell Campus of Memorial University, who has worked with Cranston on a number of community-based initiatives, including a conference in 2019 held at the Old Cottage Hospital called the New Rural Story Forum and a co-authored publication based on his PhD research focusing on sustainability narratives on the Great Northern Peninsula, to which Cranston contributed significantly (Lowery et al. 2021). Jennifer Charles is a social entrepreneur based on Fogo Island and a research assistant with Memorial University's Faculty of Business Administration. In these roles, she and Cranston collaborated on a case study on the BBCHHC for Memorial University's Centre for Social Enterprise in support of students and practitioners seeking a model of resilient place-based social enterprise in rural Newfoundland and Labrador. Lowery contributed to this chapter by drafting several sections of the manuscript, helping to coordinate authors' contributions, and overseeing revisions based on editorial team and peer reviewer comments. Cranston and Charles co-authored the section outlining the story of the Old Cottage Hospital, and each authored different sections of the chapter and contributed to the revision process.

A More Inclusive Vision of Community Leadership

Engaging a Wider Group of Community Leaders and Entrepreneurs

Academic research on rural community development, community engagement, and social enterprise has a tendency to focus on a predictable roster of local leaders. Engagement efforts undertaken by researchers from external institutions often seek visible and vocal community leaders, but if they are not informed by a deep knowledge of local dynamics, their efforts may merely reinforce local elites and exacerbate inequalities within communities (Shaw 2006), while maintaining power imbalances between communities and institutions such as the government and the university (Post and Ruelle 2021). Despite the best efforts of engagement practitioners to include a diverse set of local actors, stakeholder-based engagement strategies often define participants by the sectors or organizations they represent and fail to engage participants beyond the small group of individuals in official positions of authority (Reed et al. 2009). In contrast to this narrow focus, a more nuanced understanding of leadership seeks to engage those who play the essential role of bridging between community members with different world views and priorities (Selsky and Smith 1994), who in many cases do not occupy formal leadership roles in local government, non-profits, or businesses. In rural communities, these boundary spanners often are the links between locals and external groups and institutions (Steiner, Farmer, and Bosworth 2020; also Chapter 3). In other words, they are community brokers whose connecting and spanning work often goes unrecognized.

Similarly, entrepreneurship research and popular media tend to focus on a small number of heroic entrepreneurs—particularly in high-tech and high-growth industries—who receive inordinate amounts of attention and study. This focus creates a narrow picture of entrepreneurship that often excludes the experiences of entrepreneurial actors like women entrepreneurs, entrepreneurs in the Global South, and Indigenous entrepreneurs (Murphy et al. 2020; Welter et al. 2017). In contrast, researchers have increasingly recognized that entrepreneurship frequently is a collaborative process that is the result of not one innovative individual acting alone, but many entrepreneurship enablers who provide invaluable but unrecognized supports (Thompson 2010; Timmons and Spinelli 2009). These unsung heroes may work in business development agencies, colleges and universities, financial institutions, or start-up incubators, or they may assist entrepreneurs through informal channels like friend and family networks.

Finally, researchers have begun to take note that entrepreneurial action can happen not only at the level of an innovative person or orga-nization, but in entire communities (Borch and Ensign 2016). A small but growing research area on community entrepreneurship has high-lighted it as an important site of entrepreneurial action (Lumpkin, Bacq, and Pidduck 2018) in which community members come together to ad-dress a common concern and create social enterprises operated and governed by local actors (Haugh and Brady 2019). Community entre-preneurs often think of value creation in a more holistic way than con-ventional entrepreneurs, seeking not only to generate private profit, but also to contribute to multiple forms of capital that create benefits for the entire community or region (Adhikari et al. 2018). These can include human capital, such as training and skills development; natural capital, such as using the community's natural assets and protecting the local environment; and cultural capital, such as preserving a heritage build-ing. This community-based social entrepreneurial action is distinct from many social enterprises which may aim to benefit a specific com-munity or region, but do not necessarily engage the people they seek to benefit directly in the governance of the enterprise (Lumpkin and Bacq 2019). Through this mission of holistic value creation and community-driven governance, community entrepreneurship can even spark a spiralling-up process to reverse socio-economic and ecological decline in communities affected by de-industrialization or environmental crises (Gutiérrez-Montes 2005; Winkler et al. 2016). In this spiralling-up pro-cess, community members identify different assets across multiple forms of community capital and strategically invest in one or two assets that can trigger a positive feedback loop of renewal. For example, in a rural county in Nebraska facing population decline and business closures, local leaders invested in youth leadership and wealth transfer from family businesses to spark a transformational process of economic, cul-tural, and social revitalization (Emery and Flora 2006). This holistic idea of value creation inherently calls for the engagement of a more inclusive network of entrepreneurial actors from across the community and beyond.

A New Language to Talk about Community Leaders

Language matters. How we speak about and define community leaders can either foster a more inclusive environment or create barriers and stifle development. Community leaders provide the passion, vision, and energy to spark social movements, create change, and contribute to the spiralling up of communities. Their success hinges on many factors. For example, they must remain present and committed to the community, rather than just riding into town, starting something, then leaving again. They also need to engage and empower a wide network of community brokers and entrepreneurial enablers in their local community. This important role underlines how everyone, regardless of formal education and community status, can contribute to building and sustaining communities. We need to look beyond the usual definitions of leadership and recognize the unsung heroes within local entrepreneurial networks who lead behind the scenes.

In this chapter, we use new language to acknowledge the varied local actors who operate in entrepreneurial networks to ignite community development. We borrow from academic and popular sources to describe this more inclusive cast of characters, identifying the skills and qualities that those individuals bring to their leadership roles, including their ability to create communities around them and nourish other leaders who will follow them.

As described in Malcolm Gladwell's *The Tipping Point*, social shifts are instigated by three categories of people: Connectors, Mavens, and Salespeople. These are the community brokers who provide local leaders with the connections and promotion required for a place-based initiative to succeed. Connectors are people who know many other people from many walks of life. They "are extraordinarily powerful. We rely on them to give us access to opportunities and worlds to which we don't belong" (Gladwell 2002, 54). Connectors span boundaries between in-groups and external actors who may have beneficial resources or connections — which corresponds to the PLACE Framework's principle of *linking divergent perspectives*, an essential competency for rural social enterprises that often rely on different resources and supports from local and external partners (Korsgaard, Ferguson, and Gaddefors 2015).

Mavens are equally important in spreading social change: "The word *Maven* comes from the Yiddish and it means one who accumulates knowledge" (Gladwell 2002, 60). Communities and social enterprises require up-to-date and accurate information to function effectively; therefore "the people with the most information must be the most important" (Gladwell 2002, 60). From a perspective of inclusive community development, Mavens can possess many kinds of knowledge, including both formal and informal learning, meaningful stories of the community's struggles and successes (Hammond 2013), and tacit knowledge about local industries that was gained not through formal training but through regular interaction with local firms (Holmen and Fosse 2017).

A third group of people who are critical to tipping social shifts are Salespeople — the people with "the skills to persuade us when we are unconvinced of what we are hearing" (Gladwell 2002, 70). Persuading community members of the value of a local development initiative requires Salespeople to be effective storytellers, enacting the PLACE Framework's principle of *conveying compelling stories* by invoking common stories and motivating others to take action (van Hulst 2012).

When these three kinds of leaders work together, communities can grow in a more inclusive manner. Instead of growing like a Christmas tree — in which the community leader sits like the star above the lower branches — the community grows like an orchard, with multiple leaders who operate at the same level. Orchard trees, such as apple trees, have strong, deep tap roots and lateral fibrous roots that can extend to more than twice the spread of the tree's canopy. Each tree in the orchard represents an enterprise that bears a unique kind of fruit: some produce the high-yield crops of traditional private enterprise, while others grow slowly and deeply to nurture community initiatives with little financial return but other valuable staples like cultural heritage or social inclusion (Lumpkin et al. 2018). To be successful, regardless of form or industry, place-based enterprises must be knowledgeable of and respectful of the past.

Each enterprise must be rooted in the soil of the community's place-based identity (Shrivastava and Kennelly 2013) and be able to absorb such nutrients as the stories of previous successes and failures in the community (Sandercock 2005). The community brokers exist in the branches — the Connectors, Mavens, and Salespeople outlined above. This group can also include researchers, policy-makers, financial supporters, government agencies, and philanthropists. The fruits of this labour represent the benefits of entrepreneurial activity that creates holistic value in communities (Lumpkin and Bacq 2019). This fruit is a renewable resource that nourishes the initiative and gives the entire entrepreneurial network the energy to continue, while also containing the seeds that create new growth. Properly nourished and tended, these seeds can become future leaders of new projects, thus ensuring the sustainability of the orchard.

In the language of spiralling-up, community leaders in each of these diverse roles represent distinct assets of knowledge and capabilities that, when brought together, can spark community transformation (Emery and Flora 2006). Thus, effective community leaders can be transformational assets by using their intimate knowledge of the capabilities of these diverse individuals to bring them together around a common vision for renewal and community resilience.

Visions of Leadership in Rural Newfoundland and Labrador

This inclusive focus on entrepreneurial leadership is highly relevant for community development efforts in rural Newfoundland and Labrador (NL). Due to colonial legacies and top-down governance structures, popular political discourse in NL often focuses on traditional leaders, who are credited with major policies or accomplishments (Vodden 2010). At the provincial level, this approach idealizes political strongmen like Joey Smallwood and Danny Williams, the latter remembered for having a big personality and championing big projects (Deshaye 2017; House 2021). In rural regions, heroes who come into a community with a mission to improve local conditions tend to be venerated. For example, William Ford Coaker and Wilfred Grenfell are celebrated for their labour organizing and medical work, and their stories are major components of tourism interpretation on the Bonavista Peninsula and the Great Northern Peninsula (GNP), respectively (Coaker Foundation 2006; Wood and Lam 2019). On the GNP in particular, stories are told of external heroes parachuting into communities to solve their problems, perpetuating a sense of external dependence. Combined with the memory of failed economic development projects in forestry and other sectors, this narrative reduces the agency of local actors to improve community well-being (Lowery et al. 2021).

The perpetuation of top-down, Christmas-tree leadership, in which the monolithic leader from outside the region shines brightly but leaves little room for other stars to find places among the branches, runs counter to the inclusive and grassroots vision of community leadership outlined above. In NL and elsewhere, community development efforts must be driven primarily by local residents who acknowledge the diverse ways they can take leadership. Although external partners and resources are undoubtedly important for rural communities to thrive (see Chapter 3), particularly when resistance to change and vested interests within the community are strong, the impetus for change must start from local residents, who then can mobilize a variety of local and external partners.

Many examples of such community-driven action across the province demonstrate the "orchard style" of leadership. For example, the Clarenville Farm and Market was created by local farmers and food processors to create a community hub for selling agricultural products. Livyer's Lot Économusée in Boat Harbour was created by the Placentia West Development Association (Chapter 4) to feature local craftspeople's work. The French Shore Tapestry in Conche was created by local embroiderers learning from artists in France but employing their own skills to tell the stories of their communities. These and other community-based enterprises rely on a diverse cast of characters, including Connectors, Mavens, and Salespeople, to sustain their initiatives and connect them to necessary resources. The BBCHHC at the Old Cottage Hospital is an especially compelling story of inclusive and community-driven leadership that we share in the next section to highlight how this inclusive view of community leaders contributes to a more sustainable way of growing communities and promoting local leaders.

The Story of the Old Cottage Hospital

The Bonne Bay Cottage Hospital Heritage Corporation (BBCHHC) began as a dream to save the Old Cottage Hospital in Norris Point, NL from being torn down once the hospital closed. The heritage building had been the anchor of health and wellness along the GNP for over 60 years. In anticipation of the building's 2001 closure, Joan Cranston, a physiotherapist working at the hospital, and a team of community leaders formed the BBCHHC to take on the challenge of preserving and repurposing the Old Cottage Hospital. For the past 20 years, the BBCHHC has been committed to "the adaptive re-use of the former Bonne Bay Cottage Hospital for the preservation of local culture and heritage (including arts, crafts, music and oral history); the promotion of health and wellness; and community

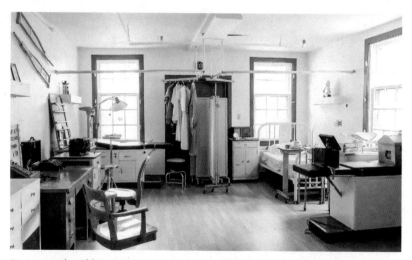

Figure 2.1. The Old Cottage Hospital is an example of a social enterprise providing tangible services for the community while preserving local culture and heritage. (Photo credit: Joan Cranston, 2022)

economic and social development" (BBCHHC n.d.). Today, the BBCHHC has become a social enterprise hub hosting a diverse array of tenants and programs including the Old Cottage Hostel; a community kitchen, gardens, and greenhouse; the Voice of Bonne Bay community radio station; the Cottage Hospital Museum Room; the Norris Point Public Library; and numerous health services and other small business tenants.

The road to resilience, however, has not been smooth. For the past two decades, the BBCHHC has struggled with infrastructure upkeep, shoestring budgets, and periods of wavering local support. However, by engaging and supporting a wide network of government, industry, academic, and community-based partners, and a tireless team of dedicated volunteers, the BBCHHC has illustrated the importance of supporting all partners and members of the team. That team has continued to persevere in their pursuit of community resilience and sustainable social enterprise in rural Newfoundland.

The BBCHHC's story can be told through the five principles of the PLACE Framework: *promoting community leaders, linking divergent perspectives, amplifying local capacities and assets, conveying compelling stories,* and *engaging both/and thinking.* Through this Framework, we can explore lessons that may assist other rural communities looking to create a better future for themselves. In this chapter, we focus on *promoting community leaders,* but we will also expand on the scope of the "P" in the PLACE acronym. From a community perspective, "P" also includes all the passionate people and partners who make up a diverse and inclusive entrepreneurial network that contributes to building and sustaining their community.

The Bonne Bay Cottage Hospital opened in July 1940. It was part of a network of cottage hospitals in Newfoundland that opened between 1936 and 1954, bringing consistent health-care services to many isolated areas for the first time. From 1939 to 1940, the people of Norris Point and surrounding areas pulled together to build the Cottage Hospital. With the government supplying only a foreman and nails, the local community contributed the land, 10,000 hours of volunteer labour, 90,000 feet of lumber, and $12,000 in cash. At its opening, the facility boasted

23 beds, a dental clinic, a nursery, and a staff of 10 medical professionals. By the time of its closure in 2001, the Cottage Hospital was one of the largest and longest-serving hospital facilities of its type and time in the province. Beyond its medical significance in the area, the Cottage Hospital was celebrated by staff and patients alike for its warm, supportive culture and home-like atmosphere.

By the early 1990s, the Newfoundland and Labrador government had set its sights on a regionalized health-care system, and cottage hospitals across the province quickly fell out of favour. Word soon came that the Bonne Bay Cottage Hospital would close. The doctors, nurses, staff, and local residents were devastated. The community banded together and lobbied the provincial government to keep health-care services in Norris Point. The government committed to building a new regionalized health-care facility in the community, but the decision to close the Bonne Bay Cottage Hospital stood.

A group of six local leaders was passionate about saving the structure and building on its legacy. Joan Cranston, her husband Gary Wilton, local dentist Marina Sexton, Colleen Kennedy with the Gros Morne Cooperating Association, speech-language pathologist Sheila Walsh, and Michaela J. Kent with Parks Canada all met around a kitchen table and began forging a plan to create a new future for the Old Cottage Hospital. Some members of the group were originally from the region, while others had moved to the area over the years, but all shared a deep connection to the Bonne Bay Cottage Hospital — an example of *linking divergent perspectives*. "It's often the people that aren't from here that see the potential," Cranston noted at the time. The BBCHHC was formed as a not-for-profit community corporation in September 2001, and the Old Cottage Hospital closed its doors for the first time in over 60 years that December.

With funding assistance, the team hired consultant David Simms of the Great Northern Peninsula Development Corporation (GNPDC), who had been embedded on the GNP, where he didn't just ride into town on a white horse but worked on place-based development for many years. Some of the initiatives that he developed still exist today, such as the

Daniel's Harbour Hatchery and GNP Crafts. Simms led the BBCHHC's board in an opportunity identification process and explored uses for the Cottage Hospital building that would both honour the past and serve the present needs of the region, *engaging both/and thinking*. A vision emerged: to transform the Old Cottage Hospital into a multi-functional community space to address current community demands, such as additional health services and a home for the public library, and to create new opportunities for the community, including an international hostel. With their long-term vision in mind, the BBCHHC adopted a gradual, "as is, where is" scope and timeline, reflecting the pragmatic approach taken to using the building in the state it was in at the time of acquisition and gradually making repairs as funds became available. They started small and built slowly, generating revenue streams for future growth.

The "as is, where is" approach enabled the BBCHHC to examine the space in creative ways. The first opportunity was converting the old medical records area into a new home for the Norris Point Public Library. Next, the former male ward was designated as a museum space to display the collection of medical equipment that remained from the hospital's early days. Patient rooms were repurposed as affordable office and clinic spaces for local organizations and health providers. The BBCHHC transformed the Bonne Bay Cottage Hospital's former staff residence area into the Old Cottage Hostel, a revenue-generating enterprise that contributed to the building's upkeep and enabled ongoing development. The hostel created valuable linkages between insiders and outsiders, *linking divergent perspectives*, while sometimes uncovering brokers and supporters in unlikely places, *promoting community leaders*. The feeling among the team was that everything was coming full circle.

In 2007, with the launch of Trails Tales Tunes, a 10-day festival of music, storytelling, and activities in Norris Point, board member Gary Wilton was inspired to create a temporary, community-based radio station to accompany the festival activities. The BBCHHC team supported his initiative, and the Voice of Bonne Bay (VOBB) community radio station was born, *promoting community leaders*. In addition to broadcasting the activities of the festival, VOBB interviewed community members to discuss current events and invited local seniors to share stories from the past. In this way, the VOBB became a Connector, spanning the boundaries between different local groups and amplifying the voices of community members whose knowledge and opinions might not otherwise have been heard, thereby *promoting community leaders*. As an Internet-based station as well as an FM broadcaster, VOBB also linked the community with the outside world, becoming a valuable tool for linking insiders and outsiders. It was a turning point for the BBCHHC. As the community gathered in the VOBB studio or tuned in to the station from home, they heard their own stories reflected in the voices of their neighbours, *conveying compelling stories*. The community realized that the transformation of the Old Cottage Hospital into a community-based social enterprise was indeed about them and for them.

The BBCHHC continued to access grants to help underemployed locals find careers and enter the workforce. The caretaker, Bob, found joy in exchanging stories with hostel visitors from all over the world and gained a renewed passion for the building, becoming an enthusiastic Maven for the overall project, *promoting community leaders*. By 2020, the BBCHHC supported a group of local parents working to establish another revenue-generating venture, the community's first daycare, truly contributing to the future of the community and growing the next generation of community builders and leaders, *promoting community leaders*. At the time of writing, the BBCHHC is also working to incubate community development initiatives in other parts of the region, working closely with a group in Port au Choix that is renovating a historic building into a community health and wellness centre called the GNP Community Place, organizing a grassroots research collective of community and academic researchers in identifying community-based research opportunities, and facilitating a health collective of health-care practitioners across the peninsula. All of these diverse partners in academia, health care, and other fields act as Salespeople by communicating the vision of the Old Cottage Hospital and related initiatives to their wide networks (*conveying compelling narratives*).

Cranston has sometimes wondered whether taking so long to grow has been a sign of the BBCHHC's failure. Ultimately, the BBCHHC's slow, organic, "as is, where is" approach and patient willingness to engage and support a broad network of entrepreneurial enablers has allowed the team to form critical partnerships, respond to the needs of the people, and fully transform an old heritage building into a self-sustaining hub for community resilience and social enterprise on the GNP.

Lessons Learned

The story of the Bonne Bay Cottage Hospital is exemplary for making the most of what and who is on the ground and leveraging those assets to spark community renewal. There are no grand heroes or legendary feats, only the persistent dedication of community members who had a vision for repurposing a cherished local asset and who patiently worked together to make that vision a reality. Although Joan Cranston and the group who formed the original BBCHHC board to save the hospital could easily be seen as the leaders perched at the top of the tree, they would be the first to say that they are just a few of many leaders who have stepped forward over the years to make the Old Cottage Hospital a thriving community-based enterprise that also nurtures a diverse orchard of leaders. We offer some brief lessons for community development practitioners and policy-makers, contributions to academic research on entrepreneurship and rural development, and guiding thoughts for a deeper understanding and application of the PLACE Framework.

Practical Lessons for Community Leaders and Entrepreneurs in Rural NL

The prolific glorification of the traditional entrepreneur can put a lot of pressure on a budding leader with a new idea. Questions like "Where to start?", "How to start?", and "What if I fail?" can paralyze a good idea before it ever has a chance to grow. These tensions escalate in rural settings where relationships are close, anonymity is absent, and the risk that business failure brings to one's personal reputation in the community is high.

As such, the foundational message of this chapter may come as a relief to community leaders throughout rural NL: "You don't have to do things alone. In fact, you shouldn't."

Community enterprise research and the story of the Old Cottage Hospital can provide new and existing community leaders with the motivation to reach out to other potential leaders in their community, share their ideas, and ask those individuals for assistance with specific tasks, such as connecting with industry experts, spreading the word about their venture, tapping into place-based values, growing the business, and discovering young leaders to carry ventures into the future. The Old Cottage Hospital example of community leadership also provides entrepreneurs with a local example of starting and growing a business in rural NL. Instead of the prominent high-growth, fast-reward stories of sole entrepreneurs in Silicon Valley, the Old Cottage Hospital is the story of a dedicated team who slowly grew a small business over 20 years with the help of a wide network, changing, learning, and evolving as they went.

Perhaps the challenge for local entrepreneurs may be that of looking at their own communities and networks with fresh eyes and seeing the valuable roles their friends, neighbours, and colleagues actually could play. The Old Cottage Hospital story encourages us to take a big-picture view of the people who are actively building community, to encourage the people already involved to have a voice, and to form the linkages necessary to make new community-based business opportunities happen.

Lessons for Policy-makers

Community leaders and the entrepreneurial networks that support them contribute their experience, skills, passion, energy, creativity, and thousands of hours of their time to making their communities better places to live. In order to acknowledge this valuable service, policy-makers need to find creative ways to recognize and support these efforts. Support can come in many forms, including, but not limited to, monetary support. Policy-makers should strive to ensure that the support achieves its intended effects and that it is equitable and rewards all who contribute, not only the leaders at the top.

Policy-makers need to recognize that one of the main barriers that community leaders face is funding programs that do not meet their needs. Programs often are designed to meet bureaucratic outcomes but stifle the community development they are supposed to enhance and support. Instead, policy-makers should work with community leaders to ensure that their programs suit community needs.

Policy-makers need to recognize that the administrative overburden of many funding programs drains the passion and energy of community leaders and their networks. Those who are immersed in community development work recognize that proper project administration is a vital element of success. However, unnecessary paperwork is a deterrent that can drain the passion and energy of community leaders and contribute to burnout.

Lessons Learned for Academic Research

In regard to increasing calls for more inclusive approaches to entrepreneurship (Murphy et al. 2020; Welter et al. 2017), the story of the Old Cottage Hospital highlights entrepreneurial action taking many forms that go beyond traditional notions of private venture creation. The efforts of the original founders of the Old Cottage Hospital, as well as the many other leaders who have developed initiatives like VOBB radio station, demonstrate that community-based entrepreneurship not only creates new businesses, but bears a wide array of fruit that is shared widely among community members. This inclusive idea of value creation reinforces growing conceptions of entrepreneurship as a vehicle for creating shared wealth to positively impact many forms of community capital (Lumpkin and Bacq 2019). The key role of the BBCHHC Board, which is comprised entirely of local residents and is accountable to the rest of the community, underlines the importance of governance that ensures local ownership and distribution of benefits in community-based enterprises (Murphy et al. 2020; Peredo and Chrisman 2006).

The story of the Old Cottage Hospital also demonstrates the need for a more inclusive language for talking about leadership in rural community development. Considering the tendency for researchers to employ stakeholder analysis tools that narrow the field of relevant stakeholders to a small group of formal leaders (Reed et al. 2009), there is a great need for more embedded and inclusive approaches to understanding leadership in communities. This need is especially pressing in community engagement processes that can reinforce local elites and maintain inequitable power relations between communities and such external institutions as universities (Post and Ruelle 2021). The journey of advocacy, lobbying, and community engagement that led to the salvage of the Old Cottage Hospital and the creation of the BBCHHC features a diverse cast of characters who embody the many facets of leadership. Over the lifetime of the BBCHHC, some leaders have acted as Connectors, bridging between local residents and external partners in creating VOBB radio; others have acted as Mavens by retaining community knowledge about the oral history of the building and collecting it from elders in the community; still others have been engaged as Salespeople, pitching the vision of the Old Cottage Hospital to policy-makers, academics, and other actors with potentially valuable resources and connections.

Overarching these leadership styles is a sense of egalitarianism. For example, a short stay at the Old Cottage Hostel will reveal that the janitor is given as much respect as the visiting scholar. Each tree in the orchard is nurtured according to its particular needs and the unique fruits that it bears. A strong emphasis on boundary-spanning is employed by leaders across the Old Cottage Hospital's initiatives as a vital strategy for connecting local priorities to resources both internal and external (Selsky and Smith 1994; Steiner, Farmer, and Bosworth 2020). In the search for more inclusive language to talk about community leadership and to frame how to engage community members, the story of the Old Cottage Hospital provides a context with a helpful vocabulary providing insights into the many ways in which community members can lead.

Finally, this chapter builds on research about spiralling-up and resilience in communities affected by socio-economic shocks. The Old Cottage Hospital story contributes new insights about the transformational potential of inclusive leaders. Researchers on sustainable community development have long been interested in the connections between different assets and forms of community capital, particularly the potential for certain assets to trigger a synergistic shift that leads to lasting, long-term community transformation (Gutiérrez-Montes 2005; Stone and Nyaupane 2018). In rural communities struck by external shocks like de-industrialization or population decline, many case studies have shown how a transformational asset like youth leadership skills or built heritage can hold the key to turning around a community's fortunes (e.g., Emery and Flora 2006; Winkler et al. 2016). This chapter demonstrates that community leaders themselves can act as transformational assets. When the decision was made to shut down the Bonne Bay Cottage Hospital, Norris Point was dealt a multi-faceted blow — to its cultural identity, health-care services, built capital, and employment — enough to trigger a deep downward spiral in a small community. However, residents mobilized their passion and persuasiveness not only to convince the government to locate the new hospital in Norris Point, but also to form a community enterprise dedicated to repurposing the old hospital building. Although the creative reuse of heritage buildings can be a powerful asset for community renewal (Kepczynska-Walczak and Walczak 2013), the account offered here shows that community leaders themselves also represent a transformational asset in grassroots movements to repurpose and revitalize beloved community spaces.

Lessons for the PLACE Framework

Through the place-based research presented here with the story of the Old Cottage Hospital, the PLACE Framework's initial principle to *promote community leaders* has been expanded. Specifically addressed are the *community leaders*, who need support so that rural businesses can thrive and communities can become effective in resisting socio-economic and ecological decline. While recognizing and honouring traditional community leaders is important, we argue that entrepreneurial success requires the input of a broader network of people who often are not recognized for the

leadership they provide. In their own ways, these members of the entrepreneurial network also are community leaders, and thus they should be
acknowledged, promoted, and celebrated alongside traditional leaders.
While it takes a concerted effort on the part of leaders and policy-makers
to seek out, engage, and appropriately nurture these additional individuals, the outcome is well worth the cost, effort, and time. The PLACE
Framework illustrates that by promoting community leaders, entrepreneurial individuals gain greater strength and motivation to create and
contribute to their community. In this chapter, we emphasize that the
more people we can promote, the more willing those individuals are to
contribute to community renewal initiatives and to be engaged in the
overall resilience and sustainability of their communities.

Further, we offer some guiding thoughts on how the first principle
of the PLACE Framework, *promoting community leaders*, can expand our
understanding of the other four principles. The Old Cottage Hospital
story deepens our perspective on the second principle, *linking divergent
perspectives*, in that many of the leaders engaged in the organization also
act as links between insider and outsider groups or between different stakeholder groups within Norris Point. As Chapter 3 describes, community-
based enterprises often build bridges between local and external actors.
For example, VOBB Radio, located within the Old Cottage Hospital, was
born from a collaborative effort between members of the BBCHHC
Board, a university professor at Grenfell Campus of Memorial University,
and rural community advocates from outside the community. The Old
Cottage Hospital enriches our understanding of the "A" in the PLACE
Framework, *amplifying local assets*, in that the many leaders engaged in
the initiative and its varied programming also showcase the rich human assets of community members. Furthermore, the Old Cottage Hospital leaders form a diverse entrepreneurial network that helps to *convey
compelling stories* about the hospital and its role in the renewal and resilience of Norris Point. Finally, the Old Cottage Hospital illustrates the
importance of the "E" in PLACE, *engage both/and thinking*, by acknowledging that community development sometimes requires a spark to

ignite it — a person or event to initiate the spiralling-up process — but many more people and skill sets are necessary to grow and sustain an initiative. Thus, the story of the Old Cottage Hospital helps to show that community leadership is not an either/or scenario dependent on a few traditional leaders, but rather a both/and concept in which many can lead in different capacities.

Conclusion

As the story of the BBCHHC demonstrates, the PLACE Framework is a useful tool for understanding the process of community enterprise development. The first principle of PLACE, *promoting community leaders*, is versatile, descriptive, and reflects the importance of people who are passionate about their place and the partners that they engage in their efforts. The broad and inclusive account of community leadership given here can guide our perceptions of who these people are, help us to redefine traditional views on leadership, and aid us in recognizing, respecting, and valuing the work of everyone who contributes to building a stronger, more resilient community. While acknowledging the benefits of involving a wide range of community members is key, the challenge of engaging, motivating, and managing such a large and varied group cannot be understated. Success hinges on community leaders' ability to engage all five elements of the PLACE Framework. It depends on the leaders' propensity to build an inclusive community around an idea or an action (*promote community leaders*), bring others into this inclusive vision (*link divergent perspectives*), recognize the valuable human assets a community has to offer (*amplify local capacities*), inspire others with the story of their vision (*convey compelling stories*), and recognize leadership in all its forms while nurturing the upcoming leaders of tomorrow (*engage both/and thinking*). All forms of leaders — traditional leaders, Connectors, Mavens, Salespeople, and future leaders — are essential to the sustainability of the whole organism, the success of the initiative, and ultimately the long-term resilience of a community.

Acknowledgements

The authors would like to recognize the Bonne Bay Cottage Hospital Heritage Corporation Board, whose members shared their time and expertise to advise on the development of this chapter. We also thank Gary Noel, who shared insights on Voice of Bonne Bay Radio, and Rachel Atkins for providing context on the GNP Community Place. Finally, we acknowledge the Centre for Social Enterprise at Memorial University for supporting the chapter's development.

References

Adhikari, Rajendra P., Laurie Bonneya, Megan Woods, Sophie Clark, Lea Coates, Andrew Harwood, Robyn Eversole, and Morgan P. Miles. 2018. "Applying a Community Entrepreneurship Development (CED) Framework." *Small Enterprise Research* 25, no. 3: 257–75. https://doi.org/10.1080/1 3215906.2018.1522274.

Arias Schreiber, Milena, Ida Wingren, and Sebastian Linke. 2020. "Swimming Upstream: Community Economies for a Different Coastal Rural Development in Sweden." *Sustainability Science* 15, no. 1: 63–73. https://doi. org/10.1007/s11625-019-00770-0.

Bonne Bay Cottage Hospital Heritage Corporation (BBCHHC). n.d. "About Us." Old Cottage Hospital (website). Accessed April 5, 2022. https://oldcottage-hospital.com/about/.

Charles, Jennifer. 2021. *The Bonne Bay Cottage Hospital Heritage Corporation's Approach to Community Resilience in Norris Point: A PLACE Framework.* St. John's: Memorial University Centre for Social Enterprise. https://www. mun.ca/social-enterprise/about/what-is-se/place-framework/related-re-search.php.

Coaker Foundation (Sir William Ford Coaker Heritage Foundation). 2006. "Sir William Ford Coaker Heritage Foundation." Historic Port Union (website). https://www.historicportunion.ca/en/foundation.html.

Deshaye, Joel. 2017. "The Hero's Energy in Newfoundland and Labrador." In *The Democracy Cookbook: Recipes to Renew Governance in Newfoundland and Labrador,* edited by Alex Marland and Lisa Moore, 113–16. St. John's: ISER Books.

Emery, Mary, and Cornelia Flora. 2006. "Spiraling-Up: Mapping Community Transformation with Community Capitals Framework." *Community Development* 37, no. 1: 19–35. https://doi.org/10.1080/15575330609490152.

Ensign, Prescott C., and Odd Jarl Borch. 2005. "Entrepreneurship and Innovation at the Edge: Creating Inducements for People and Place." In *Settlements at the Edge: Remote Human Settlements in Developed Nations*, edited by Andrew Taylor, Dean B. Carson, Prescott C. Ensign, Lee Huskey, Rasmus O. Rasmussen, and Gertrude Saxinger, 379–404. Chelthenham, UK: Edward Elgar.

Gladwell, Malcolm. 2002. *The Tipping Point: How Little Things Can Make a Big Difference*. New York: Back Bay Books.

Gutiérrez-Montes, Isabel. 2005. "Healthy Communities Equal Healthy Ecosystems? Evolution (and Breakdown) of a Participatory Ecological Research Project towards a Community Natural Resource Management Process, San Miguel Chimalapa (Mexico)." PhD diss., Iowa State University. Retrospective Theses and Dissertations. https://doi.org/10.31274/rtd-180813-15377.

Hammond, Sue Annis. 2013. *The Thin Book of Appreciative Inquiry*, 3rd ed. Bend, OR: Thin Book Publishing Company.

Haugh, Helen, and Andrew Brady. 2019. "Community Perspectives on Social Entrepreneurship." In *A Research Agenda for Social Entrepreneurship*, edited by Anne de Bruin and Simon Teasdale, 67–81. Cheltenham, UK: Edward Elgar.

Holmen, Ann Karin T., and Jens Kristian Fosse. 2017. "Regional Agency and Constitution of New Paths: A Study of Agency in Early Formation of New Paths on the West Coast of Norway." *European Planning Studies* 25, no. 3: 498–515. https://doi.org/10.1080/09654313.2016.1276159.

House, Douglas. 2021. "The Danny Williams Government, 2003–2010: 'Masters in Our Own House?'" *Newfoundland and Labrador Studies* 36, no. 1: 1719–26.

Kepczynska-Walczak, Anetta, and Bartosz M. Walczak. 2013. "Visualising 'Genius Loci' of Built Heritage." In *Envisioning Architecture: Design, Evaluation, Communication: EAEA-11 Conference 2013, Politecnico di Milano*, edited by Eugenio Morello and Barbara E.A. Piga, 23–28. Rome: Nuova Cultura.

Korsgaard, Steffen, Richard Ferguson, and Johan Gaddefors. 2015. "The Best of Both Worlds: How Rural Entrepreneurs Use Placial Embeddedness and

Strategic Networks to Create Opportunities." *Entrepreneurship & Regional Development* 27, nos. 9–10: 574–98. https://doi.org/10.1080/08985626.2015.1085100.

Kretzmann, John P., and John L. McKnight. 1993. *Building Communities from the Inside Out: A Path toward Finding and Mobilizing a Community's Assets.* Evanston, IL: Center for Urban Affairs and Policy Research.

Lowery, Brennan, Joan Cranston, Carolyn Lavers, Richard May, Renee Pilgrim, and Joan Simmonds. 2021. "Harnessing the Power of Stories for Rural Sustainability: Reflections on Community-Based Research on the Great Northern Peninsula of Newfoundland." *Gateways: International Journal of Community Research and Engagement* 14, no. 2: 1–22. https://doi.org/10.5130/ijcre.v14i2.7766.

Lumpkin, G.T., and Sophie Bacq. 2019. "Civic Wealth Creation: A New View of Stakeholder Engagement and Societal Impact." *Academy of Management Perspectives* 33, no. 4: 383–404. https://doi.org/10.5465/amp.2017.0060.

Lumpkin, G.T., Sophie Bacq, and Robert J. Pidduck. 2018. "Where Change Happens: Community-Level Phenomena in Social Entrepreneurship Research." *Journal of Small Business Management* 56, no. 1: 24–50.

Murphy, Matthew, Wade M. Danis, Johnny Mack, and (Kekinusuqs) Judith Sayers. 2020. "From Principles to Action: Community-Based Entrepreneurship in the Toquaht Nation." *Journal of Business Venturing* 35, no. 6.

Peredo, Ana-María, and James J. Chrisman. 2006. "Toward a Theory of Community-Based Enterprise." *Academy of Management Review* 31, no. 2: 309–28. https://doi.org/10.5465/amr.2006.20208683.

Post, Margaret A., and Morgan L. Ruelle. 2021. "Power in Engaged Scholarship: Dimensions and Dynamics of Knowledge Co-Creation." *Gateways* 14, no. 2: 1–9. https://doi.org/http:dx.doi.org/10.5130/ijcre.v14i2.8009.

Reed, Mark, Anil Graves, Norman Dandy, Helena Posthumus, Klaus Hubacek, Joe Morris, Christina Prell, Claire H. Quinn and Lindsay C. Stringer. 2009. "Who's In and Why? A Typology of Stakeholder Analysis Methods for Natural Resource Management." *Journal of Environmental Management* 90, no. 5: 1933–49. https://doi.org/10.1016/j.jenvman.2009.01.001.

Sandercock, Leonie. 2005. "Out of the Closet: The Importance of Stories and Storytelling in Planning Practice." In *Dialogues in Urban and Regional Planning*, edited by B. Stiftel and V. Watson, 299–321. London: Routledge.

Selsky, John W., and Anthony E. Smith. 1994. "Community Entrepreneurship: A Framework for Social Change Leadership." *Leadership Quarterly* 5, no. 3: 277–96.

Shaw, Mae. 2006. "Community Development and the Politics of Community." *Community Development Journal* 43, no. 1: 24–36. https://doi.org/10.1093/cdj/bsl035.

Shrivastava, Paul, and James J. Kennelly. 2013. "Sustainability and Place-Based Enterprise." *Organization & Environment* 26, no. 1: 83–101. https://doi.org/10.1177/1086026612475068.

Steiner, Artur, Jane Farmer, and Gary Bosworth. 2020. "Rural Social Enterprise — Evidence to Date, and a Research Agenda." *Journal of Rural Studies* 70: 139–43. https://doi.org/10.1016/j.jrurstud.2019.08.008.

Stone, Moren Tibabo, and Gyan P. Nyaupane. 2018. "Protected Areas, Wildlife-Based Community Tourism and Community Livelihoods Dynamics: Spiraling Up and Down of Community Capitals." *Journal of Sustainable Tourism* 26, no. 2: 307–24. https://doi.org/10.1080/09669582.2017.1349774.

Thompson, John. 2010. "'Entrepreneurship Enablers' — Their Unsung and Unquantified Role in Competitiveness and Regeneration." *Local Economy* 25, no. 1: 58–73. https://doi.org/10.1080/02690940903545406.

Timmons, Jeffry A., and Stephen Spinelli. 2009. *New Venture Creation: Entrepreneurship for the 21st Century*, 8th ed. New York: McGraw-Hill/Irwin.

van Hulst, Merlijn. 2012. "Storytelling: A Model *of* and a Model *for* Planning." *Planning Theory* 11, no. 3: 299–318. https://doi.org/10.1177/1473095212440425.

Vodden, Kelly. 2010. "Heroes, Hope, and Resource Development in Canada's Periphery: Lessons from Newfoundland and Labrador." In *The Next Rural Economies: Constructing Rural Place in Global Economies,* edited by Greg Halseth, Sean Markey, and David Bruce, 223–38. Oxfordshire, UK: CABI International.

Welter, Friederike, Ted Baker, David B. Audretsch, and William B. Gartner. 2017. "Everyday Entrepreneurship — A Call for Entrepreneurship Research to Embrace Entrepreneurial Diversity." *Entrepreneurship Theory and Practice* 41, no. 3: 311–21. https://doi.org/10.1111/etap.12258.

Winkler, Richelle, Lorri Oikarinen, Heather Simpson, Melissa Michaelson, and Mayra Sanchez Gonzalez. 2016. "Boom, Bust and Beyond: Arts and

Sustainability in Calumet, Michigan." *Sustainability* 8, no. 3: 284–308.
https://doi.org/10.3390/su8030284.

Wood, Gregory, and Jose Lam. 2019. *Restoring and Retelling the Story of Grenfell Gardens*. St. John's: Harris Centre, Memorial University.

CHAPTER 3

Linking Divergent Perspectives and Stakeholders: A Case Study of St. Anthony Basin Resources Incorporated

Brennan Lowery, Sam Elliot, Sara Langer,
Mark C.J. Stoddart, and Kelly Vodden

Introduction

Sustainable local development is a dynamic process that requires collaboration between multiple stakeholder groups and an understanding of their intertwined relationships. Social enterprises can play a unique role in this process by straddling the worlds of business, civil society, and local government (Tracey, Phillips, and Haugh 2005), particularly in rural communities and regions where local stakeholders often serve multiple leadership roles (Steiner and Teasdale 2019). Social enterprises can thus bridge different stakeholders, acting as "boundary spanners" by working across diverse perspectives and logics (Powell et al. 2018; Steiner, Farmer, and Bosworth 2020). As suggested by the second pillar of the PLACE Framework, place-based social enterprises can *link divergent perspectives,* navigating local and non-local partnerships while gaining access to necessary resources from both local and external sources (Korsgaard, Ferguson, and Gaddefors 2015). Place-based enterprises play a crucial connecting role, particularly in rural and remote regions where communities are separated by distance. They can also help advocate for regional development priorities by engaging provincial/state and federal decision-makers, while safeguarding the unique identity of communities within a region.

Ideally, place-based enterprises can help promote a more equitable distribution of resources between communities and stakeholders, although it is important to acknowledge that their activities can potentially create (or amplify) an uneven terrain of benefits within regions.

On the tip of Newfoundland and Labrador's Great Northern Peninsula (GNP), St. Anthony Basin Resources Inc. (SABRI) has helped to create new economic development opportunities by bringing together diverse communities and perspectives. SABRI serves a region of 16 communities by managing a shrimp quota and reinvesting revenues into regional development initiatives (Foley, Mather, and Neis 2013). Fisheries are a major pillar of the GNP's regional economy (Butters et al. 2016), even after the 1992 groundfish moratorium when fisheries largely shifted from cod to crustacean species such as shrimp, crab, and lobster (Thomas et al. 2014). Furthermore, communities on the GNP have a multitude of assets such as cultural heritage sites of national and international importance (Parill et al. 2014). However, many of these assets are overlooked in provincial discourse on rural viability, which often characterizes rural regions in terms of negative trends like demographic decline (Lowery et al. 2021).

This chapter demonstrates how SABRI works to link divergent perspectives and how these multi-stakeholder partnerships enhance local assets in pursuit of regional sustainability. We analyze publicly available documents from the region to conduct a social network analysis that maps SABRI's partnerships with actors both on the GNP and outside the region, then link these partnerships to some of the key impacts that SABRI has had on multiple forms of community capital (Emery and Flora 2006). This chapter demonstrates that SABRI's partnerships link diverse actors such as municipalities, non-profits, private-sector actors ranging from local businesses to international investors, and government agencies. However, previously identified collaboration gaps in the region persist, such as poor connectivity across sub-regions of the geographically vast GNP and a greater emphasis on local linkages than on ties to national and international partners (Stoddart et al. 2020; Tucker et al. 2011). Partnerships generate numerous positive impacts on the regional economy, while also enhancing social cohesion, cultural identity, health and wellness, environmental conservation, and other areas. By briefly outlining these positive impacts, this chapter demonstrates how SABRI's partnerships not only generate beneficial outcomes for regional sustainability, but also strengthen the asset base that can be used as inputs for future community and regional development initiatives. We also acknowledge challenges that have limited SABRI's ability to deliver greater regional benefits, such as shrimp quota cuts and gaps in local and external collaboration that could be strengthened. Thus, we highlight the dynamic nature of the PLACE Framework through the linkages between the "L" and "A" principles, as well as the interdependencies between stakeholders, partnerships, and assets in community development.

About the Authors

This chapter was the result of a collaborative process between academic researchers based at Memorial University and SABRI. The former included Kelly Vodden and Mark C.J. Stoddart, who have conducted research for nearly two decades on the GNP on relevant topics such as fisheries, innovation, network mapping, regional governance, and regional heritage and tourism development (Ommer et al. 2007; Stoddart et al. 2020; Tucker et al. 2011; Vodden et al. 2019), as well as two early-stage researchers, Brennan Lowery and Sara Langer. Stoddart is a professor in the Sociology Department at the St. John's campus of Memorial University. One of his research areas is sustainable tourism development, which has included looking at the GNP regarding tourism-related social networks. He advised and contributed to the network analysis presented here. Kelly Vodden is a professor with the Environmental Policy Institute at the Grenfell Campus of Memorial University, whose research focuses on collaborative governance and sustainable local development in rural regions, including the GNP. Both Vodden and Stoddart contributed to drafting and revision throughout the development of the chapter, drawing insights from their previous research in the region.

Early career scholars included Brennan Lowery, this chapter's primary author, whose PhD research focused on asset mapping and sustainability narratives in the region (Lowery et al. 2021), and Sara Langer, a PhD student at Grenfell Campus. Lowery had the unique perspective of living in St. Anthony from June 2021 to August 2022, allowing him to gain an in-depth understanding of community dynamics and access to SABRI staff, which informed the drafting and revision of the chapter. Langer conducted the analysis informing this chapter, including document review and social network analysis (see Methods section), as well as contributing to drafting the chapter.

Sam Elliot represented the key link to SABRI's activities, having worked as executive director of the organization from 1999 until his retirement in late 2022 and having overseen most of the regional development initiatives discussed in the chapter. During the chapter research and writing process, Elliot met several times with other co-authors to discuss the aims of the chapter, review initial drafts, and provide documents to inform the analysis.

About SABRI

Fisheries were the lifeblood of communities across rural and coastal NL and remain so in some regions, such as the GNP. Approximately 25 per cent of the regional labour force is employed in harvesting and processing fish (NL Statistics Agency 2020), with communities such as Port au Choix, Anchor Point, and St. Anthony relying heavily both on harvesting and fish plant employment. Rural regions like the GNP often are described only in terms of their deficiencies: primarily population decline and related socio-economic and ecological challenges following the groundfish moratorium (Lowery et al. 2021). Research, however, suggests that sustainable rural development often starts with the assets of a given region and mobilizes those assets to realize new opportunities (Emery and Flora 2006; Vodden, Baldacchino, and Gibson 2015).

Communities on the tip of the GNP (see Figure 3.1) came together to capitalize on a rare opportunity to acquire new quota in the then-growing shrimp fishery after the groundfish moratorium. In 1997, local fisheries advocates and the federal fisheries management agency (Fisheries and Oceans Canada) worked together to secure a 3,000-ton shrimp quota, deciding that it would be administered collectively among 16 communities

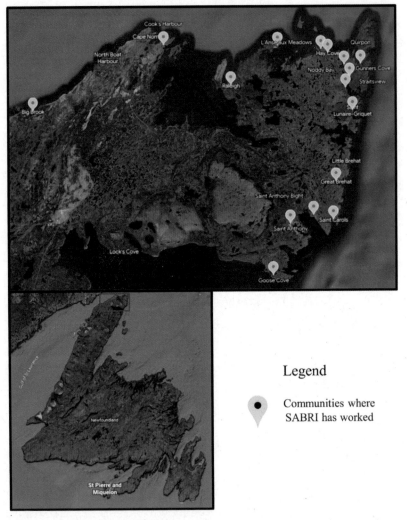

Figure 3.1. Map of communities in which SABRI has worked. (Map data from Google, 2019)

(Foley, Mather, and Neis 2013). SABRI was established with a mission to allocate this multi-ton quota to communities from Big Brook to Goose Cove to improve the region's economic base and rural livelihoods and well-being (SABRI 2021).

In the design of the organization, which was unique in NL at the time, its founders decided that these communities should participate directly in decision-making, dedicating 4 out of 15 seats on its volunteer Board of Directors to community representatives, with the remaining seats representing fish harvesters, processors, and other local organizations like the Chamber of Commerce and Rising Sun Developers, an arm's-length economic development group associated with the town of St. Anthony (Foley, Mather, and Neis 2013). Furthermore, the revenues generated from harvesting and processing activity would be invested equally into community development projects among the 16 beneficiary communities. As shown in Figure 3.1, SABRI's projects span the organization's service region, benefiting communities like St. Anthony, St. Anthony Bight, Goose Cove, St. Lunaire-Griquet, and Raleigh. Figure 3.2 provides a timeline of SABRI's community and regional development projects, which are discussed in detail below.

Many of these development projects have been made possible by a partnership in harvesting and processing shrimp with the Nova Scotia-based company Clearwater Seafoods, which generates royalties that SABRI reinvests into its projects (Daly and Chuenpagdee 2020). The cornerstone of that partnership has been the operation of St. Anthony Seafoods, a multi-species processing plant built in 1999, which was owned jointly by SABRI (with a 25 per cent ownership stake) and Clearwater (75 per cent). In 2020, a new joint venture between Clearwater and Quin-Sea Fisheries assumed ownership for the facility. SABRI has maintained harvesting contracts, however, and continues to work with for-profit fishing enterprises to ensure that ships have crews from the region and that revenues are invested into ongoing regional development projects.

Using revenue from these business partnerships, SABRI has invested in a wide range of community-based initiatives. SABRI offered business development services to local residents from 2002 to 2008, as reported by Community Services Council (2008), and has provided scholarships and bursaries to local graduates and supported local recreational activities. SABRI has also contributed to local infrastructure, such as ice-breaking and port upgrades in 2008 that were carried out by the Port of St. Anthony, and in 2014, with investment in a marine lift for fishing vessels. SABRI has carried out multi-community infrastructure initiatives

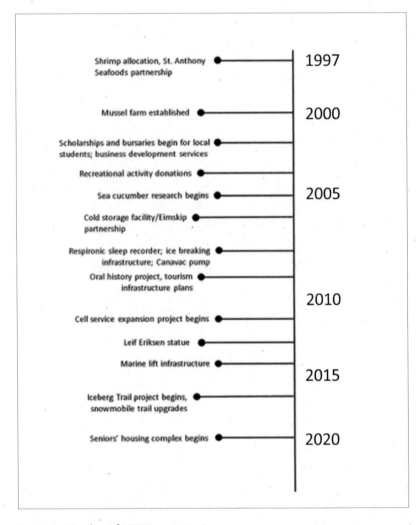

Figure 3.2. Timeline of SABRI's projects since 1997.

such as constructing a network of hiking trails called the Iceberg Trail. This work has spanned SABRI's service region (Figure 3.1). SABRI's initiatives are described in further detail below, in the context of SABRI's multi-stakeholder partnerships, after a brief outline of the conceptual foundation of our assessment.

The Importance of Linking Diverse Stakeholders and Perspectives for Rural Sustainability

Social Capital as a Critical Community Asset

This chapter approaches SABRI from a holistic perspective of sustainable community and regional development, which recognizes the importance of multiple forms of mutually supporting community assets, or "capitals" (Emery and Flora 2006). Through this lens, sustainable development is considered a delicate balance in which local actors seek to enhance economic, social, cultural, human, and built capital, while minimizing impacts on natural capital (Roseland 2012). These forms of community capital are shown in Figure 3.3, with associated examples of community assets.

In particular, social capital has been highlighted as a critical leverage point for mobilizing both local assets and actors (Emery and Flora 2006). Community renewal efforts must navigate multiple domains of social capital, including bonding (the tight-knit, affinity-based ties of people who live in close proximity), bridging (weaker ties based in professional relationships with peers in horizontal networking exchanges), and linking (vertical relations with actors in positions of power) (Poortinga 2012). By effectively navigating each domain of social capital, social enterprises in rural areas can secure access to local resources by partnering with community associations via bonding social capital, strengthening collaboration between community groups with similar goals but few existing ties via bridging, and linking with external actors like government agencies to access public and private funding sources and policy supports (Korsgaard, Ferguson, and Gaddefors 2015).

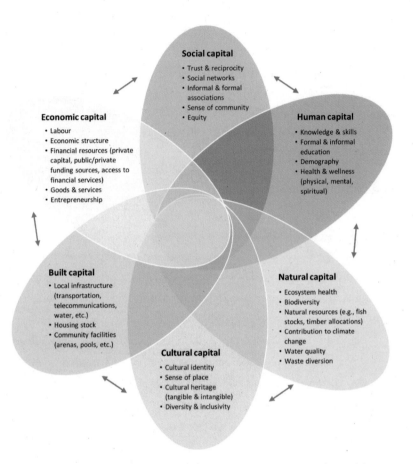

Figure 3.3. Forms of community capital and related assets. (Source: authors' elaboration)

Bridging ties are individual or organizational members of a social network that help to connect otherwise disconnected subgroups (Frank et al. 2012; Lubell et al. 2012). They can play a vital brokering role by filling gaps between distinct subgroups and ensuring that information and resources can move throughout the network. Bridging ties are well-positioned to exercise leadership or political influence, because they are central to linking divergent perspectives and connecting disparate actors to form collaboration networks. These networks stimulate creative diversity and provide avenues to access new resources from the network's periphery and external sources (Bathelt, Malmberg, and Maskell 2004; Krebs and Holley 2004; Woolcock 2001). When a network's internal connectivity is strengthened, members have increased capacity to pursue partnerships and projects that enhance linked social capital, such as joint proposals to government agencies or industry investments.

The Role of Social Enterprise in Multi-Stakeholder Collaboration

In pursuing holistic community sustainability, a wide variety of local stakeholders will have multiple, divergent perspectives regarding the direction of local development. Representatives from private, state, and civil society sectors may clash in cross-sector interactions due to conflicting priorities and values (Powell et al. 2018), which can result in one stakeholder taking unilateral action that harms the interests of other actors or collective priorities. The theory and practice of alternative dispute resolution provides numerous case studies of these multi-stakeholder conflicts (Susskind et al. 2003), while literature on regional sustainability planning emphasizes the need for stakeholders to work together to identify a shared vision (Hermans, Haarmann, and Dagevos 2011). Similarly, rural regions facing collective action dilemmas such as watershed governance or local infrastructure management may enact collaborative efforts to realize shared decision-making and mutual benefits across diverse communities and sectors (Breen and Markey 2015; Eger et al. 2021).

Social enterprises can bridge or link these divergent perspectives. Since they often act as hybrid entities straddling the worlds of traditional business and social purpose organizations (Tracey, Phillips, and Haugh 2005), social enterprises have unique competencies for understanding different and competing priorities. Social entrepreneurs face great tensions in balancing their social mission and viable business models (Smith, Gonin, and Besharov 2013), often adopting complex organizational structures to navigate different legal regimes and funding pools (Haugh and Brady 2019). Social entrepreneurs have often helped bring together stakeholders with differing priorities and logics around shared visions for change

(Selsky and Smith 1994). Furthermore, many social and community-based enterprises have wider conceptions of value creation than conventional profit-driven entrepreneurs and, therefore, can tap wider pools of local assets (Adhikari et al. 2018) that positively influence those capital stocks (Lumpkin, Bacq, and Pidduck 2018). The remainder of this chapter examines how SABRI has both contributed to and drawn from bridging and linking forms of social capital to bring together divergent stakeholders and perspectives, while strengthening multiple forms of community capital to foster more resilient and sustainable communities.

Methods

To examine SABRI's role in *linking divergent perspectives*, this study examined various documents relating to SABRI's initiatives, social networks, and the impacts of these efforts. The documents included peer-reviewed literature on SABRI and the GNP region; SABRI's reports, presentations, website, and newsletters; and publicly available news articles, government media releases, policy reports, project budgets, and other information. Documentary sources are important for signalling organizational priorities and structuring organizational practices (Prior 2008). At the same time, this reliance on secondary data has limitations, such as the tendency for official organizational documents to discuss only the formal relationships between actors and not disclose informal dynamics that may be revealed in interviews or focus groups. Although primary data collection was not feasible for the scope of this project, the author team was able to complement insights from secondary data analysis with their first-hand observation from their extensive experience in the region and through in-depth discussions with SABRI about preliminary findings, thereby helping to ensure the validity of the results (Hesse-Biber 2010).

Next, we conducted a social network analysis (SNA), a methodological approach to focusing analysis on relationships or ties between the actors within a particular social world (Prell 2012). SNA is most often used for analyzing ties among individual people, but it can also be applied to ties among organizations. Social network measures can tell us a great deal about the potential for sharing information and resources within a network, as well as which actors are well-positioned for leadership or brokerage roles in the network.

To analyze the relationships involved, we constructed a two-mode network map or sociogram, examining projects and actors associated with SABRI and the work with which the organization is involved. We coded the collected grey literature, along with academic articles that expand on some of SABRI's projects, using NVivo software. We categorized projects and coded actors (organizations, levels of government, and businesses) and beneficiaries within these project categories, identifying project-associated relationships between actors and SABRI. These data were then imported to Visone software, which we used to produce a sociogram that visualizes the actors and their ties to the projects with which they were involved (see Figure 3.4).

SABRI as a Regional Connector

Relationships and the networks they create are SABRI's means of creating community impacts and enhancing community capital. By positioning SABRI at the centre of the network and mapping their projects and the other actors connected to these projects and to the organization, Figure 3.4 illustrates how SABRI does the work of linking diverse perspectives, thereby creating positive impacts on the community and region.[1] For actors, node size was adjusted to reflect degree centrality of each actor. Thus, the bigger the node, the more connected it is to various projects as the figure illustrates.

SABRI is connected to a broad range of actors, including government agencies (from the municipal level to the federal), international organizations (UNESCO), private companies, community organizations such as sport and recreational groups, and academic researchers. Central actors within the network include the federal Atlantic Canada Opportunities Agency (ACOA), the provincial Department of Business, Tourism, Culture,

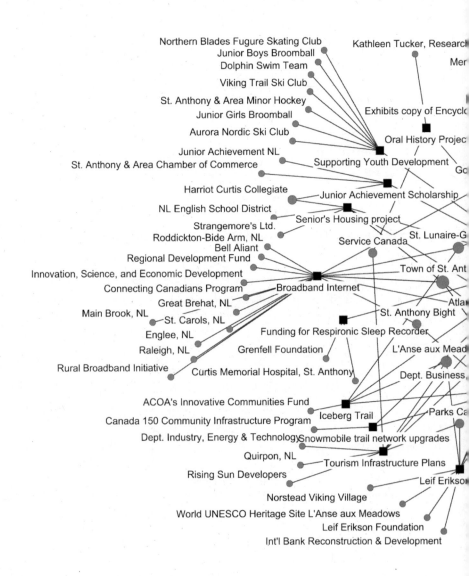

Figure 3.4. Two-mode collaboration network of actors (circles) and SABRI projects (squares).

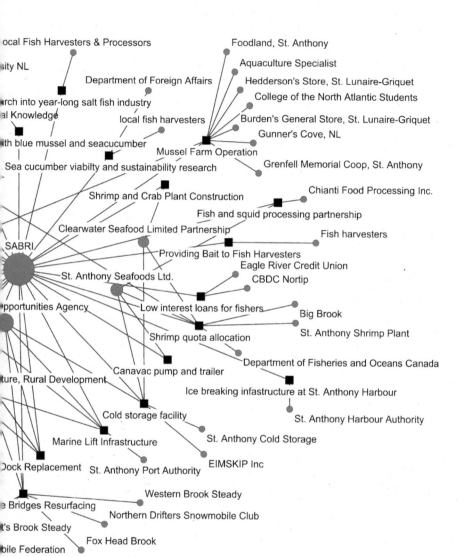

and Rural Development (now Industry, Energy, and Technology, or IET), companies like St. Anthony Seafoods Ltd. and Clearwater Seafood, and municipalities. SABRI's connections also create network bridges across economic sectors, with fisheries-oriented projects touching on other areas like tourism, recreation, information technology, housing, and education. SABRI has channelled fisheries revenues into trail development and cultural heritage initiatives, for example, which have in turn helped to foster and support the tourism industry.

In addition to a need for greater connections between regional fishing and tourism sectors, Tucker et al. (2011) found that the community and regional development networks in the region lacked external connections, particularly outside of the Corner Brook and Gros Morne area of western Newfoundland or the provincial capital, St. John's. Stoddart et al. (2020) also observed "vertical collaboration gaps" in the region, and Figure 3.4 tells a very similar story, with few external actors within the network. That said, SABRI does contribute to linking social capital through the organization's relationships with provincial and federal agencies (e.g., ACOA and IET) and externally owned firms like Clearwater, which brings significant financial resources into the region. For example, SABRI secured federal funding through a no-interest loan for a cold storage facility representing a multi-million-dollar investment to the region and intending to attract shipping companies and decrease shipping costs to Europe from St. Anthony (White and Hall 2013). SABRI's partnership with Icelandic firm Eimskip is a major pillar of this European trade link. After a decade of bringing ships to St. Anthony, Eimskip offered to take over the cold storage facility's operation, entering a 20-year lease agreement with SABRI in 2015, whereby SABRI owns the facility and Eimskip rents the space for operations (SABRI 2021). In terms of university collaborations, Memorial University's non-centrality in Figure 3.4 reflects the identification of some network ties with individual researchers or projects, rather than their aggregation into a single organizational node.

Many of these external partnerships have been initiated by SABRI, which has taken an entrepreneurial approach to seeking out opportunities and partners on many of its initiatives. SABRI staff have often found industry or research partnerships by searching online and cold-calling potential partners. In the case of local partnerships, projects have often originated from SABRI's involvement in other organizations like the Port Authority or the Chamber of Commerce.

Figure 3.4 reveals that SABRI's engagement with local and external actors varies depending on the nature of its regional development projects. Initiatives like the oral history project or youth development are focused on local partnerships, for which SABRI develops bonding and bridging social capital. Projects like the cold storage facility or cell service expansion involve national and international partners, which requires the ability to foster links to social capital. Other external partnerships are functions of policy and funding regimes, such as provincial or federal government agencies acting as funders for regional development projects or Fisheries and Oceans Canada exercising federal jurisdiction over fish harvesting. Despite these important external connections, our analysis reaffirms previous network studies in the region by identifying a much stronger emphasis on local and provincial partnerships than on national or international linkages.

Snapshot of SABRI's Impacts on Regional Sustainability

SABRI's efforts to foster multi-stakeholder partnerships have had many beneficial outcomes for regional sustainability on the GNP. Just as SABRI's projects have brought together multiple partners, they have also drawn on a wide range of local and non-local assets to generate multi-dimensional impacts across social, economic, cultural, human, and built capital, while also helping safeguard the region's natural assets. This section uses the multiple community capitals framework to show some of the impacts and outcomes resulting from SABRI's partnerships. These outcomes are often intertwined with inputs that SABRI has utilized to carry out its projects. Impacts from a single project can register across multiple capital areas. Table 3.1 provides a brief sample of these impacts.

Table 3.1. A sample of SABRI's regional development projects, partnerships, and community capital impacts.

Project	Partners Involved	Types of Capital Enhanced	Sample Contributions
St. Anthony Seafoods Limited Partnership	• Clearwater Seafoods • Quin-Sea/Royal Greenland	Economic	• Multi-million-dollar investment by SABRI, Clearwater, Quin-Sea, and Royal Greenland as contributing partners • 150+ processing plant workers at peak (now approximately 100)
		Built	• Construction and upgrading of shrimp/multi-species processing plant
Seniors' housing complex	• Government of NL • NL English School District • Local contractors	Economic	• $6M overall project budget • Local construction companies contracted
		Human	• Location promotes active lifestyles, physical and mental health
		Built	• 26 independent living units
		Social	• Increased access to affordable housing
St. Anthony Cold Storage	• Eimskip Inc.	Economic	• Multi-million-dollar investment • 30 long-term jobs created
Medical equipment	• Charles Curtis Memorial Hospital • Grenfell Foundation	Economic	• $300K investment in medical equipment
		Human	• Improved access to medical services
Oral history project	• Member communities • Service Canada	Cultural	• Documenting oral histories of 16 communities in service region
Leif Eriksen statue	• Community of L'Anse aux Meadows • Leif Eriksen Foundation • Norstead Viking Village • Parks Canada	Cultural	• Interpreting Viking history while enhancing cultural tourism offerings

Project	Partners Involved	Types of Capital Enhanced	Sample Contributions
Fisheries research and development projects	• Local fish harvesters • Memorial University • Government of NL • Fisheries & Oceans Canada	Economic	• Research on potential new species (e.g., sea cucumber, whelk, toad crab)
		Natural	• Investigating by-product innovation opportunities
Arctic char conservation	• Save Our Char Action Committee	Economic	• Investigating sustainable harvesting opportunities
		Natural	• Supporting local conservation group
Cell service expansion	• Bell Aliant • Government of NL • Parks Canada • Clearwater • International Grenfell Association • Member communities	Built	• Two cell towers constructed and funding for cell coverage upgrades
		Economic	• $1.5M investment from multiple partners
		Social	•Access to cell service expanded to 95 per cent of residents in the region
Iceberg Trail development	• Member communities • ACOA • Government of NL	Economic	• Four seasonal jobs created
		Natural	• Improved access to view natural amenities of the region

One of the most frequently highlighted outcomes of SABRI's projects is their impacts on the regional economy. SABRI's business model lays the foundation for all its work by channelling royalties from the shrimp fishery towards community development projects (Daly and Chuenpagdee 2020), which at the peak of the organization's lifetime generated roughly $1.5 million in annual revenue (Foley, Mather, and Neis 2015). These revenues come from an offshore harvesting agreement with Clearwater, currently for the harvest of approximately 430 metric tons of shrimp, which allows SABRI to leverage its own funds to secure additional funding from provincial and federal governments, foundations, banks, and other sources. As outlined in Table 3.1, SABRI has attracted millions of dollars of local and external investment into the region. Although many of these financial contributions are charitable donations, we use the term "investment" both to reflect SABRI's own language and to reflect that these financial inputs have generated non-monetary returns in other areas of community capital (e.g., human capital through improved access to specialized medical services). Health impacts could also be quantified in monetary terms by calculating the value of travel costs avoided when residents are able to avail themselves of local health-care services instead of travelling to larger centres.

Most of SABRI's projects involve a mix of their own funds and external funding sources, such as a recent cell service expansion initiative in which SABRI invested $375,000 into a $1.4 million project (25 per cent), including contributions of $35,000 from Parks Canada, $25,000 from Clearwater, and $20,000 from the International Grenfell Association. A significant limitation to SABRI's economic impact is the cuts to shrimp

Figure 3.5. St. Anthony Cold Storage, SABRI's initiative, is a major economic contributor to the region. (Photo credit: Brennan Lowery, 2020)

quotas that have occurred since the initial allocation of 3,000 tons to the region, which have greatly reduced the organization's key revenue stream for investing in development projects.

Another major economic impact has been the creation of both temporary and long-term jobs. The largest employment impact by far is from St. Anthony Seafoods, which now employs approximately 100 workers on a seasonal basis, down from a peak of about 150 (Dean-Simmons 2020; Foley and Mather 2015). The Eimskip partnership has also created about 30 long-term jobs while connecting St. Anthony to an international shipping network spanning the North Atlantic. Many other initiatives have generated seasonal or temporary employment, such as the construction of St. Anthony Cold Storage (Eimskip), which temporarily employed about 30 people.

SABRI's initiatives have also positively impacted human capital in the region. Examples include providing $230,900 in scholarships and bursaries to local graduates since 1997 and hiring local students to work on projects like the mussel farm operation. This student employment provided local youth with valuable experience and connections to regional industries. SABRI also supports community health and well-being programs, enhancing the quality of regional health-care services through investing a total of $300,000 into medical equipment at Curtis Memorial Hospital, with support from the Grenfell Foundation. Some of SABRI's other projects have promoted active lifestyles, such as improvements to local snowmobile trails in collaboration with the NL Snowmobile Federation, a provincial association that promotes snowmobiling and helps maintain snowmobile trails. These investments in recreational infrastructure contribute to tourism development and regional livability.

SABRI's projects have had a substantial impact on built capital across its service region. In partnership with St. Anthony Seafoods, it has generated continuous enhancements to a multi-species processing plant, while St. Anthony Cold Storage (Eimskip) has enhanced port infrastructure in collaboration with Eimskip Inc. and federal funding agencies, as discussed above. Beyond fisheries, initiatives like the cell service expansion project have led to the construction of LTE cellular towers in Raleigh and St. Lunaire-Griquet (Government of NL 2018), made possible through a collaboration involving the provincial government, Bell Aliant, and several local funding partners (see Table 3.1). SABRI's most recent large-scale project, the seniors' housing complex, has built 26 independent living units of 900 square feet at the site of an abandoned former high school.

SABRI's work has enhanced cultural capital by helping maintain the GNP's culture and rural lifestyle and supporting cultural heritage initiatives. For example, SABRI carried out an oral history project in 2009 in partnership with community researcher Kathleen Tucker and Service Canada, interviewing residents and documenting stories about traditional livelihoods, cultural heritage sites, and historical events. SABRI has also invested in cultural heritage initiatives like a statue of Leif Eriksen in L'Anse aux Meadows that was built in partnership with Norstead Viking Village, Parks Canada, and the Leif Eriksen Foundation. More recently, the Iceberg Trail construction involved interpretation of historically significant sites and enhanced opportunities for visitors and locals to appreciate the region's natural and cultural assets, supported by funding from provincial and federal governments.

SABRI has supported environmental initiatives in the region, such as a local conservation group called the Save our Char Action Committee dedicated to restoring habitat for a rare regional population of arctic char (Fitzpatrick 2021). SABRI assisted with the financial management of the project. It has also led research and development initiatives to identify potential new fisheries and to repurpose fish by-products. For example, SABRI has worked with small-boat fishers to investigate the potential of a toad crab fishery and has conducted surveys on species like whelk and sea cucumber. It has also pursued long-term partnerships with researchers at Memorial University and other institutions to assess new product opportunities based on fisheries by-products, seeking to ensure that fisheries resources are more fully and sustainably utilized. These partnerships involve researchers from diverse faculties such as the Marine Institute, Engineering, Environmental Policy, and

Boreal Ecosystems and Agricultural Sciences. In this instance, Figure 3.4 under-represents the value of this community–academic partnership by illustrating only a single connection between SABRI and Memorial University as a whole.

Finally, all of SABRI's work depends on partnerships enabled by social capital, which in turn further enhances the region's social capital. As shown in Figure 3.4, SABRI's projects employ all three forms of social capital described by Poortinga (2012), including bonding by partnering with local associations like the Boys and Girls Club, bridging by working with multiple municipalities on regional initiatives like the cell tower project, and linking by attracting international investment for the cold storage facility. SABRI's relationships with external actors like provincial and federal government agencies, international firms, and academic researchers have helped strengthen connections between local actors and external networks. For example, SABRI has formed a funding partnership with ACOA to provide financing for many of its community development projects. The importance of this funding relationship is illustrated in Figure 3.4, with ACOA having a high degree of network centrality. In addition, SABRI is motivated to engage in multiple long-term partnerships with some actors, such as Memorial University, that are less central. SABRI also helps strengthen bonding social capital in the region by playing an active role in local associations such as the St. Anthony and Area Chamber of Commerce and by supporting local groups, including outdoor recreation associations. Overall, the social network analysis reaffirms previous findings from the region (e.g., Stoddart et al. 2020; Tucker et al. 2011) that social network ties to local and provincial actors are stronger than national and international ones (with the exception of federal government agencies like ACOA and DFO). This situation highlights that opportunities remain for SABRI to strengthen partnerships further with actors outside the province.

Lessons Learned and Conclusion

The case study presented here demonstrates the potential for rural social enterprises to leverage partnerships to create diverse forms of value that enhance regional sustainability. SABRI has served as a bridging social network tie, connecting diverse communities and stakeholder groups — from municipalities and local associations to international investors — while realizing diverse projects with positive impacts for communities on the GNP. Thus, we contribute to previous research on the potential of place-based social enterprises to draw on and simultaneously contribute to social capital as a critical asset for community sustainability (Korsgaard, Ferguson, and Gaddefors 2015). Through multi-stakeholder collaboration, social enterprises such as SABRI can enhance the bonding capital that is often a major asset in rural communities (Reimer 2005), and also strengthen bridging social capital between actors with similar interests but few existing connections, while fostering linking social capital with vertical actors such as government agencies and external firms (Poortinga 2012). This networking includes linking "insiders" and "outsiders," which previous PLACE research has highlighted as an important function of rural social enterprises (Slawinski et al. 2019). However, as observed in previous studies on collaboration gaps on the GNP (Tucker et al. 2011; Stoddart et al. 2020), SABRI's partnerships with vertical actors at national and international levels remain relatively weak compared to its local and provincial linkages.

This analysis has shown how SABRI's partnerships strengthen collaboration across diverse stakeholder groups. Their projects have simultaneously engaged federal and provincial government agencies, local fish harvesters and plant workers, community elders, and international corporations. By acting as a key boundary spanner between local kinship and friendship networks and external linkages to powerful actors (Selsky and Smith 1994), SABRI reaffirms how social enterprises can bridge between multi-sectoral actors with differing priorities and logics (Powell et al. 2018). Thus, we highlight how social enterprises can support multi-stakeholder efforts in rural regions to address complex governance issues (Eger et al. 2021), for example, by attracting funding for regional infrastructure investments or participating in natural resource management.

This chapter shows how the bridging work of social enterprises creates diverse forms of value — monetary and non-monetary, tangible and intangible — and cuts across social, economic, cultural, and ecological domains. Strengthening previous studies on social enterprise and multi-dimensional value creation (Adhikari et al. 2018; Lumpkin, Bacq, and Pidduck 2018), we demonstrate that SABRI's partnerships have generated not only economic value, but a wide range of benefits across multiple forms of community capital (Emery and Flora 2006). As shown in Table 3.1, a single project often leverages multiple partners and generates positive impacts across multiple capital areas, such as the cell service expansion project that has created benefits far beyond the financial investment attracted. These findings reinforce existing knowledge about the interdependencies between different forms of community capital (Flora et al. 2005), while pointing to future research opportunities about the complex inputs, outcomes, and feedback loops between projects and capitals that were outside the scope of this chapter.

These findings offer lessons for regional stakeholders and policy-makers while raising questions for future research. First, given the limitations discussed with the secondary data reviewed in this chapter, an in-depth analysis based on primary data such as interviews or surveys would provide a more fulsome assessment of SABRI's impact on regional sustainability informed by deep contextual understanding and a wider range of perspectives. This future research area provides an opportunity for further collaboration between SABRI and academic researchers, from which other rural regions in NL may benefit. Future research could collaboratively examine challenges faced by the organization, such as where collaboration gaps exist in SABRI's networks and how these might best be addressed. For example, applied research and network mapping could help SABRI to identify national and international partners from the private sector, non-profits, academia, or government, while learning from existing collaborations like the cold storage partnership. Future research also could explore options to enhance the long-term resilience of SABRI by considering challenges such as shrimp quota losses and succession issues brought forward by a recent leadership transition (the latter issue was anecdotally identified as a major challenge for organizations across all sectors on the GNP due to difficulties with recruiting and retaining youth). Finally, given current debates around NL's financial sustainability and calls for drastic changes to provincial fiscal policy (Premier's Economic Recovery Team 2021), SABRI may serve as a model of rural reinvestment and regional economic development. However, caution must be taken to avoid neo-liberal prescriptions that would download public services onto social enterprises without adequate resources or local decision-making authority (Steiner and Teasdale 2019). In contrast with ongoing deficiencies-based narratives about rural regions like the GNP (Lowery et al. 2021), social enterprises can work with local stakeholders to identify existing community capacities while fostering multi-level partnerships that harness untapped opportunities for locally appropriate economic development.

In conclusion, the case presented here offers some guiding lessons for further elaboration of the PLACE Framework. We provide a contextually nuanced account of how the "L" looks in practice, building on previous findings on the importance of linking insiders and outsiders (Slawinski et al. 2019), while informing future applications of the PLACE Framework with a rich account of how rural social enterprises interact with various stakeholders. The case of SABRI can also inform the other aspects of the PLACE Framework, both in subsequent chapters of this volume and future applications. For example, we highlight how the "L" and "A" of PLACE are intimately connected, given that various stakeholders, both local and external, bring distinct sets of assets to the table, which can be combined for mutual benefit through collaborative partnerships. Previous PLACE research has shown that non-local actors can often offer new insights into existing local assets (Slawinski et al. 2019), as we found in the case of SABRI's partnership with academic researchers on marine by-product innovation opportunities. As this volume continues to elaborate the principles of social enterprises authentically embedded in place, the case study presented here can enrich ongoing efforts to understand the value of the PLACE Framework approach for rural renewal.

Note

1. The size of project nodes was left uniform, rather than adjusting for degree centrality. Tie thickness was also left uniform, thus reflecting the presence or absence of ties between actors and projects (essentially a binary 1 or 0 measure), rather than reflecting the frequency of coding references across actors and projects.

Acknowledgements

The authors offer their sincere thanks to Christopher Mitchelmore, the current Executive Director of SABRI, for carefully reviewing the chapter and sharing insights on SABRI's ongoing efforts in the St. Anthony Basin region. We also are grateful to Renee Pilgrim, a community leader in St. Anthony Bight, for providing further guidance on the regional context. Finally, we acknowledge John Dagevos, adjunct professor at the Environmental Policy Institute, Grenfell Campus, Memorial University, for providing input on the analysis that informed the chapter.

References

Adhikari, Rajendra P., Laurie Bonney, Megan Woods, Sophie Clark, Lea Coates, Andrew Harwood, Robyn Eversole, and Morgan P. Miles. 2018. "Applying a Community Entrepreneurship Development Framework to Rural Regional Development." *Small Enterprise Research* 25, no. 3: 257–75.

Bathelt, Harald, Anders Malmberg, and Peter Maskell. 2004. "Clusters and Knowledge: Local Buzz, Global Pipelines and the Process of Knowledge Creation." *Progress in Human Geography* 28, no.1: 31–56.

Breen, Sarah, and Sean Markey. 2015. "Unintentional Influence: Exploring the Relationship between Rural Regional Development and Drinking Water Systems in Rural British Columbia, Canada." *Journal of Rural and Community Development* 10, no. 3: 50–77.

Butters, Leanna, Amalie Romero, Abdul Rahim Abdulai, Shem Evans, Nazrul Islam, Abigail Oppong, Evodius Rutta, Nick Arsenault, and Ode Echik-wonye. 2016. *Our Way Forward: Sharing Knowledge and Building Capacity for Regional Development*. Corner Brook, NL: Grenfell Campus, Memorial University. http://cdnregdev.ruralresilience.ca/?page_id=462.

Cochrane, Phoebe. 2006. "Exploring Cultural Capital and Its Importance in Sustainable Development." *Ecological Economics* 57, no. 2: 318–30.

Community Services Council Newfoundland and Labrador. 2008. *Community Profits: Social Enterprise in Newfoundland and Labrador*. St. John's. http://communitysector.nl.ca/f/CommunityProfits.pdf.

Daly, Jack, and Ratana Chuenpagdee. 2020. "Facing an Uncertain Future: A Prospective Analysis of Trade Policy on Coastal Communities in Northwest Newfoundland." *Marine Policy* 117: 103890.

Dean-Simmons, Barb. 2020. "'Anxiety is Just through the Roof' in this Newfoundland Town." *Saltwire News*. August 11, 2020. https://www.saltwire.com/nova-scotia/news/anxiety-is-just-through-the-roof-in-this-newfoundland-town-483810/.

Eger, Sondra, Sarah Minnes, Kelly Vodden, Amy Hudson, Kathleen Parewick, and Deatra Walsh. 2021. "COVID-19 and Drinking Water Security in Rural, Remote Communities and Indigenous Communities: The Role of Collaboration among Diverse Actors in Responding to a Global Pandemic." *Journal of Rural and Community Development* 16, no. 4: 112–40.

Ekins, Paul, Sandrine Simon, Lisa Deutsch, Carl Folke, and Rudolf De Groot. 2003. "A Framework for the Practical Application of the Concepts of Critical Natural Capital and Strong Sustainability." *Ecological Economics* 44, nos. 2–3: 165–85.

Emery, Mary, Edith Fernandez, Isabel Gutierrez-Montes, and Cornelia B. Flora. 2007. "Leadership as Community Capacity Building: A Study on the Impact of Leadership Development Training on Community." *Community Development* 38, no. 4: 60–70.

Emery, Mary, and Cornelia B. Flora. 2006. "Spiraling-Up: Mapping Community

Transformation with Community Capitals Framework." *Community Development* 37, no. 1: 19–35.

Fitzpatrick, Ashley. 2022. "It's Special to Me: Northern Peninsula Residents Rally behind Rare Char Population." *CBC News*. January 15, 2022. https://www.cbc.ca/news/canada/newfoundland-labrador/northern-peninsula-char-1.6303705.

Flora, Cornelia B., Mary Emery, Susan Fey, and Corry Bregendhal. 2005. *Community Capitals: A Tool for Evaluating Strategic Interventions and Projects*. Ames, IA: North Central Regional Center for Rural Development. https://www.ffa.org/documents/lts_communitycapitals.pdf.

Foley, Paul, and Charles Mather. 2015. "Making Space for Community Use Rights: Insights from 'Community Economies' in Newfoundland and Labrador." *Society & Natural Resources* 29, no. 8: 965–80.

Foley, Paul, Charles Mather, and Barbara Neis. 2013. *Fisheries Allocation Policies and Regional Development: Successes from the Newfoundland and Labrador Shrimp Fishery*. St. John's: Harris Centre, Memorial University.

Foley, Paul, Charles Mather, and Barbara Neis. 2015. "Governing Enclosure for Coastal Communities: Social Embeddedness in a Canadian Shrimp Fishery." *Marine Policy* 61: 390–400.

Frank, Ken, I-Chien Chen, Youngmi Lee, Scott Kalafatis, Tingqiao Chen, Yun-Jia Lo, and Maria Carmen Lemos. 2012. "Network Location and Policy-Oriented Behavior: An Analysis of Two-Mode Networks of Coauthored Documents Concerning Climate Change in the Great Lakes Region." *Policy Studies Journal* 40, no. 3: 492–515.

Government of Newfoundland and Labrador. 2018. "First Project Announced under Cell Service Pilot" (news release). July 31, 2018. https://www.gov.nl.ca/releases/2018/tcii/0731n01/.

Haugh, Helen, and Andrew Brady. 2019. "Community Perspectives on Social Entrepreneurship." In *A Research Agenda for Social Entrepreneurship*, edited by Anne de Bruin and Simon Teasdale, 67–81. Cheltenham, UK: Edward Elgar.

Hermans, Frans L. P., Wim M. F. Haarmann, and John F. L. M. M. Dagevos. 2011. "Evaluation of Stakeholder Participation in Monitoring Regional Sustainable Development." *Regional Environmental Change* 11, no. 4: 805–15. https://doi.org/10.1007/s10113-011-0216-y.

Hesse-Biber, Sharlene N., and Patricia Leavy. 2010. *The Practice of Qualitative Research*. London: Sage.

Korsgaard, Steffen, Richard Ferguson, and Johan Gaddefors. 2015. "The Best of Both Worlds: How Rural Entrepreneurs Use Placial Embeddedness and Strategic Networks to Create Opportunities." *Entrepreneurship & Regional Development* 27, nos. 9–10: 574–98.

Krebs, Valdis, and June Holley. 2004. "Building Sustainable Communities through Social Network Development." *Nonprofit Quarterly* 11, no. 1: 46–53.

Lowery, Brennan, Joan Cranston, Carolyn Lavers, Richard May, Renee Pilgrim, and Joan Simmonds. 2021. "Harnessing the Power of Stories for Rural Sustainability: Reflections on Community-Based Research on the Great Northern Peninsula of Newfoundland." *Gateways* 14, no. 2: 1–22.

Lubell, Mark, John Scholz, Ramiro Berardo, and Garry Robins. 2012. "Testing Policy Theory with Statistical Models of Networks." *Policy Studies Journal* 40, no. 3: 351–74.

Lumpkin, G.T., Sophie Bacq, and Robert J. Pidduck. 2018. "Where Change Happens: Community-Level Phenomena in Social Entrepreneurship Research." *Journal of Small Business Management* 56, no.1: 24–50.

Newfoundland and Labrador Statistics Agency. 2020. "St. Anthony–Port au Choix Rural Secretariat Region Tables and Charts." Community Accounts (website). https://nl.communityaccounts.ca/tablesandcharts.asp?_=vb7En-4WVgbWyonL_.

Ommer, R., with the Coasts under Stress Team. 2007. *Coasts under Stress: Understanding Restructuring and the Social-Ecological Health of Coastal Communities*. Montreal and Kingston: McGill-Queen's University Press.

Parill, Erika, Kyle White, Kelly Vodden, Jacqueline Walsh, and Greg Wood. 2014. *Regional Asset Mapping Initiative: Humber–Northern Peninsula–Southern Labrador Region*. Corner Brook, NL: Grenfell Campus, Memorial University.

Poortinga, Wouter. 2012. "Community Resilience and Health: The Role of Bonding, Bridging, and Linking Aspects of Social Capital." *Health & Place* 18, no. 2: 286–95.

Powell, E. Erin, Ralph Hamann, Verena Bitzer, and Ted Baker. 2018. "Bringing the Elephant into the Room? Enacting Conflict in Collective Prosocial Organizing." *Journal of Business Venturing* 33, no. 5: 623–42.

Prell, Christina. 2012. *Social Network Analysis: History, Theory & Methodology.* London: Sage.

Premier's Economic Recovery Team. 2021. *The Big Reset: Executive Summary.* St. John's.

Prior, L. 2008. "Researching Documents: Emergent Methods." In *Handbook of Emergent Methods,* edited by Sharlene N. Hesse-Biber and Patricia Leavy, 111–26. New York: Guilford Press.

Putnam, Robert D. 1995. "Bowling Alone: America's Declining Social Capital." *Journal of Democracy* 6, no. 1: 65–78.

Reimer, Bill. 2005. "A Rural Perspective on Linkages among Communities." Paper prepared for Building, Connecting and Sharing Knowledge: A Dialogue on Linkages between Communities, Carleton University, Ottawa, March 3, 2005.

Relph, Edward. 2009. "A Pragmatic Sense of Place." *Environmental and Architectural Phenomenology* 20, no. 3: 24–31.

Roseland, Mark. 2012. *Toward Sustainable Communities: Solutions for Citizens and Their Governments,* 4th ed. Gabriola Island, BC: New Society Publishers.

St. Anthony Basin Resources Incorporated (SABRI). 2021. "St. Anthony Basin Resources Inc.: Part of Our Future . . . Part of Our Region." Presentation to Fisheries and Oceans Canada. October 10, 2021.

Selsky, John W., and Anthony E. Smith. 1994. "Community Entrepreneurship: A Framework for Social Change Leadership." *Leadership Quarterly* 5, no. 3: 277–96.

Slawinski, Natalie, Blair Winsor, Daina Mazutis, John W. Schouten, and Wendy K. Smith. 2019. "Managing the Paradoxes of Place to Foster Regeneration." *Organization & Environment* 34, no. 4: 596–618. https://doi.org/10.1177/1086026619837131.

Smith, Wendy K., Michael Gonin, and Marya L. Besharov. 2013. "Managing Social-Business Tensions: A Review and Research Agenda for Social Enterprise." *Business Ethics Quarterly* 23, no. 3: 407–42.

Steiner, Artur, Jane Farmer, and Gary Bosworth. 2020. "Rural Social Enterprise — Evidence to Date, and a Research Agenda." *Journal of Rural Studies* 70: 139–43.

Steiner, Artur, and Simon Teasdale. 2019. "Unlocking the Potential of Rural Social Enterprise." *Journal of Rural Studies* 70, no. 1: 144–54.

Stoddart, Mark C.J., Gary Catano, Howard Ramos, Kelly Vodden, Brennan Lowery, and Leanna Butters. 2020. "Collaboration Gaps and Regional Tourism Networks in Rural Coastal Communities." *Journal of Sustainable Tourism* 28, no. 4: 625–45.

Susskind, Lawrence, Mieke van der Wansem, and Armando J. Ciccareli. 2003. "Mediating Land Use Disputes in the United States: Pros and Cons." *Environments* 31, no. 2: 39-58.

Thomas, Emily, Kelly Vodden, Ratana Chuenpagdee, and Maureen Woodrow. 2014. *Fishing Policies and Island Community Development*. St. John's: Harris Centre, Memorial University.

Tracey, Paul, Nelson Phillips, and Helen Haugh. 2005. "Beyond Philanthropy: Community Enterprise as a Basis for Corporate Citizenship." *Journal of Business Ethics* 58, no. 4: 327–44.

Tucker, Amy, Ryan Gibson, Kelly Vodden, and June Holley. 2011. *Network Weaving for Regional Development on the Tip of the Northern Peninsula Project Report*. Northern Peninsula Regional Collaboration Pilot.

Vodden, Kelly, Godfrey Baldacchino, and Ryan Gibson. 2015. *Place Peripheral: The Promise and Challenge of Place-Based Development in Rural and Remote Regions*. St. John's: ISER Books.

Vodden, Kelly, David Douglas, Sean Markey, Sarah Minnes, and Bill Reimer, eds. 2019. *The Theory, Practice, and Potential of Regional Development: The Case of Canada*. London: Routledge.

White, Kyle, and Heather Hall. 2013. "St. Anthony Basin Resources Incorporated (SABRI): Expanding Regional Social and Economic Benefits." CRD Project Innovation Case Study. http://innovationnl.ca/wp-content/uploads/2013/08/SABRI.pdf.

Winkler, Richelle, Lorri Oikarinen, Heather Simpson, Melissa Michaelson, and Mayra Sanchez Gonzalez. 2016. "Boom, Bust and Beyond: Arts and Sustainability in Calumet, Michigan." *Sustainability* 8, no. 3: 284.

Woolcock, Michael. 2001. "The Place of Social Capital in Understanding Social and Economic Outcomes." *Isuma: Canadian Journal of Policy Research* 2: 65-88.

CHAPTER 4

Amplifying Local Capacities and Assets: Findings from Placentia West and Bonavista

Ario Seto and Elizabeth Murphy

Introduction

This chapter showcases the role of place-based social enterprises (PBSEs) in bringing public attention to the optimal use of local capacities and assets. Drawing examples from two PBSEs in Newfoundland and Labrador (NL), Canada, one in Placentia West (population 1,039) and one in Bonavista (population 3,190), this chapter argues that, beyond economic generation, continuously revaluing and recreating local capacities and assets is about cultural change that vigorously fosters a community's pride in place, history, culture, and livability. In turn, assets become more durable and meaningful for the communities when they are embedded in social relationships and cultural practices.

A community's ability to recreate local capacities and assets, or recognize an "old" asset's new value, is particularly helpful when the community has limited resources to recover from economic decline. Like other communities in NL, social and economic decline has haunted the communities observed for this chapter since the Canadian government imposed a moratorium on commercial cod fishing in 1992. Scrambling to generate new economic activity, the provincial government initiated several projects to diversify local economies. However, the disparity between government programs and community realities made it difficult to achieve such goals (Peters et al. 2018; Ruseski 2006). Two community activists in Placentia West recalled that their fishermen husbands were hesitant to take advantage of government-provided retraining programs because they had been fishing since they were teenagers. Furthermore, there was scarcely any suitable employment for the new skills being offered, and they would still need to move elsewhere to work. A community leader in Bonavista explained that a company approached his town with a proposal to develop a polychlorinated biphenyls incinerator there in the late 1990s. Although this new industry could have provided jobs and helped the community to recover from economic decline, locals rejected the opportunity because they feared the possible toxic waste and considered that such an approach to economic revitalization would be at odds with the community's history.

These stories illustrate that job creation in communities that have recently lost their centuries-long livelihood should not only provide opportunities for economic recovery, but also sustain community values to avoid the further erosion of local identity. These rural communities had just lost their jobs and did not want to lose their culture as well. Facing such challenges, communities in the Burin Peninsula's Placentia West region and Bonavista turned to social entrepreneurship to leverage local capabilities and find ways to rely on the local assets they already had to contribute to community revitalization. As Chapter 1 details, studies have shown that PBSEs can effectively meet a community's economic and social needs through the sale of goods and services, the profits from which can be used to subsidize costs for other services. With a particular focus on amplifying local capacities and assets, this chapter describes how such approaches helped residents relate to and take pride in the ongoing development.

Kretzmann and McKnight (1993) introduced the Asset-Based Community Development (ABCD) method three decades ago. It has since become a popular approach to increasing community self-reliance. The method entails assessing a community's resources, skills, and experience, determining its issues, and taking appropriate action. After identifying its potential assets, a community can create a capacity inventory that focuses on strengths. It emphasizes local participation and commitment to improvement rather than assessing the community's deficiencies and scrutinizing local communities as passive receivers of development aid.

However, ABCD can lead to a narrow focus on decision-making because it focuses on the community's assets and strengths rather than considering community deficiencies as part of the broader systemic and structural factors. For example, ABCD can overlook important power dynamics and imbalances within communities, such as unequal distribution of resources and decision-making authority. This can lead to decisions that benefit some community members over others and result in unintended consequences for marginalized groups (Blickem et al. 2018; Collinson and Best 2019; Daly and Westwood 2018). The ABCD approach risks excluding under-represented groups from the community's decision-making processes (MacLeod and Emejulu 2014), as it engages only those with particular skills and motivations and not the community as a whole (Blickem et al. 2018). Responding to this limitation, Collinson and Best (2019) expand ABCD to Asset-Based Community Engagement (ABCE), which pays particular attention to the inclusion of marginalized groups and populations. It is also worth noting that engagement encompasses not only participation in formalized development, but also individual roles in the construction of a community's social life, such as "involvement in interpersonal interactions outside the home, including social, leisure, community activities and work" (Goll et al. 2015, 2). Collinson and Best's approach is similar to Guyer's (1997) anthropological view on asset creation, which pays attention to its impact on the reproduction of social life. She underscores that "the study of assets would become the study not only of the assets themselves, or of asset management (in the life-cyclical sense), but of asset creation (in the active, historical sense). Both policies and popular processes create assets" (Guyer 1997, 123).

Informed by these studies, this chapter starts from the view that efforts to amplify local asset-based development and community engagement are not straightforward, as the presence of a capacity or an asset does not mean that the object will be immediately treated as something that has value. Asset creation on the community level involves the transfer of assets from individuals to the community and requires growing community interest in investing in particular capacities and assets. The transfer process is important because it attracts individuals who share collective goals and fosters deeper community participation in continuously re-evaluating old capacities and assets. Thus, asset creation is relational and involves evolving processes.

As a researcher taking part in Memorial University's project on coastal community development, Ario Seto approached Elizabeth Murphy, the chair of the Placentia West Development Association (PWDA), in late 2020 to ask her to share her insights on community-based revitalization. Since Murphy also sat on the board of directors of Heritage NL, a nonprofit Crown corporation seeking to preserve the province's architectural and intangible cultural heritage, the discussion quickly turned to the subject of heritage assets and how these can support community development. From that point, our interest grew to understand, to echo Guyer (1997), how communities with fewer resources can thrive like those with better capital. We initially assumed that capacity-building and recreating assets would be easier in a "richer" place like Bonavista, which as of January 2023 has over 50 structures listed on Heritage NL, compared to Placentia West with only two such structures (Heritage NL, n.d.). Drawing on semi-structured interviews with 26 local community leaders and volunteers between 2020 and 2021, this chapter depicts how such an assumption does not necessarily hold true in rural Newfoundland.

Bonavista and Placentia West were not selected for comparative analysis. As the two locations differ geographically, historically, economically, and culturally, we sought to look at commonalities and differences between the two distinct sites. The goal was to examine which community-led activities contribute to revaluing capacities and assets, with one community having a larger potential asset pool. We aimed to provide examples of the role that PBSEs play in rural communities with two different settings, how they are actively involved in community plans, and the processes that influence local capacities and asset management.

For Placentia West, we observed the PWDA. Murphy has been involved in the organization since its establishment in 1979, and her husband was one of its founders. Placentia West is located on the northwestern part of the Burin Peninsula and comprises eight communities: Baine Harbour, Boat Harbour, Brookside, Parker's Cove, Red Harbour, Petite Forte, Rushoon, and South East Bight. It is not a cultural region — it transcends historically significant community unifiers such as religion — but was created by the government of Newfoundland and Labrador's political map, first as part of the Burin–Placentia West electoral district and now as Placentia West–Bellevue. For Bonavista, we opted to observe the Bonavista Historic Townscape Foundation (BHTF) because of its influence in improving the town's livability through heritage asset management.

Drawing Public Attention to Place: Amplifying Local Capacities and Assets

The PWDA and the BHTF, in its initial form as historic society for the latter, had long histories of community engagement before the cod moratorium, and both organizations increased their involvement in tackling socio-economic problems after the moratorium posed new challenges. Before the moratorium, the fishery had contributed 8 per cent to the Burin Peninsula's economy (Hamilton and Butler 2001) and employed 12.2 per cent of the labour force (Statistics Canada 2023). When the fish plants closed in the peninsula's larger communities, such as Burin and Grand Bank, people in smaller communities lost jobs not only in fishing-related industries but also in supporting industries such as construction. A similar situation occurred in Bonavista (Sinclair, Squires, and Downton 1999). The economic situation went downhill from there. People began to look for work elsewhere, and NL experienced a massive wave of out-migration. By 1998, the populations of the Burin and Bonavista peninsulas had declined by 14 per cent and 13 per cent, respectively. Out-migration stressed local businesses and led to closures and empty communities (DeMont 1993; Hamilton and Butler 2001). Since the economy is embedded in other activities, economic decline left a trail of personal and public devastation and disrupted social life, making it difficult for people to maintain their optimism (Sinclair, Squires, and Downton 1999).

The Placentia West Development Association

Development associations are rooted in the grassroots movements of the 1960s. With broad support from the government, many communities established development associations hoping to better identify local problems and to develop human and material resources (PWDA 1990). At their peak in the early 1990s, there were more than 70 development associations across NL. Today, only around 25 development associations are listed as active (Government of NL 2023), having survived government funding cuts.

Founded in 1979, the PWDA is one of the few remaining development associations. It defines its goal as ensuring local people's voices are heard in local development, planning, and action (PWDA 1990). The eight communities served by PWDA are located around the centre of the Burin Peninsula, on Newfoundland's south coast, about 260 km from the province's capital city, St. John's. One founding PWDA member explained that when the government diverted its financial support from development associations to grants to directly aid individuals who lost their jobs after the moratorium, the PWDA had to pivot to secure its financial existence. Inspired by a self-conducted local capacities and assets assessment, the PWDA turned to social entrepreneurship to generate regular income and expanded their secretariat office into Livyer's Lot Heritage Site (Livyer's Lot, n.d.), which currently housed three social businesses.

Small communities like those in Placentia West have played supporting roles in the region and lack historical structures compared to the larger regional socio-economic centres, such as Burin and Grand Bank. Doing a capacity inventory after the moratorium, the PWDA found that apart from carpentry and fishing, their communities' biggest strength was the people's mastery of household or domestic skills, such as cooking, quilting, mat-making, and knitting — the region's intangible culture. The PWDA believed that such local capacities could be the foundation for a business venture. They offered a unique social entrepreneurship opportunity, as there was no restaurant or craft shop in the area, with the closest in Marystown, around 40 km away. To establish domestic skills as community capacity and assets, the PWDA faced a twofold challenge: to convince the communities that such skills could generate income, and to provide individuals with a market to sell their goods. In fishing communities, where traditionally male-dominated occupations were considered the traditional source of income, these skills, mainly mastered by women, were not viewed as valuable trade skills but as domestic tasks or hobbies. Thus, skilled individuals lacked the confidence to market their products as they had only ever produced for domestic consumption and did not consider their goods to be suitable for sale. One quilter expressed that such doubt was reasonable given that many residents did not have the opportunity to travel beyond their town, province, or country to personally witness how their work might genuinely compete with other products in the market.

Local artisans in Placentia West take their work seriously. They have perfectionist craftsmanship and use only premium materials. In several workshops that Seto attended, he witnessed how the artisans meticulously inspected every stitch. Such attention to detail is the local habitus of craftsmanship and demonstrates the potential of tradespeople's professionalism. Unfortunately, not many people are aware of this. To create a bridge between artisans, the public, and the market, the PWDA incorporated an informal local craft business previously run by the Placentia West Mat Makers and established a craft shop in 1996. Building on the mat makers' regular activities, the shop's mandate was to generate employment in the cultural tourism industry. The PWDA expanded the craft shop to become the Placentia West Mat Makers' sole direct sales outlet as part of a larger asset transfer that also included the transfer of existing stock and funds. However, the PWDA Craft Shop ensures that most profits go to the producers, not the sellers.

The shop provides a marketplace for local artisans to sell their products, mainly traditional products and crafts, such as the region's traditional and well-known hooked rugs, paintings, small wall decorations, crochet items, quilts, wool sweaters, mitts, tuques or "stocking caps," and knitted socks, which are the shop's best-sellers. Most knitting products are made from 100 per cent natural fibre, the quilts are thicker than products common elsewhere, the mats are made from recycled fabrics, and the hand paintings are not simply generic paintings of Newfoundland scenery commonly found in other heritage shops. These items are of higher quality than mass-produced products. Locals often tell similar stories about how they bought a product from the shop as a gift and the impressed recipient later ordered more products for other people. A German tourist who bought a pair of knitted socks at the shop sent an email to the PWDA to express his astonishment at the socks' quality, mentioning that he wore them on several bike tours and they were always warm and came back to their original shape after washing. Acknowledging that such appreciation would help raise local artisans' confidence in their product, PWDA printed and hung the email on the shop's wall.

To capitalize on local cooking capacities, the PWDA established the Tea Rose Restaurant in 1999. Using local recipes that were more than a century old as assets, gathered into a collection referred to as the "Bible," the restaurant specializes in traditional Newfoundland food. The head cook in the summer of 2021 claimed that people could taste the authenticity of the restaurant's food. The claim was verified by two customers eating at the restaurant who had driven from St. John's just to have lunch. The restaurant can seat 25 people with its six tables and generate a net annual revenue of around $7,000/month.

The restaurant and the craft shop are formal market spaces where local cooks, artisans, and other community members can witness and eventually be convinced that the market will absorb their product. Drawing on profits from the two PBSEs, the PWDA provides regular services for the surrounding communities, such as:

- wage-subsidy programs and apprenticeships, which ultimately provide recommendation letters as credentials for participants to enter the job market;
- arts and craft workshops, with some successful participants eventually becoming suppliers for the craft shop;
- food service training;
- seasonal festivals and family and seniors' social programming;
- children's educational programming in cooperation with the local school;
- hiking trails;
- repairing and maintaining community infrastructure, such as harbours and other facilities that support safe access for the fishery;
- a community garden, which, later in 2021, helped reinvigorate the skills needed to supply the PWDA's farmers' market;
- workshop space and equipment for the Placentia West quilters, other craftspeople, and the 50+ Club.

By saving some of the profits over time, the PWDA was able to secure matching funds for a government grant to acquire and restore the Livyers' Lot Paddle House Museum in 1997 and to erect a new building in 2014 to house its developing économusée — a registered trademark of the International Economuseum Network Society, which highlights small-scale goods production that preserves traditional skills and craftsmanship.

The Bonavista Historic Townscape Foundation

Bonavista is located about 300 kilometres from St. John's. The town is important in the province's history because it is one of the first sites where Europeans reached North America. Giovanni Caboto, an Italian explorer hired by England's Henry VII to find new lands across the North Atlantic, made landfall in Bonavista in 1497. With more than 3,000 residents, Bonavista is one of the larger coastal communities in NL. After the cod moratorium, fishermen in Bonavista turned to crab and other species, helping the fishing industry to survive (Parsons 2019). However, processing

crab is less labour-intensive than cod and requires fewer plants and workers. Thus, like elsewhere in NL, Bonavista also witnessed a steady population decline after the close of the cod fishery. Locals, as described above,
were sometimes skeptical of government projects they perceived to be
out of touch with rural realities.

Assessing the situation at that time, members of the Bonavista Historic Society (BHS) started public discussions about how the community
could take the lead to secure its own future. Founded in 1984, the society
organized regular seminars that became the town's forum for sharing
knowledge of Bonavista's rich history. BHS members expressed that the
town needed to diversify its economy by attracting new investors to support the fishing industry. Since jobs can always be relocated elsewhere,
they believed sustainable economic development should be a place-based
effort that increases people's appreciation of the community's history,
resources, capacities, and assets, creating a connection to the place where
they dwell. They agreed that if carefully identified, protected, developed,
and managed, the existing heritage buildings, structures, sites, land-
marks, and properties could contribute to the town's economy and host
new businesses and tourism (Bradley 2018).

Bonavista has a rich cultural landscape with various buildings, architectural styles, and historical narratives (Reynolds 2018). The town has
about 1,000 pre-Confederation structures that require protection and
restoration plans (see Table 4.1). To develop the aspiration of revitalizing Bonavista's heritage properties, BHS conducted a heritage property
survey and visual documentation in 1992, with funding support from
the town. In 1994, the BHS hosted a public forum on "Heritage Conservation and the Architectural Landscape of Bonavista." The forum
discussed and successfully drafted a heritage conservation plan to promote the entire town as a heritage district: the Historic Townscape
Project. This plan promoted a vision of Bonavista as a community with
greater agency, where residents could decide their economic future by
amplifying their use of historical and heritage buildings and properties
as local assets.

Table 4.1. A shortlist of historical structures in Bonavista.

Structures	Year Built	Description
The Big Store at Mockbeggar	ca. 1733	Features an asymmetrical gable roof. Possibly the oldest fisheries building in the province.
Alexander Bridge House	ca. 1811	The oldest documented residential property in Newfoundland.
Keough building	ca. 1860	The oldest commercial structure on Bonavista's harbourfront.
Ryan Premises	ca. 1869–88	A mercantile building complex built and owned by James Ryan Ltd.
Orange Hall	1907	The hall, with its five-storey domed-roof tower, was one of the largest Orange Lodges in North America at the time.
Memorial United Church	1918	One of the largest churches in Newfoundland. It can seat more than 1,200 people.
Garrick Theatre	1945	The oldest community theatre in Newfoundland.

With an inventory and plan on hand, the BHS was ready to improve Bonavista's livability. To better undertake its tasks, the Bonavista Historic Society (BHS) was incorporated in 1999 as the Bonavista Historic Townscape Foundation (BHTF), a non-profit organization dedicated to the conservation and development of Bonavista's built heritage. Securing funding from the public through fundraising and government grants, the BHTF has contributed to restoring various heritage structures, including a church, a school, and about 100 houses and buildings.

Among the various completed projects, the renovation of the Garrick Theatre was fundamental for community buy-in and convinced the public of the value of heritage renovation projects for the town and community. The Garrick Theatre was opened in 1945 and, as the only theatre on the Bonavista Peninsula, became a popular cultural activity destination for locals and people from the surrounding communities. Local residents had a strong sentimental attachment to the facility. A young engineer who moved back to Bonavista from St. John's mentioned that many people who grew up in Bonavista shared the collective memory of going to the theatre when they were younger to watch Saturday film matinees. However, with the decline of moviegoers in the 1990s, it had to close in 2000. Three years later, the theatre's founder, John Bradley, and his family, donated the property to the BHTF. Residents of Bonavista collected 1,500 signatures to mount pressure on key politicians and senior officials to support the reopening of a year-round theatre facility. After years of fundraising, the Foundation secured several million dollars in public and private investment to start the restoration. The Garrick was reopened in April 2010, and it is now the oldest functioning theatre in NL with year-round programming.

The BHTF also sought to mainstream heritage conservation in Bonavista through the Historic Property Investment Program. It provides financial assistance to historic property owners for the exterior restoration of their structures. Although using public funding to help private property owners maintain their heritage houses might raise concerns, a member of the BHTF and a social entrepreneur explained that it would provide a "nice face for a town where young people and all Newfoundlanders could enjoy and learn about their heritage." As a heritage property owner himself, he explained that if a private owner has the sole responsibility to maintain a heritage property, the public has no control over the property's upkeep, and deteriorating houses will become eyesores for the town.

Significant economic renewal became visually evident in Bonavista as heritage revitalization projects progressed. Church Street welcomes locals and visitors alike with new artisanal restaurants and shops. A tourist interviewed for this project mentioned that he and his sportscar club had driven to Newfoundland from Halifax to visit Bonavista and see "a beautiful, traditional NL town." Although it has maintained the fishery as its economic backbone, Bonavista has diversified its economy by growing its tourism sector and launching new businesses that leverage the arts and artisanal food and beverage products (Beaudette 2021; Samson 2018). Bonavista's economy has thus come out of the moratorium stronger than before (NLSA 2016, 2018), with more than 40 businesses established between 2013 and 2018 alone (Samson 2018).

The Processes of Rebuilding Place

In 2015, the Minister of Seniors, Wellness and Social Development, Clyde Jackman, praised PWDA's resilience in providing services to the community (Government of NL 2015). In 2010, Minister of Innovation, Trade, and Rural Development Shawn Skinner applauded BHTF's ingenuity as a social enterprise in "translating local culture" into new business opportunities (Government of NL 2010). These praises capture how PBSEs can take a role in improving the quality of community life. As the leaders of the PWDA and BHTF explained, it can be a long struggle to reach that point since communities often overlook the value of existing capacities and assets. One of the hardest parts of starting a project during a crisis is persuading the affected communities that they have not lost everything. An effective way to address this problem is to increase public awareness of the value of asset-based collaborative work by pooling all available knowledge on local capacities and assets to encourage the evolving processes of asset re-creation and relate them directly to the improvement of collective well-being.

Pooling Knowledge

Those involved in the PWDA and BHTF often expressed that one of the greatest challenges in amplifying local capacities and assets in rural communities in a province with a declining population is to secure the labour needed to support a PBSE. Yet in their experience, paradoxically, such pressure has taught them the art of networking and initiating collaborations. The PWDA and BHTF actively recruited local community members with various professional backgrounds to become volunteers or serve on their boards, including educators, business owners, council members, town officials, fish plant workers, and union leaders. Members with diverse backgrounds can enhance an organization's creativity during decision-making (Torchia, Calabrò, and Morner 2015). They are essential to realizing projects that require mobilizing community support and resources. For example, for the Historic Church Street Revitalization Project, the BHTF proposed that Church Street be reorganized from a one-way to a two-way street. The proposal was initially met with skepticism since it would reduce space for vehicle traffic. However, the business owners and a member of the fire department who sat on the board convinced the public that such a change was needed to encourage more visitors to establishments in the surrounding areas. By drawing on its diverse and influential board members, the Foundation has emerged as a "movement player," that is, an agent that has built "networks of collaboration with players across different sectors" (Stoddart, Mattoni, and McLevey 2020, 194).

It is not that outside knowledge is irrelevant — both PBSEs in this study actively form networks with actors outside the community, such as artists, entrepreneurs and social entrepreneurs, scholars, government representatives, and other actors related to rural community development — but local knowledge deserves particular attention because it informs the public specifically about who on site can do what (capacities), and which (assets) can be further developed (see also Keikelame and Swartz 2019, and a similar discussion in Chapter 3). Knowing the community creates a better inventory of the community's potential. Such local knowledge informed the PWDA and BHTF to utilize previously undervalued assets, such as domestic skills and dilapidated structures. Revamping local capacities and assets is therefore relational, involving many actors, resources, and activities. Exactly because of this relational dimension, more community members become engaged as more local capacities and assets are amplified.

Local, place-based knowledge can also help when, as described in the introduction to this chapter, the government or outsiders cannot grasp a full picture of a community because their observations might have overlooked local values. Had the PWDA and BHTF not raised locally specific issues, the government would have missed opportunities to support the communities in Placentia West and Bonavista in incubating new economic activities, for example, through government-funded heritage revitalization and skill development workshops. As community-based organizations, the PWDA and the BHTF play a role in countering emerging challenges they witness in their communities and initiating public discussions about how such problems can best be addressed.

Any community-based organization could do all the above, but PBSEs like the PWDA and the BHTF can become development drivers for two reasons. First, unlike municipalities, they are allowed to gain profits from the capacities and assets they manage. They can use these profits to kickstart other development activities. Second, to strengthen their local capacities, PBSEs tend to find support from everyone and everywhere: people from different municipalities, public and private sectors, and outsiders and insiders (for a similar finding, see Chapter 3 on the linking role of SABRI). With such "inclusive entrepreneurship" (Baskaran, Chandran, and Ng 2019), social entrepreneurs have more flexibility to engage different ideas and possibilities. They can informally chat about new ideas about optimizing local assets and directly kick off projects without dealing with complex organizational decision-making. "Every minute, we have to think about creating something, to attract people to come. We have different ideas coming from different kinds of people, and then we're hanging out [to generate new ideas], which helps so much," said one of PWDA's managers.

As participation grows, PBSEs can increase product and project development. That is why PWDA plans to expand its craft shop. Many of those who participated in its craft workshops are now able to become suppliers, and the product stock continues to increase. In Bonavista, more than 10 entrepreneurs we interviewed were previously directly or indirectly involved with BHTF and credited the BHS with spiking their interest in jumping into heritage-related businesses through its discussion series.

Evolving Projects

Using their profits, the PWDA and the BHTF could regularly organize concerts, festivals, training seminars, workshops, and various activities for different groups. Because of these socially oriented activities, the communities began to see the organizations as community hubs. The place-based social enterprises of both the BHTF and PWDA have become new local destinations where local families bring their visiting extended family or friends. The Garrick Theatre's program has expanded from movies to concerts, drama and other cultural performances, trivia, and karaoke nights. The PWDA organizes various traditional festivals at Livyer's Lot, such as summer and winter festivals, concerts, and a community garden used by seniors and primary/elementary students. These events provide spaces where older and younger generations can mingle, and their sites became cultural hubs where residents socialize, take wedding pictures, and attend must-see events for the local communities and the entire region. As public spaces, the PWDA's Livyer's Lot and BHTF's Garrick Theatre are the community's monuments to livability.

With the presence of the hubs, communities in Placentia West and Bonavista have also experienced "community upscaling" (Seto 2020) in which the growing local participation has inspired other projects. In the 1990s, the PWDA's main activity was limited to job training and public infrastructure maintenance. Today, the PWDA has two social enterprises and a museum and is home to various local clubs. The BHTF started with a few thousand dollars for renovation projects and now deals with millions of dollars in townscape revitalization involving participation from the town, local entrepreneurs, and people with various backgrounds. Such growth was made possible by the organizations' ability to partially finance newly identified needs in the communities. Murphy stated that since the establishment of the restaurant and craft shop, women's participation in the PWDA has increased, for example, through the quilting club, public kitchen, and community garden. Participation also increased through collaboration with other organizations, for example, the local 50+ club. The 50+ club had the idea to plant a communal garden in the backyard of Livyer's Lot. The PWDA then cooperated with the local school to introduce students to gardening and eventually built a greenhouse at the back of the school. The students and members of the 50+ Club can move their plants to the greenhouse in the fall and back to Livyer's Lot for spring and summer. As interest grew, the PWDA revisited an idea it originally had 30 years earlier to start a farmers' market, and in 2021 the organization constructed a building for it. As community hubs, PBSEs create projects that provide space for democratic training of community engagement.

Figure 4.1. As community hubs and public spaces, Livyer's Lot hosts summer music concerts (top), and the Garrick Theatre regularly presents performances (bottom). (Photo credit: Ario Seto, 2021)

While these specific developments might not have been anticipated, innovative ideas coincide with increasing community involvement. Accordingly, capacities and asset-based community development should be seen as a process because it is related to PBSEs' "expansion of capabilities" through delivering more community services (Scarlato 2013). The process requires identifying which capacities and assets can be capitalized on first, through asset mapping (Fuller, Guy, and Pletsch 2013), and working with local capacities and assets is seldom linear. PBSEs work in stages, as each project's success helps them define the next stage of work.

Relating Capacities and Assets to Collective Well-Being

The activities described above might not always bring an adequate economic return for a PBSE, but they foster collective well-being and community pride. As traffic increases in the community or region, their confidence in the long-term survival of their community grows. For PBSEs, community revitalization is not simply an effort to generate individual wealth but also a way of activating other activities that nurture a community's social life. Relationships are a fundamental part of an individual; they precede the definitions of people and collectives, tangible objects and immaterial values, places and histories (Donati and Archer 2015). This requires further collaboration, engagement, and regular conversations with the public to determine what might contribute to residents' well-being. To identify such needs, the PWDA and BHTF rely on local actors who know what the community members would like to have or experience. In Placentia West, PWDA hired local musicians to host summer music courses at almost no cost. This serves the community as the local school does not have a music teacher although folk music has been part of the NL community's oral history and identity. One of BHTF's leaders explained that it is sometimes difficult for the Garrick to break even beyond the tourist season. Nonetheless, the BHTF was convinced that the theatre needed a year-round and consistent program to enhance community livability. He assured that a livable town is not simply a beautiful place, but also a lively place that enhances individual lives. Livability is a prerequisite to maintaining individual and community well-being (Atkinson et al. 2020).

A community leader in Bonavista stated that funding for community heritage activities and projects is important for developing an identity of a place that can be marketed to millennials, the fastest-growing demographic moving to rural communities. Unique identities enhance community pride (see also Jennings 2015; Shannon and Mitchell 2020). Augmenting the connection between place and community is important, as a young volunteer at the PWDA proudly mentioned, "every time my friends from town come to visit, I bring them here to taste our food and see the museum, and they're amazed by how original it is."

Future Strategies for Managing Local Capacities and Assets

Success creates new challenges that require PBSEs to navigate paradoxes, a message also echoed in Chapter 6 of this volume. One key challenge is maintaining control of the environment where the asset is growing. Despite the rising demand for local crafts, the PWDA's inventory is only slowly growing due to its suppliers' limited production capacity. With the successful town beautification, Bonavista is now becoming a major tourist destination. The town is lively in the summer, but businesses still close for several months beginning in October, for "winter hibernation." The BHTF has tried to avert the situation by finding tenants willing to keep their businesses open year-round, but it cannot control the situation if all the other businesses close during the off-season. With Bonavista's beauty and tourism industry, housing prices have increased, making it difficult for locals to access the housing market (*CBC News* 2023). Leaders of both social enterprises also described how their planning and townscape enhancement projects often take on duties that should be government-led initiatives, such as the case of PWDA's annual summer music program. Dealing with local capacities and assets, therefore, comes with a caveat: rural PBSEs sometimes rise to meet the responsibilities of government when the latter's capacity is limited or reduced due to policy changes (Steiner, Farmer, and Bosworth 2020).

However, these challenges are part of the process of amplifying local capacities and assets, and the challenges themselves can actually generate new ideas. Creating long-term plans can help increase a place-based social enterprise's agency, such as when community members formed the BHTF and developed its 20-year plan for the Historic Townscape Project. The plan was later incorporated into the town's municipal development goals. A retired councilman explained the importance of council support: "The BHTF has a [Townscape Management] plan that the public approved in 2001. The work is not yet done and has to go through several [project] phases. The council support directs the town to provide its utmost support so that the Foundation could get it done." People embed their decisions in both short- and long-term frameworks that need to extend beyond the life cycles of individual projects. When such strategies are embedded in a long-term plan, other institutions can adopt them, such as the town council, which allows for succession planning. Only then can local assets become further embedded in the community's life.

Every plan requires operators to see it through. Maintaining adequate labour to manage growing assets in rural areas with declining populations is a tough job. Outsiders, returning former residents, and newcomers can help by supplementing the local labour force or by bringing new ideas from projects or activities they know from elsewhere. With current technology, place-based social enterprises should be able to expand the notion of local capacity beyond physical and geographical limitations. A young volunteer at the PWDA who was going to leave her community for university explained that she would like to continue to support the organization, but that it would be impossible since she physically would not be there. "I wish I could somehow help online," she said. Care for and a connection to local assets and capacities can extend beyond physical geography. Those who leave their communities still have the right and the capacity to love the place and to contribute to its advancement through new avenues, such as online support. Long-term development of capacities and assets cannot be secured without adequate support, and online engagement allows PBSEs to extend their pool of possible supporters.

Concluding Remarks

Amplifying local capacities and assets furthers rural community development because it prioritizes place by bringing together the place's actors, knowledge, and material and non-material culture. This approach is not only about community self-reliance, but also about cultural change; that is how the actors in community-based organizations, like place-based social enterprises, create evolving strategies to optimize their local capacities and assets because of their limited resources. Rather than viewing local capacities and assets simply as the objects of economic development discussed in the ABCD approach, we consider them to be relational matters that shape and activate community initiatives.

The case studies described in this chapter offer at least four lessons. First, since asset recognition is relational, amplifying local assets empowers local capacities. PBSEs can play a role here by inviting more actors to be involved and generating relatable activities for the communities. Second, revisiting and revaluing old assets are processes related to local knowledge, which is needed to discover what is valuable and doable. Although cultural heritage is part of everyday life, how its value is recognized can differ among community members. In Bonavista, community leaders and the BHTF first needed to raise public awareness and convince the community of the value of revitalizing old buildings. In Placentia West, household skills were not considered a means to contribute to the economy until the PWDA formalized such skills through a restaurant and a craft shop. As processes, recreating local assets can lead to unforeseeable outcomes; two decades ago, it was unimaginable that Bonavista would become one of NL's artistic centres. Since the experience of recreating local capacities and assets differs from place to place, supporting policies and mechanisms should be locally contextualized.

Third, the PWDA and the BHTF were able to become stewards of these processes because they generated revenue and used it to expand into other projects. These activities provide signs of community life, creating an impression for locals that there is a future in those places. Through engaging in economic development, catalyzing a new ecosystem of participation, and ensuring year-round community liveliness, PBSEs show how particular attention to local assets and capacities can enhance people's connection to their community and sense of ownership. Fourth and finally, while PBSEs offer many benefits, neither capacities nor assets at the local level can completely solve major community problems such as out-migration and the lack of public services described earlier. These problems require actions from the state through robust policies and programs. However, amplifying local capacities and assets could help the community as a "first-aid kit" that stimulates other social and economic activities and contributes to revitalizing community life. Such engagement is a democratic method that invites more participation, including from the state, through funding and support programs. Therefore, it is the state's responsibility to fully support communities experimenting with what works for them based on their collective aspirations. As this chapter shows, communities require the agency, such as place-based social enterprises can provide, to *amplify local capacities and assets* since local involvement becomes indispensable to shaping effective community development.

Acknowledgements

This research was funded by Future Ocean and Coastal Infrastructures, a project of the Ocean Frontier Institute funded by Canada First Research Excellence Fund, the Atlantic Canada Opportunities Agency, and the Government of Newfoundland and Labrador's Department of Industry, Energy and Technology. We sincerely thank those interviewed and members of the Placentia West Development Association and the Bonavista Historic Townscape Foundation for their deep insights.

References

Atkinson, Sarah, Anne-Marie Bagnall, Rhiannon Corcoran, Jane South, and Sarah Curtis. 2020. "Being Well Together: Individual Subjective and Community Well-being." *Journal of Happiness Studies* 21: 1903–21. https://doi.org/10.1007/s10902-019-00146-.

Baker, Melvin. 2014. "Challenging the 'Merchants' Domain': William Coaker and the Price of Fish, 1908–1919." *Newfoundland and Labrador Studies* 29, no. 2: 189–226.

Baskaran, Angathevar, V.G.R. Chandran, and Boon-Kwee Ng. 2019. "Inclusive Entrepreneurship, Innovation and Sustainable Growth: Role of Business Incubators, Academia and Social Enterprises in Asia." *Science, Technology and Society* 24, no. 3: 385–400. https://doi.org/10.1177/0971721819873178.

Beaudette, Catherine. 2021. "Bonavista Biennale — Art Encounters on the Edge: Contemporary Art in Rural Newfoundland." In *Cultural Sustainability, Tourism and Development*, edited by Nancy Duxbury, 69–84. London: Routledge.

Blickem, Christian, Shoba Dawson, Susan Kirk, Ivaylo Vassilev, Amy Mathieson, Rebecca Harrison, Peter Bower, and Jonathan Lamb. 2018. "What Is Asset-Based Community Development and How Might It Improve the Health of People with Long-Term Conditions? A Realist Synthesis." *SAGE Open* 8, no. 3. https://doi.org/10.1177/2158244018787223.

Bradley, David. 2018. "Case Study on Bonavista Historic Townscape Foundation: Laying the Foundation for the Revitalization of a Historic Community." In *Adapting Heritage Toolkit*, 17–23. St. John's: Heritage NL.

CBC News. 2023. "Bonavista Is Looking to Shut Out Airbnb as Long-Term Housing Gets Swallowed Up by Investors." February 6, 2023. https://www.cbc.ca/news/canada /newfoundland-labrador/bonavista-housing-market-1.6736419.

Collinson, Beth, and David Best. 2019. "Promoting Recovery from Substance Misuse through Engagement with Community Assets: Asset Based Community Engagement." *Substance Abuse: Research and Treatment* 13. https://doi.org/10.1177/1178221819876575.

Daly, Mary, and Sue Westwood. 2018. "Asset-based Approaches, Older People and Social Care: An Analysis and Critique." *Ageing and Society* 38, no. 6: 1087–99.

DeMont, John. 1993. "Waiting, and Praying, for Cod." *Maclean's*. June 28, 1993.

https://archive.macleans.ca/article/1993/6/28/waiting-and-praying-for-cod.

Donati, Pierpaolo, and Margaret S. Archer. 2015. *The Relational Subject*. Cambridge: Cambridge University Press.

Fuller, Tony, Denyse Guy, and Carolyn Pletsch. 2013. *Asset Mapping: A Handbook*. Guelph, ON: University of Guelph.

Goll, Johanna C., Georgina Charlesworth, Katrina Scior, and Joshua Stott. 2015. "Barriers to Social Participation among Lonely Older Adults: The Influence of Social Fears and Identity." *PLOS ONE* 13, no. 7: e0201510. https://doi.org/10.1371/journal.pone.0201510.

Government of Newfoundland and Labrador. 2010. "Bonavista's Garrick Theatre Leverages Culture to Target New Business Opportunities." May 7, 2010. https://www.releases.gov.nl.ca/releases/2010/intrd/0507n01.htm.

Government of Newfoundland and Labrador. 2015. "Investing in Health Care Infrastructure for Families and Communities: New Community Clinic Officially Opened on the Burin Peninsula." March 6, 2015. https://www.releases.gov.nl.ca/releases/2015/health/0306n03.aspx.

Government of Newfoundland and Labrador. 2023. "Digital Government and Service: Companies and Deeds Online." January 30, 2023. https://cado.eservices.gov.nl.ca/CadoInternet/Company/CompanySearchViewAll.aspx.

Guyer, Jane. 1997. "Endowments and Assets: The Anthropology of Wealth and the Economics of Intrahousehold Allocation." In *Intrahousehold Resource Allocation in Developing Countries: Models, Methods, and Policy*, edited by Lawrence Haddad, John Hoddinott, and Harold Alderman, 112–29. Baltimore: Johns Hopkins University Press.

Hamilton, Lawrence C., and Melissa J. Butler. 2001. "Outport Adaptations: Social Indicators through Newfoundland's Cod Crisis." *Human Ecology Review* 8, no. 2: 1–11.

Heritage NL. n.d. "Protecting, promoting and preserving Newfoundland & Labrador's built and intangible heritage." Heritage Property Search. Accessed July 21, 2023. https://heritagenl.ca/discover/heritage-property-search/?search=Bonavista&type&region

Jennings, Andrew. 2015. "The Old Rock's Rockin': A Cultural Anatomy of Shetland." In *Place Peripheral: Place-Based Development in Rural, Island, and Remote Regions*, edited by Kelly Vodden, Ryan Gibson, and Godfrey Baldacchino, 156–79. St. John's: ISER Books.

Keikelame, Mpoe Johannah, and Leslie Swartz. 2019. "Decolonizing Research Methodologies: Lessons from a Qualitative Research Project, Cape Town, South Africa." *Global Health Action* 12: 1–7. https://doi.org/10.1080/165497 16.2018.1561175.

Kretzmann, John P., and John L. McKnight. 1993. *Building Communities from the Inside Out.* Evanston, IL: Northwestern University Press.

Livyer's Lot. n.d. Livyer's Lot Heritage Site (website). Placentia West Heritage Committee. Accessed July 28, 2023. https://livyerslot.ca

MacLeod, Mary Anne, and Akwogu Emejulu. 2014. "Neoliberalism with a Community Face? A Critical Analysis of Asset-based Community Development in Scotland." *Journal of Community Practice* 22, no. 4: 430–50.

Newfoundland and Labrador Statistics Agency (NLSA). 2016. "Bonavista: Census 2016 and National Household Survey 2011: Employment by Occupation." Community Accounts (website). https://nl.communityac-counts.ca/table.asp?_=vb7En4WVgaauzXZlS6rIxpuixqOVko7Lqomyv4yyk-M2yo6DMxLmauZ-D.

Newfoundland and Labrador Statistics Agency (NLSA). 2018. "Bonavista Profile: Personal Income per Capita." Community Accounts (website). https://nl. communityaccounts.ca/profiles.asp?_=vb7En4WVgaauzXZl.

Parsons, Jonathan. 2019. "A Banner Year for Bonavista Ocean Choice International Fish Plant." *Saltwire News.* November 15, 2019. https://www.saltwire. com/newfoundland-labrador/ business/a-banner-year-for-bonavista-ocean-choice-international-fish-plant-376503.

Peters, Paul, Dean Carson, Robert Porter, Ana Vuin, Doris Carson, and Prescott Ensign. 2018. "My Village Is Dying? Integrating Methods from the Inside Out." *Canadian Review of Sociology* 55, no. 3: 451–75. https://doi.org/10.1111/ cars.12212.

Placentia West Development Association (PWDA). 1990. *Organization Profile.* March 27, 1990.

Reynolds, Matt C. 2018. "Maintaining the Character of a Place: Critical Approaches to Built Heritage in Newfoundland." Master's thesis, Dalhousie University.

Ruseski, Goradz. 2006. "Subsidies and the 2003 Cod Fishery Closure in Canada." In *Subsidy Reform and Sustainable Development: Economic, Environmental and Social Aspects, OECD Sustainable Development Studies,* 109–22.

Paris: OECD Publishing. https://doi.org/10.1787/9789264025653-en.

Samson, Alyson. 2018. "How a Historic Newfoundland Town Is Moving from Fishing Hub to Hipster Mecca." *CBC News*. July 29, 2018. https://www.cbc.ca/news/canada/newfoundland-labrador/bonavista-transformation-1.4743972.

Scarlato, Margherita. 2013. "Social Enterprise, Capabilities and Development Paradigms: Lessons from Ecuador." *Journal of Development Studies* 49, no. 9: 1270–83. https://doi.org/10.1080/00220388.2013.790962.

Seto, Ario. 2020. "After Community: Upscaling and the Flux of Online Civic Engagement in Indonesia."*Asiascape: Digital Asia* 7, nos. 1–2: 42–68. https://doi.org/10.1163/22142312-bja10003.

Shannon, Meghan, and Clare J.A. Mitchell. 2020. "Commercial Counterurbanites' Contribution to Cultural Heritage Tourism: The Case of Brigus, Newfoundland and Labrador." *Journal of Tourism and Cultural Change* 18, no. 4: 421–36.

Sinclair, Peter R., Heather Squires, and Lynn Downton. 1999. "A Future without Fish? Constructing Social Life on Newfoundland's Bonavista Peninsula after the Cod Moratorium." *Fishing Places, Fishing People: Traditions and Issues in Canadian Small-Scale Fisheries, edited by* Dianne Newell and Rosemary E. Ommer, 321–39. Toronto: University of Toronto Press.

Statistics Canada. 2023. "Labour Force Characteristics by Industry." https://www150.statcan.gc.ca/t1/tbl1/en/tv.action?pid=1410002301&pickMembers%5B0%5D=1.2&pickMembers%5B1%5D=2.1&pickMembers%5B2%5D=4.1&pickMembers%5B3%5D=5.1&cubeTimeFrame.startYear=1990&cubeTimeFrame.endYear=2000&referencePeriods=19900101%2C20000101.

Steiner, Artur, Jane Farmer, and Gary Bosworth. 2020. "Rural Social Enterprise: Evidence to Date, and a Research Agenda." *Journal of Rural Studies* 70: 139–43.

Stoddart, Mark C.J., Alice Mattoni, and John McLevey. 2020. *Industrial Development and Eco-Tourisms: Can Oil and Nature Conservation Co-Exist?* London: Palgrave Macmillan.

Torchia, Mariateresa, Andrea Calabrò, and Michèle Morner. 2015. "Board of Directors' Diversity, Creativity, and Cognitive Conflict: The Role of Board Members' Interaction." *International Studies of Management & Organization* 45, no. 1: 6–24.

CHAPTER 5

Conveying Compelling Stories: The Revitalization of Battle Harbour

Mark C.J. Stoddart and Gordon Slade

Introduction

Battle Harbour National Historic District is a historic site located on Battle Island, a small island off the coast of Labrador near the communities of Mary's Harbour, St. Lewis, and Lodge Bay. Of note, Battle Harbour was not named for any battle. Rather, the name is believed to be derived from the Portuguese "batal" for "boat." Today, it serves as a regional tourism anchor and space for historic preservation that is promoted based on its remoteness, simple beauty, and appeal to history buffs and ecotourists. Like most rural and relatively remote communities in Newfoundland and Labrador, this region was hard hit by the cod fishery collapse and moratorium in 1992. We turn to Battle Harbour as an example of revitalizing place by *conveying a compelling story* (the "C" principle in the PLACE Framework) about Battle Harbour as historically significant because it was known as the unofficial capital of the Labrador fishery. The Labrador fishery saw thousands of fishers and their families travel seasonally to the region from the island of Newfoundland. Many coastal communities that were active in the 1880s–90s are now abandoned, which leaves Battle Harbour as a particularly significant site for carrying the story of the Labrador fishery into the future. We look closely at the period 1990–2013 to show how this compelling story was constructed through academic–community collaboration and supported by social enterprise principles.

Both authors have been involved with Battle Harbour. Gordon Slade served in a variety of public service roles in his career in the Canadian government and in the government of Newfoundland and Labrador. He was the initiator and a key figure in redeveloping Battle Harbour as a National Historic District and a regional tourism anchor during the period 1990–2000. As founding chair and managing director of the Battle Harbour Historic Trust (BHHT), he had a hand in all the developments in Battle Harbour and was a first-hand witness to the restoration of the community into a beautiful example of an important era in Newfoundland and Labrador's history. Based on this experience, he subsequently advised Parks Canada on the development of other historic sites in the province.

Mark Stoddart is a sociology professor at Memorial University. He led an academic research project in 2013 on Battle Harbour that was initiated through conversations with Slade and was supported by the Harris Centre Applied Research Fund. The project included a survey of nearby communities on the social, cultural, and economic impacts of Battle Harbour for the region, as well as fieldwork — including observation and formal interviews — at the site. This research found a high level of consensus on the positive social and cultural impacts of Battle Harbour for surrounding host communities. It also found generally positive — though less consistent — views of the economic benefits of Battle Harbour, including contributions to training and skill development in the community and avenues for people to stay in their communities instead of going elsewhere to work and live (Ramos, Stoddart, and Chafe 2016; Stoddart, Catano, and Ramos 2018).

After providing an overview of Battle Harbour prior to 1990, we discuss how a compelling story was crafted through academic–community partnerships and supported by three related pillars: (1) the protection of material culture and heritage; (2) the ongoing practice of intangible culture and heritage; and (3) the importance of doing "history in place" (Barber and Peniston-Bird 2020) by emphasizing the relationship between the historic buildings and artifacts and the surrounding landscape/sea-scape within which they are situated. We then discuss the process for increasing community buy-in to the compelling story of Battle Harbour through the adoption of social enterprise principles.

The revitalization of Battle Harbour in the wake of the cod fishery col-lapse demonstrates the potential for using academic–community part-nerships and social enterprise principles to respond to social-ecological crisis and the decline of natural resource economies by transitioning to development centred on historic preservation and tourism. This chap-ter builds on other research that argues for incorporating social enter-prise principles to help ensure that tourism development advances the social well-being of host communities through positive economic, cultural, and social impacts (Higgins-Desbiolles et al. 2019; Murphy et al. 2020; Reggers et al. 2016; Slawinski et al. 2021; Spenceley and Meyer 2012). In the conclusion of the chapter, we also reflect on tensions between varying perspectives on Battle Harbour in terms of how to balance inter-ests in historical preservation, tourism development, and community accessibility.

Overview of Site to 1990

Battle Harbour has a long history. The island is part of the NunatuKavut Inuit traditional territory. It was also used by Basque fishers in the six-teenth century. When Basque fishers moved to Spitsbergen, Norway, to continue whaling, French migratory cod fishing and Canadian seal hunt-ing began to increase. These remained seasonal occupations until the nineteenth century, when methods for utilizing resources throughout the year were developed. Other seasonal occupations, such as fur trapping, were used to keep people going through the winter until the spring and summer seal and cod could be fished. With this shift in practices, small settlements took root along the headlands of the Labrador coast, one of the earliest being Battle Harbour (Figure 5.1). Because of its location between the island of Newfoundland and the north of Labrador, Battle

Harbour was considered a gateway to the Labrador fishing grounds and was integral to that industry.

In the 1770s, sometime before this new settlement pattern began, John Slade of Poole, England, chose Battle Harbour as the site for his northern trading post, having been well established in Twillingate, NL, before this. Although the area had been largely ignored by the fishery before then, Mr. Slade had made a good choice, because his site on Battle Island could easily avail itself of both offshore and mainland resources,

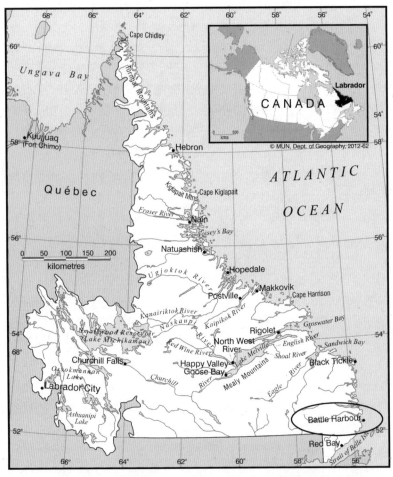

Figure 5.1. Map of eastern North America, showing the location of Battle Harbour. (Courtesy of Charles Conway, 2012)

being in the mouth of St. Lewis Inlet. His ships also had a sheltered port in the channel between Battle and Great Caribou islands.

There were several developments in the nineteenth century that helped to cement Battle Harbour as the "unofficial capital" of Labrador (Pearson 2022). First, the Labrador fishery evolved into a family-operated industry, with merchants becoming intermediaries between the fishers and the companies. Second, the Newfoundland fishery grew enormously, and ports and merchants in Newfoundland supplanted those in Devon and Dorset, in the west country of England. This process was completed in Labrador when the St. John's firm Baine, Johnston and Company bought the Battle Harbour site from Mr. Slade in 1871. A third factor that encouraged settlement in places like Battle Harbour was the discovery that great numbers of seals could be hunted in the early spring, using the same vessels that would be used for the cod fishery. This meant that cod fishers had reason to stay longer, and that they did not have to make a huge investment to take part in the new fishery that included cod and sealing.

The growing population of Battle Harbour drew other sorts of attention as well. Bishop Edward Feild — the first Newfoundland Anglican bishop to visit Labrador — went to the area in the fall of 1848 and was surprised by the number of people there. He wrote that there were some 100 ships from all over in the tiny tickle, and that 350 people permanently resided there. He estimated the summer population to be around 10,000. On this basis, he had a school built in 1850 and an Anglican church was consecrated in 1857. The Church of St. James the Apostle still stands, and the Battle Harbour Historic Trust restored the building in 1994. It is the oldest church of its kind in NL and is the only extant example of the work of William Grey, a noted ecclesiastical architect.

Dr. Wilfred Grenfell also had a large impact on Battle Harbour. Grenfell was a British doctor and head of the International Grenfell Association (IGA), who later supported the cooperative movement to create fishers' co-ops. The IGA was a mission dedicated to improving the health of people in coastal Labrador and the Northern Peninsula through international fundraising efforts and hospital construction. Being concerned for the health of the large number of fishers who were not being cared for at Battle Harbour, he made a trip for what would become the International Grenfell Association in 1892. In 1893, using buildings donated by a local merchant, he built a hospital as well as a doctor's cottage (Rompkey 2009). This hospital was the first in the province outside of St. John's.

Further development came to the area in a short time. A Marconi wireless station was built in 1904. This was the only wireless station in the region left open all year, and it acted as a feeder station for all the others during the active season (Crummey 2021). In 1930, a fire destroyed the old hospital and general store, along with several homes. The cryptic message from the Marconigram was simply "Battle Harbour Burning." In 1935, the Newfoundland Rangers built a detachment at Battle Harbour, which became a Royal Canadian Mounted Police (RCMP) post in 1950 after the province joined Confederation with Canada.

The explorer Robert E. Peary frequently visited Battle Harbour during his expeditions to the Arctic, and in 1909 he used the wireless station at Battle Harbour to send a message to the *New York Times* that he had finally reached the North Pole. On 17 September he held two press conferences in the local salt store concerning this expedition and addressed the counterclaim of Dr. Frederick Cook to have reached the Pole first. For 10 days the controversy claimed the attention of the world's newspapers, pushing Battle Harbour into the public eye. The issue was never really settled and can still cause heated debate today.

Battle Harbour's importance grew over about 200 years, but its decline took less than 100. The salt fish industry collapsed in the early 1900s, causing many residents to move inshore to places like Mary's Harbour. The hospital was relocated to that community in 1929, taking its prestige with it. Then in the 1940s, the newly established Canadian Forces Base Goose Bay encouraged new settlement in central Labrador. However, the government-sponsored resettlement programs of the late 1960s delivered the final blow (Loo 2020). Battle Harbour was resettled along with many other small and isolated communities in this province. This spelled the end of permanent, year-round occupation of the site as many residents moved to other nearby communities. Many families initially kept their homes at Battle Harbour and returned every summer, and a few still do. The mercantile premises were sold to Earle Freighting Service Limited of Carbonear in 1955, which operated it basically unaltered until the groundfish moratorium in the early 1990s. In 1991, the Earles donated the site to the Battle Harbour Historic Trust and a new era for the community began. After a period of restoration work, the site was opened to the public in 1997.

Conveying Compelling Stories through Battle Harbour

Crafting a Compelling Story

In the wake of the 1992 cod moratorium, the search for alternative regional economic drivers led to the idea of historical preservation. At Battle Harbour, the question of whether there could be an alternative economic driver for this region in the wake of the moratorium was also raised (Applin 2010). As Pollak (2017) notes, many of the stories told about rural places are stories of decline and struggle. By contrast, telling compelling stories that value rural places, traditions, and ways of being is a vital part of rural revitalization. A large part of the work of the Battle Harbour Historic Trust and the revitalization of Battle Harbour was to craft a compelling narrative of the island as the capital of the Labrador fishery. This narrative was developed through collaboration and leadership across BHHT and several academic researchers from Memorial University and beyond. Historian and former Memorial University president Dr. Leslie Harris was instrumental in initially gathering people to serve on the BHHT board. He chaired the board for some time and contributed his expertise on rural Newfoundland and Labrador. Labrador Institute director and anthropologist Carol Brice-Bennett and geographer Dr. Gordon Hancock also served on the BHHT board. Dr. Shane O'Dea contributed expertise in vernacular architecture, while archaeologist Dr. Peter Pope assisted with dating the properties on the Battle Harbour site. Dr. Ches Sanger prepared the Battle Harbour case study for Historic Sites and Monuments of Canada. Joyce Yates, a Halifax-based graduate of the University of Edinburgh, Scotland, provided the necessary early engagement with expertise in cultural preservation and management. The early development of the project benefited from the contributions of this wide range of researchers who helped fill gaps in the local community resources and skill base. Memorial University's active participation and collaboration with BHHT was more pronounced than in many other provincial economic development projects.

In early conversations about the project, Parks Canada resisted the idea of telling the Labrador fishery's story on site in Battle Harbour because of its perceived remoteness and transportation challenges for visitors. However, the historical work done by university academics helped to strengthen and elaborate the compelling story that BHHT had articulated of Battle Harbour as the capital of the Labrador fishery. Academic participants helped do the foundational work that helped justify why Battle Harbour deserved recognition as a national historic site, as well as why the story of the Labrador fishery needed to be told at Battle Harbour as a form of "history in place" (Barber and Peniston-Bird 2020).

These key actors were influential in the early stages of establishing a compelling story about Battle Harbour and making the case for redevelopment and revitalization based on historical preservation and tourism. They bought into the idea of Battle Harbour as the place to tell the story of the Labrador fishery, as well as the idea that this storytelling could be accomplished successfully in a relatively remote part of Newfoundland and Labrador. To a large extent, the local community did not have the capacity on its own to initiate or carry out this project. Without political connections or the capacity to navigate relationships with politicians and decision-makers, as well as expertise in cultural heritage preservation and interpretation, it would have been very difficult for the local community to get this project off the ground. This chapter's second author, Gordon Slade, played an important bridging role in connecting BHHT with his experience as a senior member of the civil service with the government of Canada. The involvement, professional investment, and outsider leadership of the university community and others were therefore critical to getting the project moving.

Pillar 1: Protecting Material Culture and Heritage

The revitalization of Battle Harbour through historical preservation and tourism development was rooted in a compelling story of Battle Harbour as the historic capital of the Labrador cod fishery. This story is supported by three pillars that are integrated into the Battle Harbour historic site. First, there is the protection of material culture and heritage. This includes a collection of historical buildings, including a restored church and private residences that are among the oldest in Labrador, as well as the province's last intact salt fish mercantile premises. The wharf has also been restored and a wide range of 400 historical artifacts are housed for display on site. Battle Harbour is arguably the most complete example of mercantile premises that still stand in North America (Sanger 1996). Many similar sites were allowed to fall into ruin or were destroyed for replacement by more modern fish plants. Battle Harbour did not meet this fate because Earle Freighting used it as-is until the premises were gifted to the Battle Harbour Historic Trust to be restored as an example of a nineteenth-century fishing port and settlement.

The site is also set apart by visitors' ability to rent rooms and stay in the historical buildings, something that cannot be done at other federally recognized historic sites in Canada. The kitchen building has also been adapted into a restaurant as an amenity for visitors. The richness of material culture at Battle Harbour stands in contrast with that at Red Bay, which is another key historic site and tourism anchor for coastal Labrador. The Red Bay National Historic Site tells the story of Basque whaling in the region. In Red Bay, however, Parks Canada has had to tell the story of the site with much more limited access to material culture that can inform visitors' experience.

Pillar 2: Enacting Intangible Culture and Heritage

Battle Harbour provides a setting for the ongoing enactment of intangible culture and heritage. This adds to a sense of "performative authenticity" (Zhu 2012) that is created in the relationship between visitors and site workers who continue to transmit the traditions of Battle Harbour. The intangible culture of the region is performed for/with tourists through heritage carpentry, storytelling and tours of the site, and cooking.

The integration of heritage carpentry is particularly noteworthy. Work at Battle Harbour provided opportunities for skills training in heritage carpentry, through restoration projects and ongoing maintenance. BHHT engaged other educators to help develop the capacity for heritage carpentry training, including from Algonquin College in Ottawa and the community college in Happy Valley-Goose Bay, as well as heritage carpenters from Newfoundland and Labrador who were working elsewhere in Canada. When the Battle Harbour Historic Trust took over the site, many of the buildings were thought to be beyond repair. Since then, however, local people trained by the Trust in heritage carpentry, with the guidance of historians and architects, have restored more than 20 buildings, as well as wharves and walkways, with painstaking attention to authentic design and materials. Being local gave the craftspersons an appreciation for the site, and their pride in personal connections to the community shows in the quality of their work.

Tours of the site are guided by staff with long-term personal connections to Battle Harbour who have a rich knowledge of the site and surrounding communities. Many historic sites employ guides or interpreters with historical or academic subject knowledge of the sites; but at Battle Harbour, the guided tours emphasize a strong storytelling dimension informed by the personal experiences of the tour guides, which enriches visitors' experience of moving through the historic buildings and viewing the material artifacts on display. In part, this reflects the guiding logic of the early phases of the project, where the major focus was not primarily on catering to tourists, but rather on preserving the story of the Labrador fishery for the surrounding communities. Tourism development initially followed as a way of supporting historic preservation and telling history as a community amenity. As community members work with tourists through the site, they build links between Battle Harbour visitors and surrounding communities.

Opportunities to experience traditional foodways are often valued as tourism experiences (Alonso, Kok, and O'Brien 2018; Chen and Wu

2019; Lowitt 2012). Cooking at Battle Harbour is also a form of intangible heritage that supports its compelling story. The menu is based on traditional Labrador food and has been further developed through training with a visiting chef. Furthermore, there are often opportunities for visitors to join kitchen staff for short cooking workshops. This approach to local cuisine appears to be paying off. During fieldwork in 2013, several visitors commented that the food at Battle Harbour is among the best they have experienced in rural Newfoundland and Labrador.

The quality of historical restoration and protection of material and intangible culture at Battle Harbour also contributes to area residents' positive perceptions of the site's social and cultural impacts. For example, in our 2013 survey, 97 per cent of respondents either agree or strongly agree that Battle Harbour is a source of community pride, while 96 per cent agree or strongly agree that Battle Harbour is a must-see destination for visitors to the region (Stoddart, Ramos, and Chafe 2014). Of course, an important qualification of these results is that the survey draws on those who opted to remain in these communities, rather than those who out-migrated. The experiences and perspectives of the latter may be quite different.

Pillar 3: Doing History in Place

Battle Harbour demonstrates the value of doing "history in place," or creating meaning by allowing visitors to experience historical architecture and artifacts in the context of the landscape where they were built and used (Barber and Peniston-Bird 2020; Stoddart and Knott 2020). Early discussions about preserving Battle Harbour's material culture included proposals to remove artifacts from the site and tell the Battle Harbour story elsewhere. However, the BHHT asserted the importance of telling the Battle Harbour story on site by maintaining the buildings and site-specific artifacts in the context of the island, its ocean environment, and the surrounding communities (Figure 5.2). This allows visitors to better understand the spatial and temporal dimensions of Battle Harbour's story by learning the history of the Labrador fishery while moving through the buildings — the church, salt store, dining hall, and others

— and landscapes that are part of that history. Doing history in place at Battle Harbour also provides an arena to bring together outsiders to engage with site employees and guides who often have long-term family connections to the island and St. Lewis Inlet communities. This creates space for different forms of interaction and learning that would be impossible if the history of Battle Harbour were told only through material artifacts at a faraway site, divorced from their ecological and social contexts.

Visitors' experience of Battle Harbour as a collection of historical artifacts and buildings or as a performance of intangible heritage is inseparable from the sensations of travelling on the ferry to Battle Harbour and experiencing its history surrounded by smells, sounds, and physical proximity to the ocean, rocks, and vegetation of the island. A journey to Battle Harbour also brings potential encounters with icebergs, orcas, humpback whales, dolphins, seabirds, shorebirds, and other marine wildlife. The island thus connects visitors to the native fauna, flora, and geology of southeastern Labrador.

During fieldwork at the site, visitors talked about the opportunity to experience the region's natural environment, which is seen as appealingly remote and rugged, but also peaceful and magical (Stoddart and Knott

Figure 5.2. Battle Harbour as history in place: the salt store, which was the largest in Labrador, was the most important building on the site because of the value of salt to the traditional fishery. (Photo credit: Mark C.J. Stoddart, 2013)

2020). This recalls Baldacchino's argument that "remoteness" can be used strategically as part of the appeal of rural tourism sites, especially when tourism experiences are woven into "the existing cultural mesh of the place" (Baldacchino 2015, 55). Visitors to the site also directly observe the key narrative element that traditional life in Battle Harbour required a high level of creativity and resilience to prosper in this challenging natural environment, without ready access to firewood or fresh water. The fusion of human history and ecological space also facilitates discussion about social-ecological relationships, from historical strategies for survival in this harsh environment to contemporary discussions about climate change and ocean health.

By grounding the story of Battle Harbour in its ecological place, the historic site generates opportunities for a form of tourism that draws connections between visitors, site workers, architecture and artifacts, and the non-human environment (Stoddart and Knott 2020). By cultivating a more "relational" and "collaborative" form of tourism (Ren 2021), the Battle Harbour story engages visitors in learning, using multiple senses and with human and non-human companions. As Slawinski et al. (2021, 608) similarly show in their research on Fogo Island, these types of relational and immersive tourism experiences lead "to positive word-of-mouth and word-of-mouse (i.e., digital peer-to-peer) communication" that further benefits host communities and organizations like BHHT.

Gaining Community Buy-In for the Battle Harbour Story

BHHT implemented the compelling story of Battle Harbour through the adoption of social enterprise principles, which helped the story resonate with local communities. The social enterprise model was important from the early days of BHHT, because it created a revenue model for donations to help get the project off the ground. Most importantly, the social enterprise model channelled reinvestment into the built infrastructure of Battle Harbour for heritage preservation, thereby materializing the compelling story. This created a virtuous cycle in which tourism revenues were reinvested into revitalizing the historic site, which enabled the site to attract more visitors.

As the Battle Harbour project proceeded, the social enterprise model was also important for increasing community buy-in to the project of historical preservation and tourism for revitalization and economic development. Initially, there was skepticism among nearby communities because of fears that Battle Harbour would be transformed into something unrecognizable or subjected to the "cultural counterfeiting" (Fürst 2015) that is often part and parcel of tourism marketing and promotion. This skepticism, coupled with the lack of local capacity, indicated a need for external partnerships and the involvement of people and expertise from outside the region. However, by applying social enterprise principles, BHHT was able to address much of the initial skepticism, and local support for the compelling story of Battle Harbour increased.

BHHT emphasized the importance of local hiring above minimum wage, reflecting the principle of paying what the social enterprise can afford to pay, rather than the minimum that is required. There was also an emphasis on integrating skill development, such as heritage carpentry, as part of working at Battle Harbour, as well as maintaining a continuity of employment for workers season after season. In the wake of the cod fishing moratorium when there were limited job opportunities in the St. Lewis Inlet, Battle Harbour Historic Trust was able to take people who had been in the fishery and train them in heritage carpentry, which was a vital factor in building community buy-in. During fieldwork in 2013, several staff members described how their work at Battle Harbour has allowed them to remain embedded in their communities, rather than leaving the region for work. For many rural communities, stemming out-migration is key to community revitalization, and Battle Harbour thereby makes some contribution to the viability of the St. Lewis Inlet communities. For example, an interview participant noted during fieldwork:

> Well, if I wasn't here [at Battle Harbour], I would have had to take the job [outside the region]. So, I would have had to leave

my community. . . .We're seasonal workers, but every year, you know, you got your job to come out to here. So, some of those people have been here since the site opened. (Battle Harbour informant interview #2)

There were also efforts to ensure that Battle Harbour could be used as a community amenity for the area through ferry access and electricity provision for seasonal homes. As such, the Battle Harbour project was carried out as a heritage-based tourism business that provided community co-benefits. This contribution to infrastructure with tourism and community co-benefits also helped build local support for the project.

In 2013, co-author Stoddart and colleagues carried out a telephone survey of residents of Mary's Harbour (some 17 km away from Battle Harbour), St. Lewis (12 km away), and Lodge Bay (19 km away). These are the three communities closest to Battle Harbour, though they are separated from Battle Harbour by the St. Lewis Inlet and require boat access. The survey examined various possible impacts of Battle Harbour for surrounding communities (Ramos, Stoddart, and Chafe 2016). In total, 95 people responded to the survey (41 per cent response rate). While this response rate may be lower than ideal, it is important to note that response rates have been in decline for all survey modalities over the past few decades (Nulty 2008). Furthermore, a response rate of 41 per cent is comparable to telephone-based surveys published in journals that have a similar focus on rural and regional development, including *Society & Natural Resources* (e.g., Green and Jones 2017; Willits, Luloff, and Theodori 2014) and *Island Studies Journal* (e.g., Randall et al. 2014).

Figure 5.3 gives a summary of our findings about the impacts of the site. As this figure shows, there is a high level of agreement among respondents that Battle Harbour tells important stories about the history of the region, that the site helps to give visitors an appreciation for the natural environment of the region, that the site accurately reflects the culture of the region, and that the site brings cultural and social benefits to the region.

THE BATTLE HARBOUR SITE...

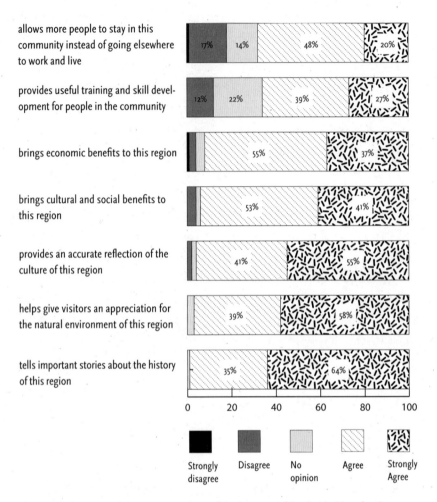

THE BATTLE HARBOUR SITE...	Strongly disagree	Disagree	No opinion	Agree	Strongly Agree
allows more people to stay in this community instead of going elsewhere to work and live	17%	14%		48%	20%
provides useful training and skill development for people in the community	12%	22%		39%	27%
brings economic benefits to this region				55%	37%
brings cultural and social benefits to this region				53%	41%
provides an accurate reflection of the culture of this region				41%	55%
helps give visitors an appreciation for the natural environment of this region				39%	58%
tells important stories about the history of this region				35%	64%

Figure 5.3. Survey participant perceptions of the impacts of Battle Harbour for the surrounding region. (n = 95; adapted from Ramos, Stoddart, and Chafe 2016 and Stoddart, Ramos, and Chafe 2014)

Questions of economic benefit elicit less consensus but are still predominantly positive about the site securing economic added value to the region, providing training and skill development opportunities, and allowing more people to stay in the community. It is difficult to speculate on *why* there is less consensus around economic benefits on the basis of our close-ended survey questions. However, the open-ended critical comments offered by some participants help illuminate the possible reasons for the more diverse views about economic benefits. We received a few open-ended comments along the lines that the financial impacts benefit a relatively small number of people and do not adequately spread out to surrounding communities. This point seems to be one of the reasons that there is less consensus around economic benefits. At the same time, when research participants raised concerns about the site through their open-ended comments, these mostly focused on the ability to ensure the long-term maintenance of infrastructure restoration work with available resources, ensuring adequate storage and protection of historical artifacts, and ensuring that the sense of historical authenticity of the site is not sacrificed for the sake of tourism development.

Taken as a whole, the survey data speak to the overall success of BHHT in crafting a compelling story for visitors that is also valued by members of surrounding communities. Of course, there also have been challenges throughout the development of this project. In the early days of the project, the big challenges included convincing people in the surrounding communities of the value of what the BHHT was trying to do, as well as convincing Parks Canada that the status of a national historic site was deserved. The quality of road infrastructure and accessibility to the site was another big challenge. Other challenges included securing funding for heritage carpentry for restoration work at Battle Harbour, as well as planning and making difficult decisions about the priority and order of restoration on a building-by-building basis. The early board of BHHT was vitally important as a forum for bridging academic expertise (particularly from Memorial University) with community partners, thereby providing organizational leadership to engage with community members, Parks Canada, and potential funders. The work of navigating these big challenges in the early phases of the project led to the generally positive community views of the site that are reflected in our 2013 survey data.

Conclusion

The renewal of the Battle Island heritage site provides an example of how academic–community partnerships and social enterprise principles can be leveraged for the purpose of conveying a compelling story about Battle Harbour as the historically significant capital of the Labrador cod fishery. This story is supported by the three pillars of: (1) protecting material culture and heritage; (2) practicing intangible or non-material culture and heritage; and (3) doing history in place. In the wake of the 1992 cod fishing moratorium, this story facilitated the transition of Battle Harbour towards redevelopment based on historical preservation and tourism. Battle Harbour itself is an abandoned community that has not had a year-round population in several decades. Nevertheless, the revitalization of Battle Harbour has had positive social and economic impacts for nearby host communities, particularly Mary's Harbour.

The Historic Sites and Monuments Board of Canada recognized the community as a national historic site in 1995 and declared it a national historic district in 1997. In 2002, Battle Harbour was designated a Signature Attraction of Atlantic Canada, along with L'Anse aux Meadows National Historic Site and Grenfell Historic Properties in St. Anthony. The site has received several awards, which also help to promote this story by drawing attention to Battle Harbour. In 2002, Conservation International and *National Geographic* magazine awarded the site the World Legacy Award for environmental and responsible tourism. In 2003, it received the Manning Award for Excellence from the Historic Sites Association of Newfoundland and Labrador. By 2010, the site was drawing approximately 2,500 visitors per year (Fennelly 2011), making it one of the anchor attractions for southern Labrador.

We conclude by noting that our description of Battle Harbour focuses on a particular period, from the beginning of its transition towards becoming a historic tourism site up to 2013, when survey research and fieldwork was carried out by co-author Stoddart and when there was a major transition in the composition of the BHHT board. There have been, and continue to be, tensions between different visions of Battle Harbour, which were evident during fieldwork in 2013. One of these tensions is between Battle Harbour as primarily a historic site that serves to protect the material and intangible heritage of the region, wherein tourism plays a supporting role, versus Battle Harbour as primarily a tourism attractor and economic driver for the region, wherein accommodating the expectations of tourists may take priority over ensuring the historical authenticity of the site. As it has been a decade since the fieldwork and survey data that inform this chapter were pursued and collected, it would be extremely valuable to replicate the survey and fieldwork to see whether there have been longitudinal changes in local residents' interpretations of community impacts, as well as whether there have been changes in how the site is balancing different interests in tourism, economic development, and historical preservation.

The tension between the competing logics of heritage preservation and tourism development is a recurring theme in studies that examine history and heritage as foundations for tourism and economic development (e.g., Antonova and Rieser 2019; George, Mair, and Reid 2009; Kimmel et al. 2015; Overton 2007; Rothman 1998). Place-based tensions between preserving tradition and introducing modern elements are also identified in research by Slawinski et al. (2021) on social enterprise and tourism development on Fogo Island (see Chapter 1). Along similar lines, Saburo Horikawa's (2021) research on the movement to protect the historic canal district of the Japanese city of Otaru identifies an important paradox and serves as a cautionary tale. Over time, the historic environment that was the basis of tourism development was reconfigured to meet the expectations of tourists to the point where it lost its sense of authenticity for visitors. This resulted in a decline of interest and visitation and is leading to a "post-tourist" era for Otaru. As Horikawa puts it, "by becoming a tourist city, Otaru lost the very environment that originally represented such a vital resource for tourism" (Horikawa 2021, 329). Relatedly, concerns around maintaining Battle Harbour as a community amenity and as an accessible space for community members to visit, use, and seasonally inhabit are coupled with anxieties about potential loss of access to the site if it is enclosed solely for tourism and paid visitors. Future research on Battle Harbour and other historic sites would benefit from greater attention to how or whether the tensions between the logics of historical protection, tourism development, and community access are navigated. When historical authenticity is the basis of a *compelling story* that also drives tourism development, what are the possibilities of — or challenges to — *linking divergent perspectives* or *engaging in both/and thinking* that supports place-based development?

Battle Harbour's transformation into a tourism and historic site was grounded in a compelling story of the Labrador fishery. We emphasize that crafting this story and redeveloping Battle Harbour as a tourism and historic site could not have happened without leadership to initiate the project and carry it through. Leadership can come from within or outside the community. If local communities lack the resources or political capital to navigate government and get projects moving, then outsider leadership and academic–community collaboration can play a vital bridging role in transforming the seeds of a gripping story into a fully realized project. Thus, while we use this case primarily as an exemplar of the PLACE Framework's *convey compelling stories* principle, this project also embodies the principles of *linking divergent perspectives* (the "L" principle in the PLACE Framework), including vital contributions from outside the local communities, and *amplifying capacities* (the "A" principle in the PLACE Framework).

Acknowledgements

This chapter draws on research that was supported by the Applied Research Fund of the Harris Centre at Memorial University. We thank research collaborator Howard Ramos for his contributions, as well as David Chafe and Christine Knott for their research assistance. We thank Douglas House for his comments and insight during the development of this project, and David Tindall for helpful comments during revisions to this chapter.

References

Alonso, Abel Duarte, Seng Kok, and Seamus O'Brien. 2018. "Sustainable Culinary Tourism and Cevicherías: A Stakeholder and Social Practice Approach." *Journal of Sustainable Tourism* 26, no. 5: 812–31.

Antonova, Anna S., and Alison Rieser. 2019. "Curating Collapse: Performing Maritime Cultural Heritage in Iceland's Museums and Tours." *Maritime Studies* 18: 103–14.

Applin, M. 2010. *Strategic Analysis and Sustainability Planning*. Battle Harbour Historic Trust.

Baldacchino, Godfrey. 2015. "Placing Identity: Strategic Considerations for Rebounding Peripheries." In *Place Peripheral: Place-Based Development in Rural, Island, and Remote Regions*, edited by Kelly Vodden, Ryan Gibson, and Godfrey Baldacchino, 41–62. St. John's: ISER Books.

Barber, Sarah, and Corinna M. Peniston-Bird. 2020. "Introduction." In *Approaching Historical Sources in Their Contexts*, edited by Sarah Barber and Corinna M. Peniston-Bird, 1–9. London: Routledge.

Chen, Yeong-Shyang, and Shou-Tsung Wu. 2019. "Social Networking Practices of Viennese Coffeehouse Culture and Intangible Heritage Tourism." *Journal of Tourism and Cultural Change* 17, no. 2: 186–207.

Crummey, Michael. 2021. "Across the Tickle." *Canadian Geographic* 141, no. 3: 78–85.

Fennelly, J. 2011. *Economic Impact Assessment: Battle Harbour National Historic District*. St. John's: Atlantic Canada Opportunities Agency.

Fürst, Bojan. 2015. "Newcomers at the Gates: Place and Space in Small Island Context." In *Place Peripheral: Place-Based Development in Rural, Island, and Remote Regions*, edited by Kelly Vodden, Ryan Gibson, and Godfrey Baldacchino, 63–85. St. John's: ISER Books.

George, E. Wanda, Heather Mair, and Donald G. Reid. 2009. *Rural Tourism Development: Localism and Cultural Change*. Bristol, UK: Channel View Publications.

Green, Brandn, and Kristal Jones. 2017. "Place and Large Landscape Conservation along the Susquehanna River." *Society & Natural Resources* 31, no. 2: 183–99.

Higgins-Desbiolles, Freya, Sandro Carnicelli, Chris Krolikowski, Gayathri Wijesinghe, and Karla Boluk. 2019. "Degrowing Tourism: Rethinking Tourism." *Journal of Sustainable Tourism* 27, no. 12: 1926–44.

Horikawa, Saburo. 2021. *Why Place Matters: A Sociological Study of the Historic Preservation Movement in Otaru, Japan, 1965–2017*. Cham, Switzerland: Springer.

Kimmel, Courtney, Andrew Perlstein, Michael J. Mortimer, Dequn Zhou, and David P. Robertson. 2015. "Sustainability of Tourism as Development Strategy for Cultural-Landscapes in China: Case Study of Ping'an Village." *Journal of Rural and Community Development* 10, no. 2: 121–35.

Loo, Tina. 2020. "Development's Travelling Rationalities: Contextualizing Newfoundland Resettlement." In *Resettlement: Uprooting and Rebuilding Communities in Newfoundland and Labrador and Beyond*, edited by Isabelle Côté and Yolande Pottie-Sherman, 43–78. St. John's: ISER Books.

Lowitt, Kristen. 2012. "The Reinvention and Performance of Traditional Newfoundland Foodways in Culinary Tourism in the Bonne Bay Region." *Newfoundland and Labrador Studies* 27, no. 1: 1719–26.

Murphy, Matthew, Wade M. Danis, Johnny Mack, and (Kekinusuqs) Judith Sayers. 2020. "From Principles to Action: Community-Based Entrepreneurship in the Toquaht Nation." *Journal of Business Venturing* 35, no. 6.

Nulty, Duncan. 2008. "The Adequacy of Response Rates to Online and Paper Surveys: What Can Be Done?" *Assessment & Evaluation in Higher Education* 33, no. 3: 301–14.

Overton, James. 2007. "'A Future in the Past'? Tourism Development, Outport Archaeology, and the Politics of Deindustrialization in Newfoundland and Labrador in the 1990s." *Urban History Review* 35, no. 2: 60–74.

Pearson, Katie. 2022. "Discover the Unofficial Capital of Historic Labrador – Battle Harbour." National Trust for Canada (website). July 4, 2022. https://nationaltrustcanada.ca/online-stories/discover-the-unofficial-capital-of-historic-labrador-battle-harbour

Pollak, Angela. 2017. "Idea Tourism: Modelling a Social and Human Capital Tourism Product." In *From Black Horses to White Steeds: Building Community Resilience*, edited by Laurie Brinklow and Ryan Gibson, 279–301. Charlottetown, PEI: Island Studies Press.

Ramos, Howard, Mark C.J. Stoddart, and David Chafe. 2016. "Assessing the Tangible and Intangible Benefits of Tourism: Perceptions of Economic, Social, and Cultural Impacts in Labrador's Battle Harbour Historic District." *Island Studies Journal* 11, no. 1: 209–26.

Randall, James E., Peter Kitchen, Nazeem Muhajarine, Bruce Newbold, Allison Williams, and Kathleen Wilson. 2014. "Immigrants, Islandness and Perceptions of Quality-of-Life on Prince Edward Island, Canada." *Island Studies Journal* 9, no. 2: 343–62.

Reggers, Amy, Simone Grabowski, Stephen L. Wearing, Paul Chatterton, and Stephen Schweinsberg. 2016. "Exploring Outcomes of Community-Based Tourism on the Kokoda Track, Papua New Guinea: A Longitudinal Study of Participatory Rural Appraisal Techniques." *Journal of Sustainable Tourism* 24, nos. 8–9: 1139–55.

Ren, Carina. 2021. "(Staying with) the Trouble with Tourism and Travel Theory?" *Tourist Studies* 21, no. 1: 133–40.

Rompkey, Ronald. 2009. *Grenfell of Labrador: A Biography*. Montreal and Kingston: McGill-Queen's University Press.

Rothman, Hal K. 1998. *Devil's Bargains: Tourism in the Twentieth-Century American West*. Lawrence: University Press of Kansas.

Sanger, Ches W. 1996. *Historic Sites and Monuments Board of Canada Agenda Paper on Battle Harbour, Labrador*. Ottawa: Historic Sites and Monuments Board of Canada.

Spenceley, Anna, and Dorothea Meyer. 2012. "Tourism and Poverty Reduction: Theory and Practice in Less Economically Developed Countries." *Journal of Sustainable Tourism* 20, no. 3: 297–317.

Slawinski, Natalie, Blair Winsor, Daina Mazutis, John W. Schouten, and Wendy K. Smith. 2021. "Managing the Paradoxes of Place to Foster Regeneration." *Organization and Environment* 34, no. 4: 595–618.

Stoddart, Mark C.J., Gary Catano, and Howard Ramos. 2018. "Navigating Tourism Development in Emerging Destinations in Atlantic Canada: Local Benefits, Extra-local Challenges." *Journal of Rural and Community Development* 13, no. 2: 57–75.

Stoddart, Mark C.J., and Christine Knott. 2020. "Landscape: Consuming Natural Places." In *Approaching Historical Sources in Their Contexts: Space, Time and Performance*, edited by Sarah Barber and Corinna M. Peniston-Bird, 32–47. London: Routledge.

Stoddart, Mark C.J., Howard Ramos, and David Chafe. 2014. *The Intangible Impacts of Tourism: The Battle Harbour National Historic District as a Tourism Anchor*. St. John's: Harris Centre, Memorial University.

Willits, Fern K., A.E. Luloff, and Gene L. Theodori. 2014. "Monitoring Controversial Environmental/Natural Resource Issues: Differential Effects of Telephone and Mail Surveys." *Society & Natural Resources* 27, no. 12: 1355–58.

Zhu, Yujie. 2012. "Performing Heritage: Rethinking Authenticity in Tourism." *Annals of Tourism Research* 39, no. 3: 1495–513.

CHAPTER 6

Engaging Both/And Thinking: A Case Study of Fishing for Success

Jennifer Brenton and Kimberly Orren

Introduction

Fishing for Success is a non-profit social enterprise in Petty Harbour (population: 947),[1] founded to share and promote the fishing heritage and culture of Newfoundland and Labrador (NL). Following the cod moratorium of 1992, many communities across the province faced economic and cultural devastation when thousands of fish harvesters lost their livelihoods and a core connection to part of their culture as a fishing people. As a coastal outport with deep fishing roots, Petty Harbour was one such community facing a crisis of culture and identity in the years following the moratorium. The co-founders of Fishing for Success, Kimberly Orren and Leo Hearn, recognized that younger generations both in Petty Harbour and across the province were becoming increasingly disconnected from their heritage, as they were presented with few opportunities to practice and share traditional fishing skills and knowledge. Orren and Hearn felt compelled to start a social enterprise rooted in the community of Petty Harbour. It would be designed to teach youth and traditionally marginalized groups, including women and new immigrants, about fishing in an effort to revitalize local knowledge and to bring traditional cod fishing back to Petty Harbour.

Many rural communities like Petty Harbour are experiencing increasingly complex challenges, including ecological destruction and economic decline related to global issues such as climate change and poverty. These places face depletion as populations relocate to more urban contexts, resulting in fewer social and economic resources for small communities (Hertel, Bacq, and Belz 2019). These complex environments for economic development nevertheless can offer unique opportunities for social enterprise creation (Johnstone and Lionais 2004). Social enterprises are organizations that pursue "business-led solutions to achieve social aims" (Haugh 2006, 183). Social enterprise is demonstrably a driver of community regeneration and building local resilience, as these organizations are able to tune into place-based needs and tap into local assets to create economic and social value for their own communities (McKeever, Jack, and Anderson 2015; Murphy et al. 2020). When social enterprises are created to address "locally situated social needs" (Seelos et al. 2011, 337), they are often considered to be place-based or embedded in communities. However, the work of place-based social enterprise can be full of tensions and contradictions, which this chapter discusses. These organizations need to engage with such complex and competing forces as honouring tradition while fostering innovation (Slawinski et al. 2021). These interrelated and sometimes contradictory elements create challenging tensions for social enterprises rooted in local places, and how these organizations choose to respond to these tensions can shape their social and financial outcomes (Smith and Besharov 2019).

This chapter extends research on social enterprise to show how social enterprises rooted in place respond to tensions that arise from competing forces (Slawinski et al. 2021). We use the case of Fishing for Success to explore how place-based social enterprises can address these tensions through an integrative and holistic approach. In this way, Fishing for Success embodies the *engaging both/and thinking* principle of the PLACE Framework by balancing multiple and sometimes conflicting goals to promote and revitalize local fishing heritage. This organization showcases how place can be leveraged to facilitate integrative thinking that produces innovative and holistic solutions to organizational and community-based problems.

Navigating Tensions of Place-Based Social Enterprise

Social enterprises are characterized by their ability to generate social impact through commercial means (Haigh and Hoffman 2012; Haugh 2006). As such, these organizations actively bridge the divide between non-profit and business worlds to create both social and financial value (Dees 2001). Social enterprises are a type of hybrid organization because they combine multiple organizational logics and goals (Battilana and Lee 2014). These logics establish the core beliefs and practices of an organization and shape its actions. A hallmark of social enterprise is that it often balances logics of both social welfare and business (Grimes, Williams, and Zhao 2019). However, carrying these dual logics simultaneously can be challenging, as these organizations must attend to multiple and sometimes contradictory or inconsistent goals and values (Smith, Gonin, and Besharov 2013). Social enterprises can also pursue multiple social goals at once, resulting in additional tensions that arise due to competing stakeholder demands (Siegner, Pinkse, and Panwar 2018). Therefore, "effectively understanding social enterprises depends on insight into the nature and management of these tensions" (Smith, Gonin, and Besharov 2013, 408).

In management research, paradox theory has been used to extend our understanding of how social enterprises experience and attend to tensions that arise from carrying multiple logics and goals (Smith et al. 2012). Paradox exists when there are "persistent contradictions between interdependent elements" (Schad et al. 2016, 6). At first glance, these elements may appear dichotomous and seemingly incompatible, like lightness and darkness (Poole and Van de Ven 1989), yet they are inextricably linked and bound in a state of mutuality where they inform and define one another (Schad et al. 2016). In a paradoxical relationship, one element cannot be chosen over the other to create a resolution; both must operate simultaneously (Quinn and Cameron 1988). For social enterprises, their dual goals can be contradictory, but they are equally mutually reinforcing (Smith, Gonin, and Besharov 2013). Financial goals promote "efficiency, performance, innovation, and growth," while social goals drive "passion, motivation, and commitment," and together these qualities can foster long-term sustainability for organizations (Smith et al. 2012, 466). The core challenge for social entrepreneurs lies not only in developing the skills required to both achieve social impact and build a financially viable organization, but also in managing the tensions that arise from conflicting social and financial demands (Smith et al. 2012).

Research on hybrid organizing and social enterprise has highlighted different ways that these organizations address paradoxical tensions and create a "workable certainty" where tensions are not resolved but navigated through various strategies and approaches (Jay 2013). Some social enterprises employ organization-level strategies and structures to mitigate conflict and work through tensions that arise when pursuing social and financial goals simultaneously. For example, Pache and Santos's (2013, 973) study of work integration social enterprises finds that organizations used "selective coupling" to pick and choose elements from each logic to "manage the incompatibility between logics." Battilana and colleagues (2015) highlight the use of "spaces of negotiation" to work through tensions between social and business goals. These spaces took the form of meetings and formal processes where members of subgroups could interact and discuss the issues they were facing. These interactions did not resolve the tensions entirely but allowed organizational members to maintain a "productive tension" (Battilana et al. 2015, 1678) between them. In their study of an information technology social enterprise, Smith and Besharov (2019, 8) found that the organization employed the use of "guardrails" or "leadership expertise and formal structures associated with each mission" to maintain organizational hybridity over time. Whenever tensions became more salient and organizational members veered towards one logic over another, they bumped against these "guardrails," which prevented the organization from straying too far from hybridity.

Aside from highlighting these various strategies to work through tensions, research shows that some organizations adopt a traditional approach that attempts to resolve tensions by forcing a choice between the competing demands, while others work to engage with the tensions in a more nuanced way (Smith et al. 2012). An either/or approach is a typical response to avoid the complexity and ambiguity created by paradox (Martin 2007). However, this attempt to force clarity and simplicity can stunt the innovative potential of engaging with these tensions. By moving from a mindset of either/or to both/and, actors can reframe challenges and "build skills in collaboration, support, and community" (Smith et al. 2012, 469).

Three key skills have been shown to enable social enterprises to navigate the tensions associated with competing demands: acceptance, differentiation, and integration (Smith et al. 2012). *Acceptance* involves recognizing that tensions are an inherent part of organizing and that engaging with these tensions can allow organizations to innovate and build resilience. Acceptance also requires social enterprises to adopt an "abundance mindset" where resources are seen as "plentiful, regenerative, and enabling rather than scarce and limited" (Smith et al. 2012, 468). When social enterprises are situated in resource-constrained environments, social-financial tensions become particularly prominent, and an abundance mentality can help these organizations focus on finding new opportunities rather than ruminating on the challenges and obstacles they face (Miron-Spektor et al. 2018).

Differentiation allows social enterprises to recognize the unique values of their social and financial demands and how each is distinctly important to the organization (Andriopolous and Lewis 2009). By contrast, *integration* involves finding synergies between the demands and seeking new and creative solutions to conflicts that arise between competing goals (Andriopolous and Lewis 2009; Smith et al. 2012). Ultimately, social enterprises are tasked with learning to embrace these tensions by valuing their distinctions and the synergies that exist between them (Andriopoulos and Lewis 2009).

Due to the persistent nature of paradoxical relationships, social enterprises must work with and through tensions on an ongoing basis. If they choose to avoid tensions or to engage with them only using an either/or approach, these organizations risk drifting away from their core social mission or facing financial demise (Siegner, Pinkse, and Panwar 2018; Smith and Besharov 2019). Learning to work through tensions and embrace ambiguity is difficult and requires constant sense-making by individuals and organizations (Jay 2013). However, if managed effectively, paradox can catalyze innovation and ensure long-term sustainability in social enterprises (Smith and Lewis 2011).

In addition to the tensions brought to the surface by the dual nature of social enterprises, these organizations can also experience additional tensions when they are embedded in communities. Research has shown that social enterprises are often locally embedded to achieve greater social impact (Lumpkin, Bacq, and Pidduck 2018; Seelos et al. 2011; Vedula et al. 2021). These organizations have been known to seek opportunities and establish themselves in places characterized by limited resources and institutional voids, which create additional challenges for organizing (Di Domenico, Haugh, and Tracey 2010) and can also generate specific place-based tensions (Slawinski et al. 2021). Increased globalization has resulted in the formation of certain organizations deemed "placeless." They remain at arm's length from the places in which they operate (Shrivastava and Kennelly 2013). According to Thomas and Cross (2007, 40), these organizations view themselves as independent occupants of place that "are not committed to the well-being of place and will only maintain the relationship as long as it benefits their shareholders." In contrast, place-based organizations have a "rootedness in the physical, social, and human capital of a place, possessing a sense of place and a social mission," as Shrivastava and Kennelly describe (2013, 90). This close human connection to the place's many facets can cause tensions to arise due to the need to balance multiple goals simultaneously, including ecological, social, and economic goals (Shrivastava and Kennelly 2013; Siegner, Pinkse, and Panwar 2018). Slawinski and her team underscore that such place-based tensions also involve insider-versus-outsider and traditional-versus-contemporary points of view, which come into play as these organizations grapple with an overarching "tension between global uniformity and local uniqueness" (Slawinski et al. 2021, 610).

Research has begun to explore how place-based organizations engage with these tensions using a both/and approach to regenerate the communities in which they are embedded (Slawinski et al. 2021). Studies have also explored how entrepreneurs can engage with place to build organizations and contribute to local communities (Johnstone and Lionais 2004; McKeever, Jack, and Anderson 2015; Murphy et al. 2020). These organizations often leverage local assets and networks to create social and financial value (McKeever, Jack, and Anderson 2015). Despite these insights into place-based organizations, we still have a limited understanding of how these organizations navigate place-based tensions and how place shapes the ways in which these organizations engage with their ingrained tensions.

To address this gap and explore these ideas in more depth, we draw upon the case of Fishing for Success, a non-profit social enterprise located in Petty Harbour, NL. Fishing for Success uses integrative, both/and thinking to balance tensions between its seemingly oppositional goals and to find creative and holistic solutions to its challenges. The findings of this case study are based on three years of ethnographic fieldwork conducted by the first author and the lived experiences of the second author as a co-founder of Fishing for Success. The first author became a member of Fishing for Success's Girls Who Fish program in 2018, has continued attending regular meetings and events, and serves as a volunteer for the organization's Women Sharing Heritage (WiSH) program. In addition to this fieldwork, formal, semi-structured interviews were conducted with organization members and community residents to gain a deeper understanding of how Fishing for Success engages with its social and financial goals and navigates the tensions of place-based organizing. This research offers new insights into the literatures on social enterprise and place-based tensions while presenting key takeaways for place-based social entrepreneurs looking for practices and strategies to embrace tensions and find new ways forward through both/and thinking.

Fishing for Success: A Place-Based Social Enterprise

Fishing for Success was created by Kimberly Orren and Leo Hearn in 2014 out of a desire to keep the fishing heritage of Newfoundland and Labrador alive. After the cod moratorium of 1992, the province faced both economic and cultural devastation. Orren and Hearn both grew up in Newfoundland and saw that, as the fishery became more industrialized and almost disappeared entirely when the cod fish moratorium came into effect, traditional fishing knowledge was becoming less accessible to younger generations. This drove them to launch a social enterprise and to design programs to make fishing more accessible to groups who traditionally were excluded from the fishery, including youth, women, and new immigrants.

Orren spent her childhood in Grand Falls-Windsor, NL, and moved to Florida with her family when she was a teenager. She fell in love with fishing at the age of eight when she caught her first mud trout. After that day, she spent her life learning about nature, fishing, and the ocean and decided to turn that passion into a teaching career. After completing her university degree, she taught science at the high school level for 13 years. Whether she was teaching chemistry, biology, or physics, she always looked for opportunities to bring her students outside and connect them to the plants, animals, and natural world they were studying (Barrett 2015). By 2006, she felt a need to reconnect with her childhood passion of fishing and to share that passion with students. To do so, she returned to university to pursue a graduate degree in fisheries and aquatic sciences. In 2009, she retired from her teaching position to move back to Newfoundland with a plan to start a social enterprise dedicated to teaching people, and youth in particular, about the fishing heritage and culture of the province (Barrett 2015).

Throughout her teaching career, Orren believed that children were becoming increasingly disconnected from nature, not just in Florida, but also back in NL. The moratorium called on northern cod fishing due to declining cod stocks in 1992 had catastrophic impacts for the economy and culture of the province. She felt that after this event, there was a marked change in how the children of the province interacted with nature, the fishery, and their culture. She saw great value in heritage and the way it could contribute to building personal connections and attachments to place, so she knew this disconnect could have real implications for the future of NL. She felt that if the youth of the province grew up without a deep attachment to place, they would be less likely to stay, or leave but return, and contribute to the development of the province. She wanted to do something about this; so, armed with her education, teaching skills, and love of fishing, she started scoping out possible locations for her social venture.

Orren chose Petty Harbour, a town with a population of 947 nestled along a section of coastline just 15 kilometres south of St. John's. This community is accessible to those living in the nearby urban centre, but it also has a small-town, outport atmosphere. Moreover, Petty Harbour is a Protected Fishing Area, meaning that those who fish within the limits of the community's waters can do so only with hook and line. This protection was put in place in the late 1800s by the families of Petty Harbour who saw more industrial methods of fishing, like gill nets and trawlers, as unsustainable and threatening to the jobs of local fish harvesters (Bryant and Martin 1996). By the 1960s, these unsustainable methods were being adopted in many other fishing communities across the island, and indeed globally, because of their efficiency. However, efficiency came at a cost to marine ecosystems, as these methods damaged the sea floor and encouraged the overfishing that had led to the cod moratorium (Barrett 2015). By contrast, the handline fishery in Petty Harbour has always been small-scale and family-run and prioritizes the quality of fish over quantity. Orren believed that this sort of sustainable fishery would be an ideal environment for teaching people about fishing and the sustainability of the oceans.

Hearn, a retired fish harvester, spent his whole life on the water. For over 200 years, his ancestors fished for cod in Petty Harbour, and he followed his family's tradition (Nolan 2017). Growing up in Petty Harbour, he could remember a time when fishing was a family affair and even the children of the community were tasked with cutting out the tongues of the cod their fathers brought ashore. From a young age, he was immersed in the culture of a fishing community, and as he grew he learned the necessary skills to become a fish harvester. After fishing for 25 years, tracking the movements of cod and finding fishing grounds off Petty Harbour became second nature to Hearn (Nolan 2017). When the moratorium was called in 1992, thousands of fish harvesters from across the province, including Hearn, lost their livelihoods and a central piece of their cultural identity. He was able to find work at the dockyards in St. John's in the years that followed, but he missed his life on the water (Nolan 2017).

While working to gain the necessary capital to launch Fishing for Success, Orren met Hearn, who shared the same passion for preserving their fishing heritage. They decided to partner together to make Fishing for Success a reality. Orren purchased Island Rooms, a historic section of land around the inner harbour where the community's fishing families had traditionally "roomed" (Barrett 2015). "Rooms" were wooden sheds perched along the shore and overhanging the water where families would gather and process their catch. Orren and Hearn used traditional building methods and materials to rebuild the sheds and fishing stage needed to recreate traditional fishing premises (Delisle 2016). Over the next several years, they self-financed the land and boats they needed and officially launched Fishing for Success in 2014.

Fishing for Success works towards its social mission of promoting fishing heritage by offering experiential social programs targeted towards specific groups, including youth, women, and new immigrants. One of their core programs is Girls Who Fish, which is designed to expose women and girls to the fishery and encourage their involvement in the traditionally male-dominated industry. Participants in all Fishing for Success programs can take part in seasonal activities like cod fishing, ice fishing, boat maintenance, hiking, berry-picking, weaving, painting, and cooking. These activities are designed to be immersive and to connect participants to nature and local culture. They also create opportunities for sharing culture with those who are visiting the province or who have recently immigrated. All of these programs are offered at minimal or no cost to participants, to ensure that they can be as accessible as possible. To offset the costs of the programs, Fishing for Success generates revenue by offering tourist excursions during the summer months. These excursions often include a mixture of activities on land and on the water, such as cod-fishing trips and lessons in fish processing and cooking.

Leveraging Place to Facilitate Both/And Thinking

As a place-based social enterprise, Fishing for Success grapples with numerous tensions that arise from the plurality of its goals and its rootedness in place. While some individuals and organizations may approach such tensions using an either/or perspective, where a choice is made between competing forces, Fishing for Success is an example of how tensions can be engaged using a both/and mentality. This approach requires organizations to recognize the distinctiveness and interdependence of competing demands, to embrace the tensions they create, and to find new ways forward. Fishing for Success also highlights how place, including its built, natural, cultural, and social elements (Shrivastava and Kennelly 2013), can be leveraged to navigate tensions between competing demands of old and new perspectives, social and financial goals, insiders and outsiders, and overarching tensions between local and global forces.

Even in the formation stages of their organization, Orren and Hearn used an integrative approach by drawing on traditional local assets in new ways. They were committed to honouring the history and heritage of Petty Harbour, but also repurposed them for use by new groups of people in modern and innovative ways, as their programs are designed to teach fishing skills to those traditionally excluded from the local fishery, including youth, women, and newcomers. This process was aided by the integration of the different backgrounds and complementary knowledge sets that they possess. By combining Hearn's knowledge of Petty Harbour and local fishing with Orren's teaching experience and understanding of fishing in different contexts, the two were able to create an organization that appreciates both the old and the new, as well as both local ways of knowing and global influences.

The primary mission of the organization is to promote heritage fishing; therefore, the use of traditional practices, tools, and spaces is highly important to the work of Fishing for Success. Island Rooms is a place-based asset that carries historical and cultural significance in the community. This piece of land that hugs the harbour was once used by fishing families in Petty Harbour for processing fish, and now it is home to several fishing sheds full of gear and the equipment needed to teach groups of people how to fish. One of the challenges Fishing for Success faces is how to balance the historical and heritage significance of these types of assets with the need to adapt them to modern-day uses. Fishing for Success has found strategies to engage both opposing factors in a way that promotes innovation while still honouring the history and heritage of the community. For example, they have found ways to use traditional place-based assets in new ways to advocate for and create a more inclusive fishery.

After Orren and Hearn had established their social enterprise on Island Rooms, one of the traditional fishing stages on the property was severely damaged by high winds in 2018 and was blown into the harbour. This stage was historically important for the community, as it had been the first stage to be rebuilt in Petty Harbour after a great storm in 1966 destroyed much of the community's previous fishing infrastructure. Fishing for Success worked to rebuild the stage using wood reclaimed from the old stage and other abandoned properties around Petty Harbour. They stayed true to the historic integrity of the building but decided to incorporate a wheelchair ramp into the design, making it possible for wheelchair users and others with mobility challenges to access the boats more easily.

Another tension concerns the very practice of fishing in NL, recognizing the wave of industrialized fishing that resulted in the collapse of cod stocks and the deterioration of aquatic ecosystems. Fishing for Success has had to find ways to teach the value of fishing for connecting to heritage, nature, and community in a way that is not harmful to ocean ecology, especially when cod stocks are still recovering from overfishing. To achieve this balance, they only use traditional handline techniques for fishing, actively work to minimize waste in the organization, and search for equipment with a limited environmental footprint. They also draw upon Indigenous ways of knowing, through partnerships with Indigenous groups, to connect with traditional fishing practices that are respectful of the land and the sea. These partnerships allow Indigenous youth and Elders to access fish and create opportunities for sharing culture between Indigenous and non-Indigenous groups. Fishing for Success believes that these kinds of collaborations are important to keep the practice of heritage fishing alive and also promote a more diverse and inclusive sustainable fishery.

Figure 6.1. In 2020, Fishing for Success launched a Pride dory that was painted in rainbow colours as a symbol to advocate for greater diversity and inclusion in the fishery. This boat also serves as a visual representation of the organization's core values and mission to make fishing more accessible and inclusive. (Photo credit: Kimberly Orren, 2021)

Another core tension Fishing for Success faces is between their social and financial goals. As a social enterprise that works to achieve a social mission while remaining financially viable, it faces unique challenges due to the interdependent and sometimes contradictory nature of these goals. Fishing for Success's business model makes these tensions particularly salient, as their primary stream of income — tourist outings — is predominant, separate from their social programming. This means that Fishing for Success sometimes has to choose between making money and working towards their social goals. Gaining access to fish has also been a challenge for Fishing for Success, and this challenge has perpetuated these tensions between their social and financial goals. The fishery in NL is highly regulated with strict quotas, even 30 years after the moratorium was called. A recreational fishery is open to the public for approximately 30 days each year, and a commercial fishery is available only to those who are licensed fish harvesters. Without a commercial licence, Fishing for Success can spend only a limited amount of time on the water, and so they have to carefully manage the schedules for their programs and their tourist outings. They want to allow the participants in their programs to have as many opportunities as possible to go fishing, but they also need to generate income to support those initiatives. This institutional constraint prompted Fishing for Success to lobby the government for increased access to fish, and after years of persistence they were granted a special educational fishing licence in 2021. This licence gives them additional fishing days during the year, allowing them to take more of their social programming participants out fishing. Despite this advantage, Fishing for Success still has to carefully allocate their time on the water between their economic activities and those that generate social value, as they have limited human resources and frequently are hindered by Newfoundland and Labrador's precarious weather.

One way that Fishing for Success manages the tensions between its social and financial goals involves finding ways to integrate them, so that they can be achieved simultaneously. It is not a perfect balance, but this approach allows the organization to work towards both aims without favouring one over the other. For example, Fishing for Success has involved its Girls Who Fish members in assisting with tourist outings. This creates opportunities for their program participants to gain exposure to fishing activities while still generating revenue from the outing. These tourist outings also focus on teaching heritage skills, promoting awareness about ocean conservation, and encouraging the sharing of culture. While these outings target customer groups over the organization's beneficiaries, Fishing for Success still uses these revenue-generating opportunities to share their social mission with others and promote the work of their other programs. This highlights that, while Fishing for Success has to occasionally make decisions between *either* generating revenue *or* creating their intended social impact, these decisions are made with the ultimate understanding that the organization is still working to achieve *both* financial sustainability *and* social impact. Keeping an overall both/and mindset allows the organization to make necessary either/or choices that keep the organization moving forward without compromising the integrity of their social and financial goals.

Fishing for Success also faces tensions between insiders and outsiders. All of their programming draws "outsiders" to the community of Petty Harbour, meaning those who grew up and/or reside in places outside the community. Some community residents do not always see the value of bringing these groups of people into local community life. Especially in a community as small as Petty Harbour, these outsiders may be seen as intruding or using resources that should be reserved for locals. Outsiders also often bring divergent views and perspectives that can be construed as negative and disruptive to the community's traditions (Slawinski et al. 2021). However, outsiders also bring fresh perspectives, and they are often key drivers of economic development, as they bring new business to the community.

Fishing for Success has had to find ways to manage these complex tensions that are inherent to the work of place-based social enterprise. When it comes to addressing insider–outsider tensions, it can be difficult to bridge divides that separate these groups of people. Fishing for Success navigates these tensions by creating opportunities for connection and knowledge-sharing between different groups (Slawinski et al. 2021). It does this by bringing in outsiders for programs and drawing upon locals and local businesses to execute and support the programs. One example of this type of connection is the Women Sharing Heritage (WiSH) program, a partnership with the Association for New Canadians through which refugee women can come to Petty Harbour and engage in culture-sharing around fishing. This program involves many local businesses, like the local mini aquarium, café, and craft shop, to deliver an immersive cultural experience for the participants.

In 2019, Fishing for Success also partnered with academics and researchers to execute a workshop on social enterprise and community development. This workshop brought a cross-sector group of community actors from across NL to Petty Harbour and involved a series of place-based experiential activities organized with the help of local residents and businesses (Brenton and Slawinski 2023). These kinds of initiatives have created opportunities for building connections between insiders and outsiders and have allowed these groups to see past their differences to find common ground through shared experiences.

Another strategy Fishing for Success uses to work through insider–outsider tensions involves telling narratives about the social impact of its work. One such narrative arises from the WiSH program. This program has proven to be very beneficial for the mental well-being of the refugees who participate, as it allows them to connect with nature, culture, and others. The success story of this program has been shared widely by both the Association for New Canadians and the Centre for Addiction and Mental Health in their national newsletters (Centre for Addiction and Mental Health 2019). By telling positive stories about their work, Fishing for Success hopes to increase feelings of empathy in the community for its beneficiaries. These feelings of empathy and compassion can increase integrative thinking by helping people understand issues from the perspectives of others (Miller et al. 2012).

Key Takeaways and Future Research

The Fishing for Success case offers valuable insights into the tensions of place-based social enterprise. Research has highlighted that organizations rooted in place face specific, place-based tensions that emerge from competing local and global forces (Slawinski et al. 2021). However, this same rootedness in place shapes how organizations frame and respond to challenges (Shrivastava and Kennelly 2013; Slawinski et al. 2021). Studies have shown that actors who are embedded in the physical and cultural aspects of the local natural environment are, according to Whiteman and Cooper (2011, 890), "attuned to changes in ecological conditions and actively interpret material cues in different landscapes and at different times."

Being closely tied to place provides individuals and organizations with a more holistic understanding of challenges and their underlying tensions. Fishing for Success uses its strong ties to place, knowledge of the community's history, and connections to local residents to help build and sustain its own organization. This embeddedness also gives it a greater understanding of the close connections between the social, cultural, and ecological aspects of place (McKeever, Jack, and Anderson 2015), which allows the social enterprise to work towards a both/and approach to navigating tensions that is essential for its long-term sustainability. The key takeaway of this case study is that, while being rooted in place can cause tensions to surface, this same connection to place can also facilitate the adoption of a both/and approach that is needed to work through those tensions.

This idea is demonstrated through how embeddedness in place allows Fishing for Success to develop an abundance mindset despite facing limited resources. An abundance mindset involves "attending to resources as plentiful, regenerative, and enabling rather than scarce and limited" (Smith et al. 2012, 468). These authors add that adopting an abundance mindset is critical for practicing integrative thinking, as it allows social entrepreneurs to accept tensions and shift their focus from "problem solving to possibility finding" (Smith et al. 2012, 468).

Fishing for Success works to cultivate this mentality by drawing upon place-based assets. These assets include physical, built assets like traditional fishing sheds and boats, but also cultural assets, like stories and heritage skills. Even though Fishing for Success possesses limited human and financial capital, it uses its embeddedness in place to leverage place-based assets to overcome its constraints. It also develops an abundance mindset by collaborating with others. It leans into their social networks, another key asset, to gain access to additional resources, such as funding and access to new beneficiary groups. Collaboration with others, both inside and outside the community, also introduces new perspectives and ideas that encourage the kind of creative thinking needed to embrace tensions and ambiguity.

When striving for a both/and approach, Fishing for Success does not attempt to resolve the tensions that arise from its competing goals. It acknowledges that interdependent elements like tradition and modernity are integral and inherent to its work and function as a place-based social enterprise. Integrative thinking has been described as a "critical antecedent" of social entrepreneurship, as social enterprises must attend to these kinds of elements on an ongoing basis (Miller et al. 2012, 625). Embracing one element does not mean that the organization must forsake the other. For example, it is possible to honour that which is historic and traditional while embracing that which is new and modern. While it is certainly easier and quicker to adopt an either/or mindset to these situations, Fishing for Success has shown that sitting in the discomfort of these tensions, instead of striving to reconcile them, can allow for creative thinking and innovative ways forward that can strengthen not only the organization, but the community as well. Being embedded in place facilitates this process by enabling Fishing for Success to recognize the distinctions and synergies between competing forces (Andriopolous and Lewis 2009).

Orren and Hearn are surrounded by historic fishing structures, well versed in heritage fishing practices, and grounded in stories about the local fishery. They are also highly attuned to the modern-day realities of their rural community, including changing demographics, shifting economies, and emergent technologies. This close connection to place allows Fishing for Success to appreciate the value of history and heritage while also seeing a need to adapt and innovate. This demonstrates that place facilitates an iterative process wherein embeddedness draws out these distinctions between competing forces while also presenting organizations with unique opportunities to find synergies.

However, this case also demonstrates that even when striving to maintain a both/and approach to navigating tensions, organizations may still need to make either/or choices in their day-to-day operations. For example, there are instances where social enterprises may need to prioritize making money over creating social impact, or they may choose to prioritize the needs of their beneficiaries over generating the most revenue. However, being rooted in place allows organizations to keep a both/and perspective even when making these either/or choices. Research has shown that place-based organizations possess holistic understandings of local needs and challenges, allowing them to identify new opportunities (McKeever, Jack, and Anderson 2015). This case highlights that this same holistic perspective also allows organizations to engage both/and thinking to navigating tensions.

Conclusion

Fishing for Success offers insight into the tensions of place-based social enterprise and demonstrates how embeddedness in place can facilitate the adoption of a both/and approach to navigate tensions. Future research in this area could examine this phenomenon in different contexts to explore how tensions are experienced and managed by other organizations. Insights from new contexts may also uncover additional kinds of tensions faced by place-based social enterprises. Moreover, while this case shows how place can help organizations develop integrative thinking, future studies could explore how place may also constrain both/and thinking, and the types of strategies organizations may employ to manage tensions in these instances. This chapter has highlighted Fishing for

Success's both/and approach to tensions and leveraging place to facilitate integrative thinking. As a principle of the PLACE Framework, the notion of *engaging both/and thinking* represents an important process that can help social entrepreneurs and community leaders address the ambiguity and complexity that arise from community work. The case of Fishing for Success shows that even when faced with numerous conflicting demands and tensions, place-based social enterprises can lean into their deep connections to place to build innovative solutions that create social impact and revitalize communities.

Note

1.   This is the population of Petty Harbour–Maddox Cove because the two communities are amalgamated.

Acknowledgements

Our work was funded by the Social Sciences and Humanities Research Council of Canada and by the Future Ocean and Coastal Infrastructures (FOCI), an Ocean Frontier Institute project supported by the Canada First Research Excellence Fund. We would like to thank every Fishing for Success and Girls Who Fish volunteer, and Canada Summer Jobs staff who believe in the dream of making space in the boat for everyone! This gratitude extends to the tourists who, through their enjoyment of a cultural fishing experience, provided the revenue to support Fishing for Success community programs.

References

Andriopoulos, Constantine, and Marianne W. Lewis. 2009. "Exploitation-Exploration Tensions and Organizational Ambidexterity: Managing Paradoxes of Innovation." *Organization Science* 20, no. 4: 696–717.

Barrett, Terra. 2015. "Fishing for Success with Kimberly Orren." *Living Heritage*

Podcast. Episode 17, November 12, 2015. http://www.ichblog.ca/2015/11/livingheritage-podcast-fishing-for.html.

Battilana, Julie, and Matthew Lee. 2014. "Advancing Research on Hybrid Organizing: Insights from the Study of Social Enterprises." *Academy of Management Annals* 8, no. 1: 397–441.

Battilana, Julie, Metin Sengul, Anne-Claire Pache, and Jacob Model. 2015. "Harnessing Productive Tensions in Hybrid Organizations: The Case of Work Integration Social Enterprises." *Academy of Management Journal* 58, no. 6: 1658–85.

Brenton, Jennifer, and Natalie Slawinski. 2023. "Collaborating for Community Regeneration: Facilitating Partnerships in, Through, and for Place." *Journal of Business Ethics*, no. 184: 815–834. https://doi.org/10.1007/s10551-023-05365-5

Bryant, Shelley L., and Bernard Martin. 1996. *Ancient Rights: The Protected Fishing Area of Petty Harbour–Maddox Cove.* St. John's: Protected Areas Association of Newfoundland and Labrador. http://lib-lespaul.library.mun.ca/PDFs/ich_avalon/AncientRightsBooklet.pdf.

Centre for Addiction and Mental Health. 2019. *Women Sharing Heritage Program, Association for New Canadians.* https://www.camh.ca/en/professionals/professionals--projects/immigrant-and-refugee-mental-health-project/newsletter/promising-practices/2019---2020/pp-pg-nov-2019---women-sharing-heritage-program.

Dees, J. Gregory. 2001 [1998]. *The Meaning of Social Entrepreneurship*, rev. ed. Durham, NC: Center for the Advancement of Social Entrepreneurship. https://centers.fuqua.duke.edu/case/wp-content/uploads/sites/7/2015/03/Article_Dees_MeaningofSocialEntrepreneurship_2001.pdf.

Delisle, Raina. 2016. "Old Coast, New Coast: Petty Harbour, Newfoundland." *Hakai Magazine*, October 14, 2016. https://www.hakaimagazine.com/article-short/old-coast-new-coast-petty-harbour-newfoundland/.

Di Domenico, MariaLaura, Helen Haugh, and Paul Tracey. 2010. "Social Bricolage: Theorizing Social Value Creation in Social Enterprises." *Entrepreneurship Theory and Practice* 34, no. 4: 681–703.

Grimes, Matthew G., Trenton A. Williams, and Eric Y. Zhao. 2019. "Anchors Aweigh: The Sources, Variety, and Challenges of Mission Drift." *Academy of Management Review* 44, no. 4: 819–45.

Haigh, Nardia, and Andrew Hoffman. 2012. "Hybrid Organizations: The Next Chapter of Sustainable Business." *Organizational Dynamics* 41, no. 2: 126–34.

Haugh, Helen. 2006. "Social Enterprise: Beyond Economic Outcomes and Individual Returns." In *Social Entrepreneurship*, edited by Johanna Mair, Jeffrey Robinson, and Kai Hockerts, 180–205. New York: Palgrave Macmillan.

Hertel, Christina, Sophie Bacq, and Frank-Martin Belz. 2019. "It Takes a Village to Sustain a Village: A Social Identity Perspective on Successful Community-Based Enterprise Creation." *Academy of Management Discoveries* 5, no. 4: 438–64.

Jay, Jason. 2013. "Navigating Paradox as a Mechanism of Change and Innovation in Hybrid Organizations." *Academy of Management Journal* 56, no. 1: 137–59.

Johnstone, Harvey, and Doug Lionais. 2004. "Depleted Communities and Community Business Entrepreneurship: Revaluing Space through Place." *Entrepreneurship and Regional Development* 16, no. 3: 217–33.

Lumpkin, G.T., Sophie Bacq, and Robert J. Pidduck. 2018. "Where Change Happens: Community-Level Phenomena in Social Entrepreneurship Research." *Journal of Small Business Management* 56, no. 1: 24–50.

Martin, Roger L. 2007. "How Successful Leaders Think." *Harvard Business Review*. https://hbr.org/2007/06/how-successful-leaders-think.

McKeever, Edward, Sarah Jack, and Alistair Anderson. 2015. "Embedded Entrepreneurship in the Creative *Re*-Construction of Place." *Journal of Business Venturing* 30, no. 1: 50–65.

Miron-Spektor, Ella, Amy Ingram, Joshua Keller, Wendy K. Smith, and Marianne W. Lewis. 2018. "Microfoundations of Organizational Paradox: The Problem Is How We Think About the Problem." *Academy of Management Journal* 61, no. 1: 26–45.

Miller, Toyah L., Matthew G. Grimes, Jeffery S. McMullen, and Timothy J. Vogus. 2012. "Venturing for Others with Heart and Head: How Compassion Encourages Social Entrepreneurship." *Academy of Management Review* 37, no. 4: 616–40.

Murphy, Matthew, Wade M. Danis, Johnny Mack, and (Kekinusuqs) Judith Sayers. 2020. "From Principles to Action: Community-Based Entrepreneurship in the Toquaht Nation." *Journal of Business Venturing* 35, no. 6.

Nolan, Rebekah. 2017. "Fishing for Success: Making the Girls of Newfoundland the Future of the Fishery." *Journeys of Discovery with Tom Wilmer*. KCBX: Central Coast Public Radio, December 21, 2017. https://www.kcbx.org/post/fishing-success-making-girls-newfoundland-future-fishery#stream/0.

Pache, Anne-Claire, and Filipe Santos. 2013. "Inside the Hybrid Organization: Selective Coupling as a Response to Competing Institutional Logics." *Academy of Management Journal* 56, no. 4: 972–1001.

Poole, Marshall S., and Andrew H. Van de Ven. 1989. "Using Paradox to Build Management and Organization Theories." *Academy of Management Review* 14, no. 4: 562–78.

Quinn, Robert E., and Kim S. Cameron. 1988. *Paradox and Transformation: Toward a Theory of Change in Organization and Management*. Cambridge, MA: Ballinger.

Schad, Jonathan, Marianne W. Lewis, Sebastian Raisch, and Wendy K. Smith. 2016. "Paradox Research in Management Science: Looking Back to Move Forward." *Academy of Management Annals* 10, no. 1: 5–64.

Seelos, Christian, Johanna Mair, Julie Battilana, and Tina Dacin. 2011. "The Embeddedness of Social Entrepreneurship: Understanding Variation across Local Communities." In *Communities and Organizations*, edited by Chris Marquis, Royston Greenwood, and Michael Lounsbury, 333–63. Bingley, UK: Emerald Group.

Shrivastava, Paul, and James J. Kennelly. 2013. "Sustainability and Place-Based Enterprise." *Organization & Environment* 26, no. 1: 83–101.

Siegner, Meike, Jonatan Pinkse, and Rajat Panwar. 2018. "Managing Tensions in a Social Enterprise: The Complex Balancing Act to Deliver a Multi-Faceted but Coherent Social Mission." *Journal of Cleaner Production* 174: 1314–24.

Slawinski, Natalie, Blair Winsor, Daina Mazutis, John W. Schouten, and Wendy K. Smith. 2021. "Managing the Paradoxes of Place to Foster Regeneration." *Organization & Environment* 34, no. 4: 595–618.

Smith, Wendy K., and Marianne W. Lewis. 2011. "Toward a Theory of Paradox: A Dynamic Equilibrium Model of Organizing." *Academy of Management Review* 36, no. 2: 381–403.

Smith, Wendy K., and Marya L. Besharov. 2019. "Bowing Before Dual Gods: How Structured Flexibility Sustains Organizational Hybridity." *Administrative Science Quarterly* 64, no.1: 1–44.

Smith, Wendy K., Marya L. Besharov, Anke K. Wessels, and Michael Chertok. 2012. "A Paradoxical Leadership Model for Social Entrepreneurs: Challenges, Leadership Skills, and Pedagogical Tools for Managing Social and Commercial Demands." *Academy of Management Learning & Education* 11, no. 3: 463–78.

Smith, Wendy K., Michael Gonin, and Marya L. Besharov. 2013. "Managing Social-Business Tensions: A Review and Research Agenda for Social Enterprise." *Business Ethics Quarterly* 23, no. 3: 407–42.

Thomas, David F., and Jennifer E. Cross. 2007. "Organizations as Place Builders." *Journal of Behavioral and Applied Management* 9, no. 1: 33–61.

Vedula, Siddharth, Claudia Doblinger, Desirée Pacheco, Jeffrey York, Sophie Bacq, Michael V. Russo, and Thomas J. Dean. 2021. "Entrepreneurship for the Public Good: A Review, Critique, and Path Forward for Social and Environmental Entrepreneurship Research." *Academy of Management Annals* 16, no. 1: 391–425.

Whiteman, Gail, and William H. Cooper. 2011. "Ecological Sensemaking." *Academy of Management Journal* 54, no. 5: 889–911.

PART II

Case Studies Beyond Newfoundland and Labrador

CHAPTER 7

Place-Based Pursuit of Economic Self-Determination by the Toquaht Nation in Canada

Matthew Murphy, Johnny Mack, Lorenzo Magzul,
Astrid Pérez Piñan, Cloy-e-iis Judith Sayers, and Hadley Friedland

Introduction

The people of Toquaht Nation (approx. 160 citizens), one of the 16 tribes of Nuu-chah-nulth people, reside on the west coast of the land today known as Vancouver Island, British Columbia, Canada. The Toquaht have an intimate relationship to place, having lived in harmony with their Hahoulthee (traditional territory) for at least 10,000 years (Toquaht Nation 2021). After more than 150 years of European colonization and 135 years of subjugation under the Canadian Indian Act, in 2011 Toquaht Nation implemented a modern treaty, the Maa-nulth First Nations' Final Agreement (a.k.a. Maa-nulth Treaty), with the province of British Columbia and the federal government of Canada that re-established self-governance and control over a portion of its Hahoulthee. Toquaht Nation is party to the Maa-nulth Treaty along with four other First Nations communities: Huu-ay-aht First Nation, Uchucklesaht First Nation, Ucluelet First Nation, and Ka:'yu:'k't'h'/Che:k:tles7et'h' First Nation.

As a governing authority, Toquaht Nation created and ratified a constitution and accompanying laws, regulations, and policies. Text from the preamble of Toquaht Nation's constitution illustrates how the Toquaht People's connection to place and vision of sustainable development have been enshrined into the Nation's newly formed institutions.

We have existed from time immemorial and have occupied and used the lands, waters and resources of our traditional territory . . . throughout history.

We draw our identity from our relationship to our land and from our rich heritage, culture, language and our stories, myths and oral traditions.

Through the act of governing, we assume the power to preserve our natural world and enhance our identity. (Toquaht Nation 2014)

Like many First Nations in Canada, the Toquaht People are working to become economically self-sufficient through processes of economic development (Anderson, Dana, and Dana 2006; Hilton 2021). In order to pursue economic development that is not only economically viable, but also preserves and strengthens Toquaht culture and traditions and the natural environment to which Toquaht identity is strongly tied, the nation required a system for evaluating economic opportunities and measuring the impacts of economic development that was based on, and aligned with, Toquaht values that have been preserved and passed on through stories over millennia.

This chapter describes Toquaht Nation's development and use of a socio-culturally sensitive evaluation and monitoring system, called the Toquaht Project Assessment System (TPAS). The TPAS is used to estimate the potential impacts of economic development projects prior to implementation, and to monitor the actual impacts of projects that are implemented. The co-authors of this chapter worked in close collaboration with the Toquaht Nation Government and Toquaht people to develop and implement the TPAS. Johnny Mack, a University of Victoria (UVic) PhD student at the commencement of this project, and now an assistant professor in the Peter A. Allard School of Law at the University of British Columbia, is a Toquaht citizen and initiated the relationship between Toquaht Nation and the research team — in particular, the relationship with lead author, Matthew Murphy. Murphy is a settler of Irish, English, and Scottish ancestry from the United States and an associate professor of sustainability and strategy in the Gustavson School of Business at UVic, who secured a Social Sciences and Humanities Research Council Partnership Development Grant that funded this research. Cloy-e-iis Judith Sayers is a prominent Nuu-chah-nulth leader, a cousin to Johnny Mack and many other Toquaht people, and was a trusted advisor to former Toquaht Chief Burt Mack. She is also a former elected chief of Hupačasath First Nation, and at the time of writing is the president of the Nuu-chah-nulth Tribal Council. Along with Murphy, Sayers, who is also an adjunct professor at the Gustavson School of Business, served as the co-principal investigator for this research. As Nuu-chah-nulth people with strong ties to Toquaht Nation, both Mack and Sayers served the research team as essential guides for all issues related to Toquaht culture, governance, protocols, and history. Lorenzo Magzul, originally from Guatemala and of Kaqchikel Mayan heritage, joined the research team as a post-doctoral fellow and was integral to the overall project and to community engagement activities in particular. Astrid Pérez Piñán, originally from Puerto Rico, is a scholar of gender and international development and professor in the School of Public Administration at UVic. Her work on the research team was primarily focused on ensuring that the methods and analysis employed included a strong gender dimension. Together with Sayers and Hadley Friedland, a Canadian settler and associate professor of Indigenous law in the Faculty of Law at the University of Alberta, Pérez Piñán co-designed and co-facilitated a series of "Women's Circles," which served to ensure that Toquaht women's voices were heard and integrated into this research.

Ancient stories that inform the Toquaht world view reveal not only historical events, but physical, genealogical, and spiritual relationships as well as ontological and epistemological perspectives that guide individual and communal behaviour (E.R. Atleo 2004; Neville and Coulthard 2019). Coulthard and Simpson (2016, 254) refer to the ethical frameworks drawn from Indigenous place-based practices and associated forms of knowledge as "grounded normativity," pointing out that "grounded normativity houses and reproduces the practices and procedures, based on deep reciprocity, that are inherently informed by an intimate relationship to place."

Still embedded within the larger Canadian political, social, and economic context — a context in which the neo-liberal economic paradigm is prevalent — Toquaht leaders, after implementation of the Maa-nulth Treaty in 2011, sought ways to thoroughly and consistently evaluate not only the financial and employment implications of various business opportunities, but also the impacts on the environment and their culture and community. In 2013, Toquaht Tyee Ha'wilth (First Chief), Wii-tsuts-koom, Anne Mack invited our university-based research team to collaborate in the development of a system that would be used to assess the impact of economic development projects on Toquaht Nation's culture, community, natural environment, and economy. The collaborative work described here provides an example of grounded normativity and connects to the PLACE Framework underpinning this book.

The Framework's principle of *promoting community leaders* is inherent in this Indigenous, community-based research collaboration, as the project originated at the behest of the Toquaht Chief and Council and was guided by Toquaht people in both government and academic roles from start to finish. *Linking divergent perspectives* was also a regular feature of the collaboration, as Toquaht Nation sought to link its own vision of sustainable economic development to the broader Canadian and global market economic systems within which it is embedded. Likewise, the use of the assessment system developed through this project requires individuals with different roles, responsibilities, and perspectives to come together in dialogue to develop a shared understanding of each particular project's impact on well-being. Use of the TPAS relates specifically to *amplify local capacities and assets* associated with carrying out economic development projects on Toquaht territory. Meanwhile, non-Toquaht members of the research team learned about the traditional and contemporary values and visions of sustainable development held by the Toquaht

People by listening to their *compelling stories*, and the research team also used the story form in an animated video created to communicate the purpose and functionality of the TPAS to Toquaht community members. Finally, by combining methods of modern decision support science with place-based Indigenous knowledge, the TPAS itself is a model of *engaging with both/and thinking*. Moreover, use of the TPAS implies the integration of concepts and knowledge related to assessing the impacts of economic development efforts across four dimensions of well-being.

In the remainder of this chapter, we describe the origins of and approach to the project in terms of the community-based, Indigenous, feminist, and participatory action research methodologies used (Hesse-Biber 2013; Kemmis and McTaggart 2005; Kovach 2009; Smith 2012; Susman and Evered 1978). We then explain the outcomes of the project, which culminated in the development and implementation of the Toquaht Project Assessment System. This system follows the concept of grounded normativity by incorporating Toquaht Nation's place-based knowledge, values, and vision in order to assess and monitor the impacts of economic development projects.

Project Origins and Approach

This research was designed to prioritize and value First Nation interests, perspectives, and knowledge (Smith 2012). The design is consistent with a community-based approach and can reveal novel perspectives on economic development that are not often considered in the academic discourse, which is commonly embedded in and constrained by the liberal economic paradigm. The methodological approach was also guided by an ethical imperative, expressed in Canadian national guidelines for research with Indigenous communities, which calls for explicitly acknowledging and emphasizing the important role of communities "in planning and decision making, from the earliest stages of conception and design of projects through to the analysis and dissemination of results" (CIHR, NSERC, and SSHRC 2014, 110–11).

Guided by the ethical imperative that Indigenous Peoples control all research conducted within their territories — including ownership, control, access, and possession of all data and information obtained from the research (Ermine, Sinclair, and Browne 2005) — the project also employed a Participatory Action Research (PAR) method through a five-phase process that emphasized iterative cycles of co-creation and social learning (Susman and Evered 1978). The five phases include (1) diagnosing, (2) action planning, (3) action taking, (4) evaluating, and (5) specifying learning. The composition of the transdisciplinary research team, which consisted of scholars from nine different academic disciplines, reflects the diverse and participatory nature of the project itself, with half of the team consisting of Indigenous collaborators, including five members from the Toquaht community itself (Table 7.1).

Table 7.1. Research team composition.

Community-Based	University-Based
Toquaht Chief (female)	Professor — Business/Sustainability and Social Entrepreneurship (male)*
Toquaht Economic Development Officer (male)*	Professor and Former Elected First Nations Chief — Law and Business (female)
Toquaht Director of Operations 1 (female)*	Professor — Indigenous Law (male)
Toquaht Director of Operations 2 (female)	Professor — Business/Entrepreneurship (male)*
Toquaht Council Member 1 (male)	Professor — Public Admin./Gender and Development (female)*
Toquaht Council Member 2 (female)	
Toquaht Council Member 3 (female)	Professor — Indigenous Law (female)*
Tribal Resource Investment Corporation (TRICORP) CEO (male)	Post-Doctoral Fellow — Indigenous Food Systems (male)
TRICORP Business Development Officer (male)	Research Assistant — Dispute Resolution (female)*
	Research Assistant — Sociology (female)*
	Research Assistant — Engineering (female)
	Research Assistant — Computer Science (male)*

* Denotes non-Indigenous individuals.

Complementing the PAR approach, this research also incorporated literature reviews and the other qualitative methods. Building on research that has analyzed oral histories to establish key principles of Indigenous law, sustainable communities, and political thought (Borrows 2010; E.R. Atleo 2004; Friedland 2012; Harkin 1998; Napoleon 2013), this research employed a combination of oral histories, community engagement, and recently created Toquaht laws, policies, and reports to derive the guiding principles of Toquaht economic development. Contemporary Toquaht views on a range of issues related to economic development were collected through a variety of community engagement activities between July 2014 and August 2015. These included participant observation, 28 semi-structured interviews, two community-wide workshops including 56 participants, and three Women's Circles with a total of 15 participants. Approximately 43 per cent of Toquaht Nation's adult population participated in one or more of the engagement activities.

After all data were collected, analyzed, and organized, the results were presented to the Toquaht Council and government administration, who confirmed that the findings accurately reflected the values and vision of the community. Then discussions and planning began in relation to the design of an evaluation and measurement system that would ultimately be developed for use by the Toquaht Nation. Development of the assessment and monitoring system was completed in the summer of 2018.

In the sections that follow, we describe the findings of this research and the evaluation and monitoring system created for use by the Toquaht Nation and then discuss the implications of this work for economic self-determination.

Project Outcomes: Toquaht Project Assessment System

Findings from the research activities that focused on identifying Toquaht economic development principles revealed a high degree of consistency between texts related to Toquaht history and culture, laws, and regulations created by the Toquaht government and the contemporary views of

Toquaht citizens who were engaged in workshops and interviews. A description of key concepts that are pervasive throughout historical as well as contemporary Toquaht and broader Nuu-chah-nulth culture and society is provided below.

Several Nuu-chah-nulth words and concepts are accepted as indicative of the Nuu-chah-nulth world view and value system. A common phrase reflecting the Nuu-chah-nulth world view is *heshook-ish tsawalk*, which means "everything is one" or "everything is connected" (C.G. Atleo 2008). Nuu-chah-nulth scholar Umeek (Richard Atleo) stresses that this term is inclusive of all reality, including the physical and metaphysical (E.R. Atleo 2004). Moreover, Clifford Atleo explains, "*Heshookish tsa'walk* is a fundamental concept to the Nuu-chah-nulth people constantly reminding us that all life, animate and inanimate, is connected and that none of our decisions are isolated" (C.G. Atleo 2008, 11–12).

The concept of *heshook-ish tsawalk* is closely related to a second core concept in the Nuu-chah-nulth world view, *iisaak*, or "respect with caring" (Mack 2009). Personal and communal security, freedom, and happiness may be found through interconnectedness and balance (Mack 2009). Because *heshook-ish tsawalk* makes balance imperative, it is "the maintenance of balance that is the general life project" (Mack 2009, 19). *Iisaak* provides a technique to restore and maintain balance. As Umeek explains, "*Iisaak* is predicated on the notion that every life form has intrinsic value and that this should be recognized through appropriate protocols and interaction . . . . *iisaak*, as another law of life, promotes balance and harmony within creation" (E.R. Atleo 2004, 130). *Iisaak* was and is understood by Nuu-chah-nulth people to be a defining characteristic for human beings. To act disrespectfully implies a betrayal of one's humanity and risks disruption of the balance (Mack 2009).

Nuu-chah-nulth political and economic institutions traditionally were, and still are, designed to facilitate *iisaak*. This includes the system of governance within which leaders, or chiefs, called *Hawiih*, have been raised to embody the normative principle of generosity. *Hawiih* were tested throughout their upbringing to ensure they knew how to listen to the people, the land, and the spiritual world (Mack 2009). Another example of the *iisaak* ideal is found in "potlatching," a central feature of the traditional Nuu-chah-nulth economic system based on a combination of accumulation and depletion of wealth. "There was an imperative for wealth accumulation, not for personal enjoyment or luxury, but for giving away. Most of our items would be given away at our potlatches. . . . A chief left with absolutely nothing after a potlatch was a chief worthy of the utmost respect" (Mack 2009, 22). Umeek adds that Nuu-chah-nulth conceptions of generosity imply that receiving is as important as giving; therefore, "reciprocity and balance are central tenets of Nuu-chah-nulth life" (C.G. Atleo 2008, 13).

The guiding principles of interconnectedness, respect, and reciprocity are reflected in official Toquaht government laws and documents. Two examples of how present-day Toquaht values align with these concepts are shown below, in the preambles of the Toquaht Nation Environmental Protection Act (2011) and the Toquaht Nation Constitution (2007):

> The Toquaht Nation asserts that we have occupied, benefited from and governed our Hahoulthee (traditional territory) since time immemorial.
>
> The Toquaht traditional territory has in the past provided the resources necessary to sustain us and provide for our physical and spiritual needs.
>
> We value and honour our past and present connection to the lands, waters and resources of our Toquaht traditional territory and recognize that all life forms are *Hish-uk-ist-sawalk* (interconnected) and that all humanity must have *Iisaak* (respect for the earth and all life forms on it). (Toquaht Nation 2011, 6)
>
> . . . These values include:
> a belief in, and reverence for, the Creator,
> honouring our ancestors,

respecting our elders,

abiding by an internal order based on our Ha'wiih and our
    Hahoulthee

respecting our family and kinship systems,

our unique language, and

a respect for the land, air, water and environment which
    encompasses the Hahoulthee of our Ha'wiih. (Toquaht
    Nation 2007, 1)

Reflecting these values in the context of economic development, the Toquaht
Nation Government Economic Development Act (2015) affirms that:

> Toquaht businesses will engage in economic development that
> is socially, economically and environmentally sustainable and
> that respects our history and the heritage, culture and traditions
> of our people, our Hahoulthee (traditional territory) and the en-
> vironment within which we live. (Toquaht Nation 2015, 9)

The guiding principles of interconnectedness, respect, and reciprocity represent the foundation of contemporary views about what sustainability entails for Toquaht people and provide a sharp contrast to the
Western European world view that perceives objectives of environmental, social, and economic well-being to be in tension with one another.
Rather than viewing these dimensions of well-being as being in tension,
from a Nuu-chah-nulth perspective, tension arises when there is imbal-
ance between these dimensions.

In community-wide workshops, focus groups, and individual interviews, when people were asked what types of businesses they would or
would not like to see established on Toquaht territory, acceptable businesses were frequently related to ecotourism and tended to be of small
scale with low impact on the environment. Key reasons cited for proposing such types of businesses were creating employment for Toquaht

citizens, generating income for the Toquaht Nation Government, and maintaining Toquaht culture and language. By contrast, large businesses and those focused on resource extraction were commonly viewed as unacceptable. Reasons cited for opposing such businesses were that they are destructive, too big, polluting, and disrespectful.

In focus groups attended solely by women, which are both a traditional and contemporary practice that the Toquaht refer to as "Women's Circles," participant reflections on the topic of economic development related to the foundational Toquaht principle of *heshook-ish tsawalk* (interconnectedness). One participant's comment exemplifies this recurring theme: "For me, I usually think of economic development as making money, but really it is about how we take care of one another, how we preserve our language, culture, etc." Responding to this comment, another woman stated, "I feel the same way. It's not about making money; it's about becoming whole. We need to redefine what we mean by economic

Figure 7.1. Indigenous social enterprise operates based on the guiding sustainability principles: interconnectedness, respect, and reciprocity. (Photo credit: Matthew Murphy, 2022)

development." Similarly, in another women's focus group, a participant remarked, "This isn't going to be about having development that makes us lots of money — it's about having healthy businesses in the community that allow us to be sustainable."

Based on analysis of Nuu-chah-nulth literature, the Toquaht Nation's laws and official documents, and the outcomes from community engagement exercises, six recurring themes related to the Toquaht people's vision for sustainable economic development were identified:

- Holistic understanding of sustainability — all is one (*heshook-ish tsawalk*)
- Emphasis on environmental sustainability and protection
- Desire for fair and transparent political processes
- Necessity of economic health and viability
- Support for a vibrant home community and healthy citizens
- Practice and renewal of Toquaht culture and language

The evaluation and monitoring system that the Toquaht Nation would eventually use to assess and monitor business ventures was carefully designed to incorporate these themes (Murphy et al. 2020).

Assessment and Monitoring Mechanisms

A database of indicators of well-being was created to evaluate potential and actual impacts of business activity with attention to issues important to the Toquaht Nation. Many indicators emerged from the community engagement process and a review of existing Toquaht laws and government reports (e.g., Toquaht Nation 2011, 2014, 2015). Combined, these sources resulted in the identification and definition of 102 Toquaht indicators of well-being that could potentially be useful. Other factors were identified in literature on indicators of well-being used in Indigenous communities (e.g., Lewis and Lockhart 2002; Orr, Weir, and Atlantic Aboriginal Economic Development Integrated Research Program 2013; Stankovitch 2008;

Tauli-Corpuz 2008). With the close involvement of Toquaht project members, including Toquaht Nation Government staff and elected council members, a set of 79 indicators was selected for inclusion in the TPAS based on their relevance to the Toquaht context and people (see examples in Table 7.2). For the purpose of evaluating economic development projects, each indicator was associated with the various types of economic activities that the Nation considered, such as forestry, aquaculture, and tourism.

Table 7.2. Illustrative examples of indicators of well-being.

Indicator	Indicator Scale	Indicator Description	Dimension
Beach spawning areas	Percentage impact	Effect on beach spawning areas — per cent of impact	Environmental
Fauna biodiversity	Percentage or number of species impacted	Effect on diversity of fauna per unit area per hectare	Environmental
Inclusion of local knowledge	Number or percentage	Inclusion of local knowledge in decision-making and/or monitoring and evaluation	Cultural
Language learning	Number of people	Number of Toquaht citizens provided with the opportunity to learn the Nuu-chah-nulth language — disaggregated by gender	Cultural
Toquaht citizens employed	Number of people	Number of Toquaht citizens employed — disaggregated by gender and sector	Community
Improved infrastructure	Percentage efficiency	Maximally efficient use of all infrastructure to service Toquaht citizens currently living or returning to live on Toquaht territory	Community
Net Income	Dollar amount per accounting period	Income minus cost of goods sold, expenses, and taxes	Economic
Person years of employment	Number of person years	Person years of employment generated by the business — disaggregated by gender	Economic

In addition to identifying relevant indicators of well-being, the Mauri Model Decision Making Framework (MMDMF) (Morgan 2006) was selected as a practical and adaptable framework that closely adheres to principles of sound, sustainability-based decision-making (Pintér et al. 2012) as well as the Toquaht's own guiding principles of interconnectedness, respect, and reciprocity. The MMDMF is a system created by a Māori (Indigenous) scholar, Dr. Kepa Morgan, in collaboration with Māori communities in New Zealand/Aotearoa. Similar to the Toquaht, the Māori People's identity and knowledge systems are grounded in specific landscapes (Keenan 2012). At the project team's request, Dr. Morgan travelled to Vancouver Island to meet with the entire community- and university-based team to share how the MMDMF works and discuss how it could be customized for use by Toquaht Nation.

The MMDMF provides an overall assessment of well-being through a combination of assessments related to the environmental, cultural, social, and economic dimensions of well-being (Morgan 2006). The economic dimension relates to the financial impact of a project, measuring the extent to which the project will generate economic wealth and jobs while also taking into consideration any risk to the nation's financial base. For the Toquaht, the environmental dimension of well-being is best understood through the Nuu-chah-nulth concept of Ha'hoolthlii, meaning "the land" or "Chiefly territories." The term embraces more than just land, however. It includes the lands, waters, air, animals, plants, people — in short, everything within the territory. The health of the Ha'hoolthlii is seen as foundational to all other dimensions of well-being.

The community dimension of well-being is concerned with the Toquaht people and their quality of life in Macoah, the only currently occupied village on Toquaht territory. Considerations for community well-being include questions such as, "Will this project bring Toquaht people home to the territory?", "Will this project improve infrastructure or housing in Macoah?", and "How will this project affect the health and safety of the people of Macoah?"

Finally, cultural well-being is related to the vitality and resurgence of Toquaht culture, including the use of the Nuu-chah-nulth language. Considerations for the cultural dimension include questions about a proposed project's effect on traditional sites, food-gathering, or cultural ceremonies. The cultural dimension also considers ways in which an economic development project might have positive effects on Toquaht cultural practices, such as funding language or cultural programs, using Nuu-chah-nulth language in signage and naming, and including traditional knowledge in the project itself.

The assessment of projects works in two stages. The first involves determining the relative weight placed on each dimension of well-being through a procedure known as Analytic Hierarchy Process (AHP), a technique for analyzing complex problems that uses pair-wise comparisons to establish the relative importance of each dimension (Saaty 1980, 2008). The resultant priority scale of well-being dimensions is referred to as a "world view setting." World view settings can be created from the perspective of any particular group or individual, thus allowing projects to be assessed and compared based on a variety of different world views.

The second stage involves selecting indicators related to each of the four dimensions of well-being and assessing them on a five-point scale, where the values selected represent the expected impacts of the project on well-being for the relevant indicators, ranging from extreme harm to extreme improvement.

The MMDMF approach allows a project with identified indicators and related impact evaluations to be viewed comparatively from the perspectives of various world views. For example, a project assessment that results in a positive score for overall well-being based on a world view that places high priority on the economic dimension may be determined to have a negative score for overall well-being when assessed with a world view setting that places a lower priority on the economic dimension.

After completion of a piloting phase, the TPAS was used to evaluate five projects included in the Toquaht Nation's *Five-year Economic Development Plan: 2018–2022*. All projects were assessed to estimate impacts during each year covered by the five-year plan. Monitoring and evaluation of the actual impacts of these projects began in 2019.

In 2018, a short, animated video was produced to explain and demonstrate how the TPAS works. The video is set on Toquaht territory and narrated by a Toquaht community member, with the Toquaht people as its intended audience. Two fictional business opportunities — a large hotel-casino project and a small development of cabins — are compared using the TPAS. Taking into account the Toquaht's objectives related to the development of a healthy and sustainable community and the revitalization of Toquaht culture, the small development of cabins is favoured over the hotel-casino development, although the latter would have created more jobs and economic profit.

While it is premature to evaluate the long-term outcomes of using the TPAS for the Toquaht Nation, in the section below we offer observations regarding how this project and the resultant TPAS relates to Toquaht Nation's pursuit of economic self-determination.

Reflections and Conclusion

Reflecting the Indigenous, place-based concept of grounded normativity (Coulthard and Simpson 2016), developing the TPAS through community-based action research involved community, organizational, and individual reflection, dialogue, and learning about what sustainable development means to the Toquaht people and what sustainability looks like in practice (Murphy et al. 2020; Pérez Piñán et al. 2022). Through collaboration among the Toquaht community, university-based researchers in British Columbia, and Dr. Kepa Morgan, the TPAS represents the collaborative integration and co-creation of place-based knowledge across multiple Indigenous and academic communities, and across Indigenous and Western knowledge systems.

At the organizational level, the Toquaht government and Toquaht-owned businesses have used the TPAS to evaluate business opportunities related to aquaculture, forestry, clean energy production, and tourism.

The use of the TPAS implies both organizational and individual-level dialogue, learning, and planning. The Toquaht government and businesses brought their plans, resources, and knowledge into their work with the TPAS. Together, these representatives in their various roles engaged in what we refer to as a "learning dialogue" to select indicators of well-being relevant to specific projects and to evaluate how each project would affect the associated indicators at particular points in time.

The conversations that took place throughout this dialogic process led to learning that informed the evaluation and (re)design of projects. Along the way, individual participants developed a more holistic and balanced understanding of the possible impacts and various design possibilities for the projects evaluated, and by extension so did the involved organizations. For example, in one conversation about selecting indicators of cultural well-being for a renewable energy project, a representative of the Toquaht government commented, "I never imagined how cultural practices could be related to a renewable energy project." However, upon discussion with the cross-functional group assessing the project, it was recognized that the location of the energy project would create opportunities for Toquaht community members to get back out on the land to engage in gathering traditional foods from areas that were otherwise difficult to reach. Likewise, supporting the Toquaht's objective of cultural revitalization, the project would create opportunities to hold cultural ceremonies at key project milestones. Had they not been discussed and incorporated into the TPAS and project plans, it is possible that these opportunities would have been overlooked, neither planned for nor managed to ensure their realization, and not monitored or accounted for as benefits arising from the project.

Another example relates to the gender-sensitive nature of indicators used in the TPAS. From the outset, Toquaht leaders and the university-based research team aimed for the community engagement process and resultant assessment system to be gender-sensitive. Workshops and individual interviews addressed how sustainability and economic development were perceived and embodied from women's perspectives (Pérez

Piñán et al. 2022). Subsequently, for all indicators within the TPAS related to the number or percentage of people affected by a particular activity, it was decided that this information would be disaggregated by gender. Later, when assessing a project for the five-year plan using the TPAS, a business manager who predicted the creation of five jobs was asked, "How many of those positions will be filled by men and how many by women?" The manager reflected for a moment and realized that he had not considered this question or its importance before. He asked the group: "Should I create job descriptions that would make it more likely that both men and women would apply?" Heads nodded affirmatively and the answer came back from the group, "Yes." The manager then said, "I haven't thought about that before. I'm not sure how I would do it." Others in the group offered to convene a separate meeting, including individuals with human resources and social services responsibilities, to work on development of job descriptions with the manager. Meanwhile, a target was set and recorded in the TPAS for hiring a gender-balanced group of employees for this project and, when monitoring the actual impacts for this project, the manager will be asked to report on how many men and women were hired. Later, this information will be shared with the community when progress updates are provided about Toquaht Nation's business activities. Both successes and setbacks will be noted and discussed among community members and organizational representatives, leading to further opportunities for learning and adaptation.

Insights drawn from the development and use of the TPAS may be useful to both advance and challenge thinking about the PLACE Framework. Critically, for Indigenous Peoples whose very identities are closely tied to their traditional territories and whose self-determination is bounded within settler-colonial contexts, the PLACE Framework includes key principles that support self-determination and contribute to sustainable community development. In particular, the PLACE Framework's principles of *promoting community leaders* and *amplifying local capacities and assets* are closely aligned with the concept of self-determination.

This research also highlights elements that the PLACE Framework does not explicitly encompass, but that might be integrated into some of its principles. For example, early community engagement activities undertaken in this research revealed that the voices of women were not being heard, so a concerted effort was required to design and facilitate activities that would directly engage Toquaht women and elicit their perspectives. This explicit approach to ensuring that women's voices were integrated into development of the TPAS could be considered an integral part of the PLACE Framework's *engaging both/and thinking* principle. Meanwhile, creating spaces and opportunities for women's participation also provoked *compelling stories* that contributed to *amplifying local capacities and assets*.

Finally, while the PLACE Framework offers a set of guiding principles, it does not offer a way of operationalizing them or assessing the potential or actual impacts of development efforts. While we do not propose that a system such as the TPAS provides a one-size-fits-all approach, it is a highly adaptable system that offers a concrete framework for strategically deciding among different potential development pathways and evaluating the impacts of development efforts that are undertaken. Systems such as this are important complements to the guiding principles offered by the PLACE Framework.

Despite its usefulness, the TPAS has important limitations. Foremost among these is that Toquaht Nation's pursuit of self-determination occurs within a context where the Toquaht are embedded within the wider Canadian and global capitalist political-economic system. As such, most of the economic activities in which the Toquaht might engage — including aquaculture, forestry, and tourism — are connected to global industries and shaped by market forces as well as state-based and multilateral institutions. In particular, these industries are heavily regulated by the Canadian government. Therefore, although Toquaht Nation has implemented a modern treaty and developed laws, regulations, and management systems to enact the community's vision and objectives, the extent of self-determination and place-based community development is bounded. Beyond the Indigenous context, this important limitation highlights the need for further exploration of how communities can successfully navigate the tensions between more local processes of planning, assessment, and evaluation for community development and the more macro-scale structures of settler colonialism, federal government bureaucracies, and global flows of capital, resources, and people associated with industry.

In summary, the collaborative project that resulted in the creation and implementation of the TPAS illustrates how place-based values and objectives identified at the community level can become operationalized at the organizational level and then lead to learning, through dialogue, at the individual and team levels. Over time, this process works iteratively, so that the Toquaht government, its businesses, and the staff involved throughout these organizations continue the work of learning, planning, and evaluation in a holistic manner. As Toquaht people engage with the TPAS as leaders, staff members, managers, or simply as citizens, dialogue triggered through use of the TPAS positively reinforces learning related to Toquaht Nation's pursuit and enactment of economic development. Use of the TPAS, therefore, represents action taken by the Toquaht Nation to determine and pursue its own place-based vision of sustainable economic development.

Acknowledgements

This research was funded by a Partnership Development Grant, File Number 890-2013-0077, awarded by the Social Sciences and Humanities Research Council of Canada (SSHRC). We are grateful to the government of Toquaht Nation and to the Toquaht people who collaborated in this research.

References

Atleo, Clifford G. 2008. "Nuu-chah-nulth Economic Development and the Changing Nature of Our Relationships within the *Ha'hoolthlii* of Our *Ha'wiih*." Master's thesis, University of Victoria.

Atleo, E. Richard/Umeek. 2004. *Tsawalk: A Nuu-chah-nulth Worldview*. Vancouver: University of British Columbia Press.

Anderson, Robert B., Léo-Paul Dana, and Teresa E. Dana. 2006. "Indigenous Land Rights, Entrepreneurship, and Economic Development in Canada: 'Opting-in' to the Global Economy." *Journal of World Business* 41, no. 1: 45–55.

Borrows, John. 2010. *Canada's Indigenous Constitution*. Toronto: University of Toronto Press.

Canadian Institutes of Health Research, Natural Sciences and Engineering Research Council of Canada, and Social Sciences and Humanities Research Council of Canada. 2014. *Tri-Council Policy Statement: Ethical Conduct for Research Involving Humans*. Ottawa: Government of Canada.

Coulthard, Glenn, and Leanne Betasamosake Simpson. 2016. "Grounded Normativity/Place-Based Solidarity." *American Quarterly* 68, no. 2: 249–55.

Ermine, Willie, Raven Sinclair, and Madisun Browne. 2005. *Kwayask itôtamow-in: Indigenous Research Ethics*. Saskatoon: Indigenous Peoples' Health Research Centre.

Friedland, Hadley. 2012. "Reflective Frameworks: Methods for Accessing, Understanding, and Applying Indigenous Laws." *Indigenous Law Journal* 11, no. 1: 1–40.

Harkin, Michael. 1998. "Whales, Chiefs, and Giants: An Exploration into Nuu-chah-nulth Political Thought." *Ethnology* 37, no. 4 (Autumn): 317–32.

Hesse-Biber, Sharlene N., ed. 2013. *Feminist Research Practice: A Primer*. Thousand Oaks, CA: Sage.

Hilton, Carol A. 2021. *Indigenomics: Taking a Seat at the Economic Table*. Gabriola Island, BC: New Society.

Keenan, Danny, ed. 2012. *Huia Histories of Māori: Ngā Tāhuhu Kōrero*. Wellington, NZ: Huia.

Kemmis, Stephen, and Robin McTaggart. 2005. *Participatory Action Research: Communicative Action and the Public Sphere*. Thousand Oaks, CA: Sage.

Kovach, Margaret. 2009. *Indigenous Methodologies: Characteristics, Conversations, and Contexts*. Toronto: University of Toronto Press.

Lewis, Mike, and R.A. Lockhart. 2002. *Performance Measurement, Development Indicators and Aboriginal Economic Development*. Port Alberni, BC: Centre for Community Enterprise.

Mack, Johnny. 2014. "Turn Sideways: Intimate Critique and the Regeneration of Tradition." Unpublished manuscript.

Morgan, Te Kipa Kepa Brian. 2006. "Decision-Support Tools and the Indigenous Paradigm." *Proceedings of the Institution of Civil Engineers: Engineering Sustainability* 159, no. 4 (December): 169–77.

Murphy, Matthew, Wade M. Danis, Johnny Mack, and Judith Sayers. 2020. "From Principles to Action: Community-based Entrepreneurship in the Toquaht Nation." *Journal of Business Venturing* 35, no. 6.

Napoleon, Val. 2013. "Thinking about Indigenous Legal Orders." In *Dialogues on Human Rights and Legal Pluralism,* edited by René Provost and Colleen Sheppard, 229–45. Dordrecht: Springer.

Neville, Kate J., and Glenn Coulthard. 2019. "Transformative Water Relations: Indigenous Interventions in Global Political Economies." *Global Environmental Politics* 19, no. 3: 1–15.

Orr, Jeff, Warren Weir, and Atlantic Aboriginal Economic Development Integrated Research Program. 2013. *Aboriginal Measures for Economic Development.* Halifax: Fernwood.

Pérez Piñán, Astrid V., Hadley Friedland, Judith Sayers, and Matthew Murphy. 2022. "Reclaiming Indigenous Economic Development through Participatory Action Research." *Journal of Human Development and Capabilities* 23, no. 1: 30–49.

Pintér, László, Peter Hardi, André Martinuzzi, and Jon Hall. 2012. "Bellagio STAMP: Principles for Sustainability Assessment and Measurement." *Ecological Indicators* 17: 20–28.

Saaty, Thomas L. 1980. *Analytical Hierarchy Process: Planning, Priority Setting, Resource Allocation.* New York: McGraw-Hill.

Saaty, Thomas L. 2008. "Decision Making with the Analytic Hierarchy Process." *International Journal of Services Sciences* 1: 83–98.

Smith, Linda T. 2012. *Decolonizing Methodologies: Research and Indigenous Peoples,* 2nd ed. London and Dunedin, NZ: Zed Books and University of Otago Press.

Stankovitch, Mara, ed. 2008. *Indicators Relevant for Indigenous Communities: A Resource Book.* Baguio City, Philippines: TEBTEBBA Foundation, Indigenous Peoples' International Centre for Policy Research and Education.

Susman, Gerald I., and Roger D. Evered. 1978. "An Assessment of the Scientific

Merits of Action Research." *Administrative Science Quarterly* 23, no. 4: 582–603.

Tauli-Corpuz, Victoria. 2008. *Indicators of Well-Being, Poverty and Sustainability Relevant to Indigenous Peoples.* United Nations Permanent Forum on Indigenous Issues. E/C.19/2008/9.

Toquaht Nation. 2011. *Environmental Protection Act.* TNS 15/2011. http://www.toquaht.ca/wp-content/uploads/2015/06/TNS-15-2011-Environmental-Protection-Act-OC.pdf

Toquaht Nation. 2014. *Toquaht Nation Constitution.* http://www.toquaht.ca/wp-content/uploads/2015/06/TN-Constitution-as-amended-2014-01-27-00848419.pdf

Toquaht Nation. 2015. *Economic Development Act.* TNS 3/2012. http://www.toquaht.ca/wp-content/uploads/2015/06/TNS-3-2012-Economic-Development-Act-Official-Consolidation-01119384.pdf

Toquaht Nation. 2021. "Our Culture." Accessed October 11, 2021. http://www.toquaht.ca/our-culture/

CHAPTER 8

Revitalizing an Urban Core: The Case of TulsaNow

Rebecca J. Franklin and Jamie Jamieson

This work is dedicated in loving memory to Larry Silvey, founding member of TulsaNow and brainchild behind the TulsaNow name. Larry, we will always miss your laughter, and the way it seemed to slowly bubble up from a deep well of soulful joy. When your beautiful soul left Tulsa, we all became the poorer for the loss. But the positive impact you made on our lovely city will last for generations.

The Scene

The year is 1999, and Tulsa, Oklahoma, has a population of around 387,000. Once the "oil capital of the world," by the mid-1980s the oil world has decamped to Houston, Texas, leaving behind a trail of conspicuously empty downtown offices and buildings. Many are art deco buildings, echoing Tulsa's oil-fuelled heyday. The architecture remains a source of local pride. Yet the downtown and its inner neighbourhoods are in decay. Decades of white flight, closing schools, "urban renewal," underinvestment in civic infrastructure, and counterproductive zoning rules have taken their toll. Ghosts of the past are present, too: in 1921, Tulsa's north downtown saw the worst race massacre in United States history, in which 300 African Americans were killed by a violent white mob, and the homes of 10,000 Black people were incinerated.

Downtown is quiet after 5 p.m. The remaining tall, graceful buildings at its core gaze out in all directions across an expanse of surface
parking lots — spaces occupied in decades past by bustling buildings
and street life. Now a typical evening's street-level view includes a lone
automobile at a red light, with no other vehicles in sight. No pedestrians
cross, and a plastic shopping bag, inflated by the breeze, blows emptily
from one surface parking lot to another, like a tumbleweed across Oklahoma's western plains.

A bird's eye view shows the whole ensemble girded by a noose-like
Inner Dispersal Loop, installed in the late 1960s. This highway compounds
the blight that afflicts the neighbourhoods in its shadow. Its overpasses
provide informal shelter to the homeless. Interstate 244 is an east–west
crosstown expressway of the same vintage, funded by the federal Model
Cities program and now acting as a barrier for the impoverished, dispro-
portionately Black neighbourhoods to its north. Life expectancy there is 11
years less than in the predominantly white zip codes immediately to the
south. Seven miles south of downtown, Tulsa is fringed by expanding
white suburbs, which are connected to the city core by another new expressway to reduce commuting times. Cutting a swath through once-walkable
inner-city neighbourhoods, these noisy thoroughfares have unceremoni-
ously depopulated the city's centre and diminished its humanity.

In November 1999, Tulsa mayor Susan Savage presents an Infill
Taskforce Report to the public. The report advocates a shakeup of land-
use regulations and proposes a new task force whose job will be to produce a revitalization plan for one inner-city neighbourhood. In May 2000,
Oklahoma's first "new urbanist" mixed-use development is approved.
And in January 2001, four thoughtful, born-and-bred Tulsans meet over
coffee to reflect upon the state of their city and their dilapidated downtown in particular. Two recent bond issues for major downtown projects
— both flawed, if well-intentioned — have failed to garner the support of
Tulsa voters. The four Tulsans decide to "get something going," in one's
laconic phrase. They invite a handful of other people to brainstorm at
the home of a mutual friend on 10 April 2001. Attendees include two

journalists, a former mayor, a researcher, a Pentecostal church leader, a new urbanist real estate developer, and a non-profit leader. This group decides to set up an organization and name it TulsaNow.

Finding Our Feet

TulsaNow got off to a good start. One group member proposed and then organized a road trip to Oklahoma City on 21 December 2001 to see what, if any, lessons could be learned from Tulsa's larger regional rival. Oklahoma City had picked itself up off the floor after the devastating 1995 terrorist bombing of the Murrah Building — the worst-ever act of home-grown terrorism in the US, with 168 people killed — and had set about systematically revitalizing its downtown. Fifty people showed up for the bus trip, and they were welcomed by Oklahoma City mayor Kirk Humphreys. The event was reported by the *Tulsa World* newspaper, and TulsaNow met the public gaze for the first time. The trip was quickly followed by a second bus tour, this time of Tulsa itself, drawing attention to the few areas of nascent revival and private-sector development in Tulsa's urban core. TulsaNow was on its way.

At the time, Tulsa was among North America's least dense cities, at around 2,500 people per square mile (Fonseca and Wong 2000). TulsaNow was convinced that the city needed to be a great deal more human-centric rather than auto-centric, with walkable neighbourhoods and a vibrant urban core — and in so doing to become more equitable, more economically viable, and a better place to live. So, land-use reform became the focus of most of TulsaNow's public meetings, and emergent issues tended to revolve around aspects of land use, such as more sustainable development models, building density, parking requirements, placement of buildings in relation to the public realm, mass transit funding, parks funding, and so on. Conventional zoning entailed dependence on automobiles and needed to be overhauled to boost walkability, improve safety for cyclists, and improve air quality and other quality-of-life factors (Frank 2000). Tulsa's zoning ordinances were written in the

1960s and had hardly been altered in subsequent decades. Zoning attorneys who drafted the zoning framework earn a comfortable living helping property owners pick their way through and around it.

Local real-world events drove much of TulsaNow's momentum. They provided the grist and the focus for research, reflection, and fleshing out the organization's positions. TulsaNow's researchers looked at development models and best practices from other cities and produced materials for use in educating Tulsa residents and decision-makers on the most critical issues.

TulsaNow took root at a time when many community-focused groups, foundations, and universities were beginning to put their work online, and members took advantage of this opportunity to learn from practitioners in other cities and countries. The Rockefeller Foundation, among many others, provided a wealth of information and inspiring initiatives, while LinkedIn enabled members to join interest groups of practitioners from all over the world.

An important element in TulsaNow's intellectual underpinnings was furnished by "new urbanism," a movement born in the early 1990s, led by Peter Katz's (1994) *The New Urbanism: Toward an Architecture of Community*. Many other writings nourished discussions, among them Jane Jacobs's (1961) *Death and Life of Great American Cities*, James Howard Kunstler's (1998) *Home from Nowhere*, Joel Kotkin's (1993) *Tribes: How Race, Religion, and Identity Determine Success in the New Global Economy*, and Christopher Leinberger's (2005) *Turning Around Downtown: Twelve Steps to Revitalization*. The Popsicle Test (Congress for the New Urbanism, n.d.) and Building a Better Block (Better Block Foundation, n.d.) were influential early concepts. "Form-based" land-use codes, cycle lanes, mass transit, "complete streets," "road diets," and "transit-oriented development" became hot topics on TulsaNow's online forum. All of them featured in dialogue with the city council and mayor, and in proposals for city-wide application and for specific neighbourhoods.

The PLACE Framework

From this point on, we, the authors, seek to integrate the PLACE Framework into our narrative, to varying degrees as seems appropriate. This might create the illusion that TulsaNow members were highly organized, conceptual, and systematic from the very beginning. The reality was messier and much more organic than that — more a rough-and-tumble of improvisation and inspiration, humour and hard work, solitary research and showing up, and implementing strategies and plans while still dreaming them up. Voluntary, grassroots efforts are rarely tidy.

Promoting Community Leaders

When the goal is community revitalization, it is critical that those who step into leadership roles be able to motivate a diverse group of individual and organizational actors to collaborate towards a common vision (Selsky and Smith 1994). Although TulsaNow eventually developed a formalized board structure that included a president, leadership was always a team effort. Some members of the leadership team also had leadership positions with other organizations, including the Arts and Humanities Council, Leadership Tulsa, Young Professionals of Tulsa (YPTulsa), 6th Street Task Force, Mid-Town Coalition of Neighborhoods, Brookside Neighborhood Association, and other various neighbourhood organizations, while others had specialized skills and areas of expertise that contributed to the leadership team in unique ways. In itself the act of organizing empowers members: roles and tasks open up for various skills, aptitudes, and interests, depending on the time available and level of emotional commitment. Members develop a sense of self-assurance about the areas in which they add value, and they take the lead in those areas.

The 80/20 rule applied to TulsaNow as to most organizations: a few members did most of the grunt work. Yet every member of the leadership team, and later the board, generally numbering around 10, contributed both expertise and input to its various discussions. Those who did more work than others chose to do so from personal enthusiasm and with little, if any, resentment. In some cases, this work overlapped with a day job. For some members it was nice to have a role they enjoyed, where their work was appreciated, from which they were unlikely to be fired, and in which they worked alongside like-minded people who frequently became friends.

The emergence of TulsaNow's online forum enabled a wider group of people to participate, to engage, and to show up at public meetings where everyone had a common interest. It created the sense of a safe environment, of a "tribe" within which it was easy to start a conversation with a stranger. Forging a formal sense of vision, mission, and strategy clarifies organizational identity and contributes to growing consensus and increasing a sense of group identity (Young 2001). The authors recall the to-ing and fro-ing of emails — no texting in those days — as the words took shape. Those most interested in the process and who participate the most are heard the most, and they gravitate naturally towards positions of leadership.

The relevance and motivating nature of the organization's vision and purpose were enough to attract a steady trickle of business leaders, entrepreneurs, and volunteers. These folks had a supportive framework within which to step up confidently and assume valuable roles. Some roles were less visible — desk research and drafting discussion papers, for example — but were critical to establishing the seriousness with which the organization was increasingly taken by elected leaders and peer organizations. Everyone could find a niche in TulsaNow where their particular talents were needed. The leadership team itself, public meetings, and online lobbying all provided opportunities for members to serve the community while playing to their strengths.

As interest in TulsaNow grew and membership numbers increased, the leadership team recognized the need to become more formalized and set about the task. While undeniably tedious at times, the process enabled board members to form deeper connections to the organization. Taking time to develop operational protocols and procedures formally acknowledged that something worth tending, cultivating, sharing, and preserving was going on. So, bylaws were drafted: *inter alia*, these cover (1) purpose, mission, strategy, and core values, (2) general membership rules, (3) the board of directors and officers, (4) committees and advisory councils, (5) meetings and order of business, and assorted other items necessary to the orderly conduct of an organization's affairs. Leadership team members duly morphed into board members, and they appointed an interim administration ahead of the first election of officers in June 2004. Anyone who paid a $20 membership fee acquired the right to vote at general business meetings and elections, though the fee eventually became non-mandatory. In the fullness of time TulsaNow became a fully-fledged, 501(c)3 (i.e., non-taxable) organization, supported by tax-deductible donations and extensive volunteer work. The bylaws stated that "TulsaNow shall be defined as a charitable, educational, non-partisan, volunteer organization concerned about the well-being and prosperity of Tulsa, Oklahoma and the surrounding region, now and for future generations" (TulsaNow 2007).

Linking Divergent Perspectives

Amid TulsaNow's formation and its initial series of public events, discussed in more detail below, the group hammered out its mission:

> . . . To help Tulsa become the most vibrant, diverse, sustainable, and prosperous city of our size. We will achieve this by focusing on the development of Tulsa's distinctive identity and economic growth around a dynamic, urban core, complemented by a constellation of livable, thriving communities. (TulsaNow 2003)

TulsaNow's core values were also eventually formalized:

- A vibrant, walkable Downtown and revitalized, core neighborhoods at the heart of a regional strategy;
- Diversity: of people, cultures, the built environment, and economic base;
- Sustainable environmental and economic development policies;
- Prosperity of all citizens in all walks of life, in terms of material opportunities, livability of neighborhoods, and civic amenities;

- The role of Design — at all levels — in the physical planning and shaping of our collective future;
- Respect, civility and genuine engagement with all points of view. (TulsaNow 2003)

Just as this process helped develop TulsaNow's leadership team, it inevitably also prompted a thoughtful discussion among people with a wide array of backgrounds and perceptions of the underlying causes of Tulsa's malaise, and of potential solutions and priorities. From its inception, TulsaNow was lucky in generally attracting a thoughtful, reasonable, responsible, and articulate group of people to its cause. Meetings were rarely rowdy. Many attendees were involved in other civic enterprises and were familiar with meeting protocols. Political affiliations were across the board, which countered the risk of groupthink.

The divergences of opinion were small: the solutions to Tulsa's urban travails, which clearly zeroed in on land-use policy as a common denominator, seemed straightforward. Outside subject matter experts endorsed this at a number of TulsaNow events. Differences over tactics arose all the time among members, irrespective of their personal and political backgrounds, but these differences were easily resolved through discussion.

Amplifying Local Capacities and Assets

Members of TulsaNow and other like-minded, Tulsa-based, grassroots organizations often lamented Tulsa's apparent loss of identity (Howard-Grenville, Metzger, and Meyer 2013; Shrivastava and Kennelly 2013). A member of YPTulsa, another volunteer grassroots organization, remarked that "Tulsa is like a beautiful woman who doesn't believe she is beautiful anymore" (N. Roberts, personal communication during YPTulsa meeting, 2003). It was an apt and deft sketch: by the 1990s the city had lost confidence in itself and seemed to not know where it was going, or the future it wanted for itself. TulsaNow helped figure this out, starting with the community's sense of place — that is, a deep attachment, personal connection, and identity feelings associated with the place (Hay

1988; Proshansky 1978; Twigger-Ross and Uzzell 1996). TulsaNow should not have needed to step in: the city's mayors and councillors could have led it forward, but town politics often make progress slow and grudging, and politicians need grassroots support they can rely on in order to change things.

So TulsaNow provided much of the motivational grunt work, bringing together a variety of skill sets. These helped it formulate responses to and strategies for a range of topics quite quickly. As a result, the group rapidly acquired a degree of visibility and authority, which in turn encouraged people to contemplate investing in the core of the city, in retail enterprises, property development, exhibition space, and so on. TulsaNow's ideas were boosted by invited speakers, as mentioned earlier — a "prophet from out of town" being obligatory.

Local capacity already existed before TulsaNow, but for the most part it was latent, inchoate, and uncultivated. "When we started our housing development in 2000," commented one downtown developer, "there was only one other entrepreneur we could point to who, like us, was visibly investing in downtown. He'd opened a music venue. There was literally nothing else visible happening" (J. Jamieson, personal communication, 2009).

In consequence, projects that were proposed tended to be inappropriate and monolithic. One predictable proposal was for a super-sized Wal-Mart, which would not have been a downtown solution at all — quite the contrary. It would have required a substantial acreage of prime land for parking, further diminishing downtown's appeal to the young creative groups upon whom the city's future depended. TulsaNow members lobbied the mayor and city councillors, addressed the Planning Commission, and talked to the media alongside others, and helped to win the argument against the project. Wal-Mart accordingly went elsewhere as the developers withdrew their plans. Success in early efforts like this served to boost confidence and inspire an appetite for better ideas. Today, as in many other cities, the most characterful developments in Tulsa's downtown and inner city are being done by local people.

Local capacities grow and flourish when a common sense of purpose, pride, and confidence begin to emerge. TulsaNow's focus on sense of place helped drive community engagement (Manzo and Perkins 2006).

Conveying Compelling Stories

TulsaNow crafted and promoted a vivid and compelling vision that was easy for ordinary people to relate to. Weaving together the potential benefits of healthy, safe, walkable neighbourhoods, the relevance of a vital urban core, and the importance of building on Tulsa's strengths and sense of identity was the easy part. Institutional resistance, however, was more problematic (Scott 2001), driven by power, politics, profit, and entrenched groupthink, summed up neatly as "the old boys' network." Yet TulsaNow's vision and outreach galvanized members and like-minded groups to rally in common cause, and on a number of occasions such rallies overcame institutional resistance. Efforts by TulsaNow and other community leaders stimulated homegrown initiatives, and Tulsa's revitalization slowly began to gather pace. It helped that most early members of the TulsaNow leadership team were effective communicators, including two professional journalists: word got out quickly.

Engaging Both/And Thinking

Positive societal change happens when community members, supporters, and entrepreneurially minded agents come together to aggregate resources and build new capacities (Lumpkin and Bacq 2019).

Engaging the public: the online forum. Resources that can be used collectively, such as social media tools, can help build, nurture, and maintain community efforts (Daskalaki, Hjorth, and Mair 2015). By late 2001, TulsaNow had created a website that featured an online public forum. It is difficult to exaggerate the effect of this forum or its importance to both the community and the organization. A dedicated board member devoted hundreds of hours to building, moderating, improving, and updating the website. TulsaNow board members wrote and posted thoughtful papers and reports on various topics of concern. Members of Tulsa-Now's research task force created an eight-page report to serve as a

downtown revitalization planning resource for Tulsa, based on revitalization efforts in other cities (TulsaNow 2002c). "Renewing the Heart of
Tulsa" was another early report, focused on the factors necessary to
achieve regional competitiveness. It included principles for creating a
viable central district, advocating "development that contributes to a dis-
tinctive and attractive sense of place and reflects the history, values and
culture of the area" (TulsaNow 2002a). A third paper talked up the role
of downtown as the city's economic and social-cultural centre, the benefits of an urban lifestyle, and the problems of sprawl (TulsaNow 2002b).

The forum became the primary vehicle of TulsaNow's engagement,
and hundreds of Tulsans gathered online for active and, by today's standards, remarkably civil discussions. Informal polls were sometimes used
to measure the civic temperature on particular topics. People relished the
opportunity to air their concerns about the city's fabric and to propose
their own ideas. For example, one individual was passionate about street
lighting and deployed the forum to educate and guide forum users on
best practices, urging the city's engineers to adopt more sustainable and
wildlife-friendly streetlights. Such expertise was picked up and woven
into TulsaNow advocacy.

In 2001, Internet trolls were only an emerging sub-species and not
yet a serious problem, though the forum soon began to require increasingly attentive moderators. The forum's very first troll was invited to a
downtown pub for a beer with two or three of TulsaNow's board members, and actually showed up. Circumventing the anonymity of a forum
username by meeting face to face led to more constructive dialogue, and
a number of subsequent pub meetings took place, with increasing numbers of attendees. It is worth noting that the *compelling story* of revitalizing Tulsa was crafted at least in part by the participants themselves: as
the narrative evolves, people become part of something worthwhile that
puts them in the story too.

TulsaNow leaders wrote op-eds for local papers and orchestrated
letter-writing campaigns to elected representatives on topical issues. Tulsa-
Now members showed up and spoke at city council meetings, the Planning

Commission, the Board of Adjustment, and the Parks Board, as well as at other relevant events. They addressed other local place-based organizations when invited: for example, Rotary groups, neighbourhood associations, non-profit organizations, commercial real estate brokers, and local foundations. Likewise, TulsaNow invited guest speakers from other organizations to its own meetings to present and to discuss their own issues.

Local media outlets, hungry for positive stories, provided plenty of coverage, usually supportive. The reporters themselves were often young transplants, keen to see signs of grassroots energy in their adopted town. It helped that reporters are often required to create two or three stories a day for their producers, and TulsaNow, with an ear to the grassroots, became adept at preparing viable stories.

TulsaNow board members regularly joined and occasionally helped to found complementary organizations in the city, and used these opportunities to create coalitions, co-sponsorships, and networks of influence and support. YPTulsa is one such organization: an energized group of young professionals keen to restore Tulsa's vitality and entrepreneurship. The Alliance for an Accessible City is another, focusing on the needs of people in wheelchairs. Some TulsaNow members also occupied positions on various oversight committees or did double duty in complementary, place-based organizations such as neighbourhood associations, the arts community, city-led task forces, and non-profits. They took advantage of opportunities to join committees and helped spread a vision of a vibrant downtown and healthy, safe, walkable neighbourhoods, while also showing how the vision could be achieved. More people got to hear about TulsaNow as a result. The vision and the narrative around it were difficult to resist, all the more so as they resonated with the city's actual past, prior to the 1960s and within the living memory of many of those listening.

Nonetheless, that vision was difficult to resist except when it was not. As the months and years went by after TulsaNow's founding, it became evident that an urban vision of a better-integrated city was markedly less attractive to many of those living on the city's fringes and in outlying municipalities, some of whom were heavily vested in a low-density, effectively segregated, suburban way of life. This group included architects dependent on retail and institutional customers whose business models hinged on an auto-centric paradigm. Robust exchanges of opinion took place both at public, in-person meetings and online.

Engaging community and government: public forum events. During its first few years, TulsaNow organized and hosted a number of public forums, large and small, around topical matters that touched on strategic issues for the city. The forums usually featured a highly regarded guest speaker, with a lengthy period given to audience questions transmitted through a moderator. In the case of mayoral forums, the speaker's address provided a conceptual framework for audience and candidates alike. This often led to impressive barrages of questions. Less well-informed candidates floundered but ended the evenings with clearer perspectives on urban priorities. For those who like their public meetings boisterous as an indication of grassroots vitality, heckling was disappointingly rare.

Some of the events included:

- On a cold and rainy night in October 2002, TulsaNow staged a brash and successful Battle of the Plans at the University of Tulsa campus. More than 200 citizens, along with TV crews, braved appalling weather as 10 shortlisted plans were presented. So successful was the event, which included exhibits around the room, that the organizers of the City–County Vision 2025 adopted the same approach for a subsequent event at the County Fairgrounds.
- Also in 2002, TulsaNow co-sponsored with Tulsa Opera the first-of-its-kind Mayoral Forum on the Arts at the Performing Arts Center. A packed room of more than 200 area residents heard mayoral candidates Bill LaFortune and Gary Watts grapple with specific arts- and downtown-related questions. Watts, a longtime civic leader and former city councilman, noted that it was the most energetic forum of the campaign season.

- On 10 September 2003, Tulsans were invited to a meeting to generate potential action items for TulsaNow. Later referred to as the Blue
Dot meeting, it began with an open-mic discussion on the positives
of Tulsa's current situation and on concerns about where it was going. This led into a brainstorming session to develop a list of things
TulsaNow could work on. Attendees came up with 21 such items and
marked their preferred priorities with blue dots. Some were general,
others specific. The top three action items on that occasion were (1)
get TulsaNow in front of decision-makers, (2) promote the Streetlife
[downtown] project, and (3) place TulsaNow people on as many public oversight committees as possible.

- In 2003, as the contents of a Vision 2025 public funding package began to take shape, TulsaNow held an open meeting on the many projects included in the funding package, moderated by Rich Fisher of
National Public Radio's local station, KWGS. TulsaNow came out in
support of a wide-ranging package, and its own website polls supported its stance. Tulsa residents voted to approve the funding package.

- In April 2005 the group organized a public forum entitled "Passing
the Popsicle Test." The test being this: a child can safely walk to a
store, buy a popsicle, and return home before it melts. The guest
speaker was Russell Claus, director of planning in Oklahoma City,
who had been recruited to lead the reinvention of Oklahoma City's
downtown following the 1995 terrorist bombing of the Murrah Building. The forum focused on how to create neighbourhoods that can be
safely used by citizens of all ages.

- In June 2005, TulsaNow co-hosted a land-use forum with Sustainable
Tulsa and the support of other local organizations, at which a speaker
on historic preservation advocated a form-based code approach to the
protection of historic buildings within neighbourhoods.

- At a February 2006 Mayoral Forum, co-hosted with Tulsa's Arts and
Humanities Council, citizens challenged candidates on subjects including investment in the downtown; the Arkansas River, which runs past
downtown; the role of the arts in Tulsa's economic development; and

the urgency of confronting the new realities of the twenty-first century. Those attending acknowledged the need to attract and retain talent.

- In September 2006 TulsaNow hosted a public forum in Tulsa's Central Library, entitled "Time to Twilight Zoning?" This marked a purposeful step towards the city's first form-based land-use code, and alerted politicians and developers to the economic potential of more compact housing developments closer to the city centre. Alan Hart, principal of VIA Architecture in Vancouver, British Columbia, appeared as guest speaker alongside a panel that included a TulsaNow board member, followed by a question-and-answer session with the audience. The session marked another step along the slow journey towards an update of Tulsa's Comprehensive Plan and the subsequent introduction of a form-based code.

TulsaNow addressed many ad hoc issues in these years, including:

- Successfully advocating on behalf of an inspired, $20 million "Streetlife" project designed to connect downtown landmarks with a Centennial Walk and a rejuvenated downtown park.
- Opposing a suburban-style housing development that would have destroyed the efforts of locals who were working to organically revitalize that area of downtown. The project was prevented from obtaining the necessary property to proceed.
- Advocating a management approach for the city's Performing Arts Center (PAC), which convinced the mayor not to transfer management to the team administering the city's new arena, but to leave it with the PAC's in-house team.
- Supporting individual candidate projects in three successive five-year public bond issues.
- Opposing public funding in 2005 for a massive, downtown soccer stadium project, while proposing better uses for the land. The project was shelved following a November 2005 op-ed from TulsaNow's president.

- Placing members on the oversight committee of the city's 2010 comprehensive plan and participating at most public meetings during its development.

- Unsuccessfully advocating for a more appropriate location for a massive, bond-funded arena. TulsaNow lost on this one, when the city appointed a "starchitect" and located the arena where it can do little to stimulate street life and housing.

- Heading off a massive financial incentive proposed by the then-mayor to lure an American Airlines expansion to Tulsa; TulsaNow supported a much broader spread of public investment. After TulsaNow's intervention, the mayor substantially diluted the incentive to the airline such that funding was also available to other projects.

TulsaNow pursued the above efforts using a range of tactics, including letter-writing campaigns to councillors and mayors, meetings with individual councillors, providing background materials and quotes to the media on the topics in hand, writing op-eds for local newspapers and magazines, giving media interviews on television and radio and in the press, and making presentations to the mayor's staff. Direct conversations with mayors usually entailed buttonholing them at public meetings, in City Hall, or at mayoral forums.

Forces for and against change. Like many midwestern and southwestern places in the United States, Tulsa is in essence a small town in which, as they say, "everyone knows everyone." TulsaNow's members were often active in other community groups, which themselves sometimes participated in TulsaNow events. For example, at the "Passing the Popsicle Test" event in 2005, co-sponsors and participants included Sustainable Tulsa, the Mid-Town Coalition of Neighborhoods, Home Owners for Fair Zoning, MoveThat Bridge, North Tulsa County Neighborhood Association, the Urban League, the League of Women Voters, and the 6th Street Task Force. Some city planners were also discreetly supportive of TulsaNow's efforts. Others in the city were less so, most notably the agency that actually administers existing land-use regulations. In

2002 three TulsaNow leaders met privately with the agency's top staff to explore ways to work together towards real change to outdated zoning laws. Agency staff rebuffed the initiative, urging TulsaNow to leave them alone to carry on in the same old way.

Unsurprisingly, therefore, the Planning Commission's responses to TulsaNow were actively hostile for many years. Commissioners proved to be wedded to a 1950s suburb-oriented paradigm that enabled socio-economic division, a "big box" and car-oriented approach to growth, and inevitable disinvestment in the urban core. They were disinclined to change.

The city's commercial and residential real estate industries likewise regarded TulsaNow's revolutionary fervour with suspicion, as did the city's senior public works engineers. Public engineers are paid to be cautious and can be vulnerable to lawsuits if their design work proves faulty. As a consequence, they can be reluctant to embrace change, even more so, perhaps, when urged on by what they see as a motley, albeit well-informed, group of volunteers from an array of non-scientific backgrounds.

In 2004 the Tulsa Chamber of Commerce expressed interest in TulsaNow's ideas. However, due to lobbying from its influential real estate members, it ultimately rejected TulsaNow's proposals for land-use reform. Land-use attorneys also make a good living from an existing system that they thoroughly understand, and they likewise locked arms to strenuously resist change. One attorney cheerfully acknowledged in a regular public meeting of the Planning Commission that his objection to a "form-based" code was likely to work *against* his client's interests. Old habits, attitudes, and practices die hard when enshrined in tradition, established professional practice, self-preservation, and a vigorous old-boy network, topped up with generous dollops of groupthink.

This resistance to an update in zoning laws endured for over a decade, through the tenures of two more mayors, both Democratic and Republican, who themselves resisted the initiatives recommended in their predecessor's 1999 report (Infill Study Task Force 1999). Indeed, mayoral transitions from Democratic to Republican and back caused sclerosis: not only did each new mayor need to be educated anew and convinced of the importance of overhauling policy, but each was wary of embracing progress achieved by their predecessor of the opposing party. TulsaNow and progressive-minded neighbourhood groups had to pick up the pieces and start again.

Tulsa, of course, is not alone in experiencing this kind of drawn-out slugfest of institutional resistance to updating land-use laws and regulations, among many other areas of governance. Resistance to change is a common factor in every human settlement, big and small. Fortunately, many towns and cities nationwide have provided invaluable examples of success that could be used to apply pressure on Tulsa's leaders: Charleston, South Carolina; Asheville, North Carolina; Louisburg, North Carolina; Milwaukee; Chicago; New York; Dallas; and Oklahoma City have all done good, innovative things. No mayor likes being conspicuously outshone by a peer.

The both/and proposition. As we have seen, a city by its very nature is complex. There are many ways of doing things well, particularly at a granular level. TulsaNow's success in its outreach arose from its place-based vision for inclusive, well-integrated neighbourhoods. The appeal of this vision was difficult to resist: it attracted support for TulsaNow's campaigns and lent strength to the organization's advocacy. The magic arose from listening to everyone who had something constructive to contribute, weaving those ideas into a coherent whole, and then conveying that whole vividly to make such a future seem within Tulsa's reach. Although the process may have been messy and fraught with challenges and setbacks, the goal was to create a big, harmonious tent in which everyone could live healthily, with dignity, and play their own part in the city's life. Revitalizing a city is not a zero-sum game. Urban diversity, by its very nature, is a both/and proposition.

City philanthropists. Some cities are fortunate in having wealthy local patrons who recognize the need for a new direction. Downtown Fort Worth, Texas, furnished one such example in the 1990s, when the billionaire Bass brothers drew on their private fortune of investment and oil wealth to kick-start major investments consistent with humane, pedestrian-oriented urban design (Golightly 1993). Other philanthropists and investors swiftly followed, and Fort Worth's success began to attract the attention of other cities. Tulsa's George Kaiser, oil baron and banker, took an early interest and launched a series of cautious, well-thought-out investments in new buildings and cultural enterprises in a neglected but promising area of downtown Tulsa — an effort that continues to the present day and contributes to a now-burgeoning arts district. The effect of this methodical, drip-drip of investment in good, new-urbanist design has been to stimulate other investors to dip their toes in the water. By the time of its official renaming to the "Tulsa Arts District" in 2017 (formerly the Brady District), the area bore little resemblance to the desolate, tumbleweed-strewn streets of the late 1990s.

Importantly, though, families like the Basses and Kaisers are early adopters rather than pioneers: they typically tread a trail blazed by quixotic mavericks who first recognized the potential for a downtown turnaround and bet heavily with their own resources. Downtown pioneers include, for example, local Tulsan Michael Sager, who began renovating abandoned downtown buildings more than four decades ago, as well as a number of other local investors who recognized the potential of the downtown's many empty and derelict buildings (Cherry 2014; Phillips 2020). The Village at Central Park, Jamie Jamieson's mixed-use development that broke ground in May 2000, was "the first new owner-occupied housing added to downtown in decades" (Easterling 2010). March 2004 saw the opening of Elliot Nelson's McNellie's Pub, described as "an oasis in a desert of blight" that "marked a turning point in downtown's revitalization" (Overall 2022). These are just a few examples, and with similar passion for a revitalized downtown, some such mavericks became ready partners with TulsaNow's efforts.

In Retrospect: Lessons Learned

While its mission and vision have stayed alive through its community leaders, members, and like-minded, place-based organizations, TulsaNow as a formal entity eventually fizzled out. But it spawned other organizations that survive and benefit Tulsans today. More than a smattering group of alumni have gone on to other influential posts. For examples, one became a very effective city planner and another became a progressive real estate developer. A third served on the city's Economic Development Commission for several years; a fourth became chief of staff to a later mayor. Two became councillors for the city and county, respectively. Another served as chair of the city's Transportation Board for several years. Several joined the oversight committee for the city's 2010 Comprehensive Plan, the first major plan overhaul since the 1960s.

TulsaNow's members thus became agents for change from within key institutions. Tulsa today has a "complete streets" policy, a dedicated planning body representing the interests of pedestrians and cyclists, a form-based land-use code, albeit now diminished through the predations of the Planning Commission, and a more resilient planning approach to

Figure 8.1. Example illustrating the revitalizing of downtown Tulsa: Event hosted by downtown pioneer Elliot Nelson. (Photo credit: Rebecca J. Franklin, 2012)

reviving deprived neighborhoods. Crucially, the Planning Commission's resistance to progressive urban planning has crumbled. Regulatory changes made since 2010 have embedded the principle of a more compact, walkable, mass transit-friendly urban form in Tulsa. At the time of writing, the second phase of expansion of a rapid transit bus system is in process.

TulsaNow was not alone in its efforts. It was one of several agents that coincided to generate these and other improvements and public investments. But it is fair to say that TulsaNow was the first substantial and unifying catalyst. It provided a coherent, motivating vision of a livable, urban future into which others could see their lives fitting. It provided the online forum for a city-wide conversation, with a couple of thousand members signed up and participating. It gave many individuals a broader and more attentive audience for their own progressive campaigns. That single individual's concerns about street lighting, for example, went mainstream, and his expertise was taken on board in designing healthy, walkable developments.

Part of the genius of TulsaNow was to connect and weave those strands into a coherent tapestry, without fully realizing at the time that it was doing so. Those strands helped to create the sense that there were different and better ways to design a city's fabric, and that those better ways were within our grasp. TulsaNow thrived between 2001 and around 2013, before fading into the background as key members moved on to other organizations and activities. New organizations and institutions took its place. As an academic aside, consider Johannisson's (1990, 78) description of community entrepreneurship in the context of community revitalization: "The community entrepreneur replaces egocentricity with sociocentricity. Not only does the community entrepreneur take on the responsibility of integrating entrepreneurial and other values — (s)he also takes pride in making him/herself redundant by building a self-organizing community." Likewise, TulsaNow alumni are more than happy to have passed the torch to a broader community of individuals and organizations who share TulsaNow's mission and values.

TulsaNow achieved a number of its goals, and its policies became embedded within the city's first modern Comprehensive Plan, adopted in July 2010 as the outcome of a mammoth, controversial, two-year undertaking. TulsaNow members joined its oversight committee as individuals, attended most of the many public outreach sessions, and advocated for the progressive policies contained in the Comprehensive Plan. A bewildered and entrenched old guard fought back on several fronts and won some skirmishes. For the most part, though, progress was substantial. Encouragingly, TulsaNow's online discussion forum remains somewhat active as Tulsans and TulsaNow alumni continue to discuss the city's revitalization.

Conclusion

What might we learn from this recap of a brief moment in the history of a conservative American city? Perhaps the most important lesson is that the energy sparked by a sense of pride in one's own community and a concern for its future can stimulate a virtuous, upward spiral of revitalization (Slawinski and Franklin 2022). Motivated people who are willing to collaborate around an inspiring vision can "get something going." That upward spiral can have reciprocal, spin-off benefits for other organizations as well: in the case of TulsaNow, its former members continue to permeate the city's social, cultural, and political fabric.

Perhaps the most worrying learning outcome is the realization that it can take much longer than expected to bring about substantive change, even when a talented group of people get moving all at the same time. The group was called TulsaNow for a reason: impatience with an unacceptable status quo and a lively appreciation that without rapid change Tulsa could forever lose its ability to compete for residents and jobs — a sense of urgency that galvanized community members towards action. A coherent organization and energetic advocates are necessary but not sufficient. Brave, progressive people must also number among elected politicians. But to take such steps and to get things done, politicians need grassroots support from organizations like TulsaNow.

References

Better Block Foundation. n.d.. Better Block (website). Accessed July 28, 2023. https://www.betterblock.org

Cherry, Scott. 2014. "Michael Sager a Driving Force in Downtown Resurgence." *Tulsa World*, May 22, 2014.

Congress for the New Urbanism. n.d. Congress for the New Urbanism (website). Accessed July 28, 2023. https://www.cnu.org

Daskalaki, Maria, Daniel Hjorth, and Johanna Mair. 2015. "Are Entrepreneurship, Communities, and Social Transformation Related?" *Journal of Management Inquiry* 24, no. 4: 419–23.

Easterling, Mike. 2010. "Part 1 — The Arena Effect." *Tulsa People*, May 24, 2010.

Fonseca, James W., and David W. Wong. 2000. "Changing Patterns of Population Density in the United States." *The Professional Geographer* 52, no. 3: 504–17.

Frank, Lawrence D. 2000. "Land Use and Transportation Interaction: Implications on Public Health and Quality of Life." *Journal of Planning Education and Research* 20, no. 1: 6–22.

Golightly, Glen R. 1993. "Analysis of Efforts to Revitalize the Fort Worth Central Business District." PhD diss., University of Texas, Arlington.

Hay, Robert. 1988. "Toward a Theory of Sense of Place." *Trumpeter* 5: 159–64.

Howard-Grenville, Jennifer, Matthew L. Metzger, and Alan D. Meyer. 2013. "Rekindling the Flame: Processes of Identity Resurrection." *Academy of Management Journal* 56: 113–36.

Infill Study Task Force. 1999. "Report of the Infill Development Task Force." May 11, 1999. Archives of TulsaNow, Tulsa, OK.

Jacobs, Jane. 1961. *The Death and Life of Great American Cities.* New York: Random House.

Johannisson, Bengt. 1990. "Community Entrepreneurship — Cases and Conceptualization." *Entrepreneurship & Regional Development* 2, no. 1: 71–88.

Katz, Peter. 1994. *The New Urbanism: Toward an Architecture of Community.* New York: McGraw-Hill.

Kotkin, Joel. 1993. *Tribes: How Race, Religion, and Identity Determine Success in the New Global Economy.* New York: Random House.

Kunstler, James H. 1998. *Home from Nowhere: Remaking Our Everyday World for the 21st Century.* New York: Simon & Schuster.

Leinberger, Christopher B. 2005. *Turning Around Downtown: Twelve Steps to*

Revitalization. Washington, DC: Brookings Institution.

Lumpkin, G.T., and Sophie Bacq. 2019. "Civic Wealth Creation: A New View of Stakeholder Engagement and Societal Impact." *Academy of Management Perspectives* 33, no. 4: 383–404.

Manzo, Lynne C., and Douglas D. Perkins. 2006. "Finding Common Ground: The Importance of Place Attachment to Community Participation and Planning." *Journal of Planning Literature* 20, no. 4: 335–50.

Phillips, Morgan. 2020. "Man about Downtown." *Tulsa World,* September 29, 2020.

Proshansky, Harold M. 1978. "The City and Self-Identity." *Environment and Behavior* 10, no. 2: 147–69.

Scott, W. Richard. 2001. *Institutions and Organizations,* 2nd ed. Thousand Oaks, CA: Sage.

Selsky, John W., and Anthony E. Smith. 1994. "Community Entrepreneurship: A Framework for Social Change Leadership." *Leadership Quarterly* 5: 277–96.

Shrivastava, Paul, and James J. Kennelly. 2013. "Sustainability and Place-Based Enterprise." *Organization & Environment* 26: 83–101.

Slawinski, Natalie and Rebecca J. Franklin. 2022. "When Positive Community Spread Is the New Normal: A Multilevel Theory of Community Entrepreneurship." 82nd Annual Meeting of the Academy of Management, Seattle.

TulsaNow. 2002a. "Renewing the Heart of Tulsa: Principles for Creating a Viable Central District." Archives of TulsaNow, Tulsa, OK.

TulsaNow. 2002b. "The Importance of Downtown: From the Urban Models Task Force." Archives of TulsaNow, Tulsa, OK.

TulsaNow. 2002c. "Urban Models Task Force: Downtown Revitalization Planning Resource." November 30, 2002. Archives of TulsaNow, Tulsa, OK.

TulsaNow. 2003. "TulsaNow: Who We Are." November 25, 2003. Archives of TulsaNow, Tulsa, OK.

TulsaNow. 2007. "Bylaws Governing Procedure of TulsaNow, Incorporated." February 19, 2007. Archives of TulsaNow, Tulsa, OK.

Twigger-Ross, Clare, and David Uzzell. 1996. "Place and Identity Processes." *Journal of Environmental Psychology* 16, no. 3: 205–20.

Young, Dennis R. 2001. "Organizational Identity in Nonprofit Organizations: Strategic and Structural Implications." *Nonprofit Management and Leadership* 12, no. 2: 139–57.

CHAPTER 9

From Welfare to Work: Marsh Farm Outreach and the "Organization Workshop" in Luton, United Kingdom

Michelle Darlington, Glenn Jenkins, and Neil Stott

Introduction

Marsh Farm Outreach (MFO) is a community organization whose mission is to regenerate their suburb of Luton, a post-industrial town in the United Kingdom (UK). This community, left with the remnants of an industrial past, began to self-organize to reimagine their place, inspired by emancipatory philosophy. Their story speaks to the power struggles that result from conflicting definitions of community empowerment. In the political climate that emerged in the 1990s, the state's direct role in local services was receding and responsibility for local regeneration was being transferred downward to community organizations (Taylor 2007). The community dimension of British social policy was ambiguous (Lawless and Pearson 2012). What did it really mean for communities to participate in their own regeneration? Would decision-making power be transferred along with responsibility? This ambiguity led to significant tensions between local authorities, whose funding was diminishing, and community organizations, who were promised greater funding and control. All this was exacerbated by the (often unrealistic) expectation that community organizations could do more with less, while still complying with the existing bureaucratic structures and operating within conventional notions of governance.

The Cambridge Centre for Social Innovation has been interested in how community organizations have met this challenge. In our research, MFO stood out as the UK organization that embodied the power struggle most vividly. Their definition of community participation was the most radical. Their vision was for residents to take control of regenerating the most deprived neighbourhoods. They had little to lose, and they were not afraid to take risks.

This story illuminates several aspects of the PLACE Framework. While the Framework emphasizes the relationship between insiders and outsiders, these concepts are relative. We describe a clash between "done-for" and "done-by" approaches, in which — ironically enough — the local authorities were seen as outsiders, while visitors from other continents were seen as insiders, welcomed as a meaningful part of the movement because of their shared values. While the PLACE Framework emphasizes *promoting community leaders* as one of its principles, MFO saw all community members as leaders. They had a "flat" structure, meaning no hierarchy in leadership, and decisions were made by consensus. Moreover, the organization sought to empower the most marginalized and excluded people, whose life experiences predominantly had involved others taking decisions on their behalf. In this sense, Marsh Farm represents an extreme case of place-building, with sustained struggles to wrestle power from existing agencies and implement a truly participatory "done-by" approach.

MFO's success required *linking divergent perspectives* — but this can be very challenging. Despite sharing the common goal of community regeneration with the local authority, their divergent perspectives on how to get there created friction. The philosophy MFO drew on came from a radical South American tradition, alien to European community development practice and governance structures. They maintained a strong focus on emancipatory politics and critical consciousness — meaning the awareness needed to intervene and change one's own reality (Freire 2005). This helped them to empower the community, but also led to conflict. Community groups, who are relatively powerless, tend to avoid conflict, but MFO did not. For them, the means was as important as the ends, and they would not compromise their vision of community empowerment.

Our previous work has outlined the challenges community organizations face in balancing "the interests and idiosyncrasies of their many varied stakeholders" (Stott et al. 2018, 1). We have explained how, in the UK, this cross-sector work has been "increasingly 'the only game in town' and the dice appear loaded" (Stott et al. 2018, 2), meaning that community organizations must collaborate, and often compromise, to gain funding and legitimacy, and to be heard. These partnerships are often fraught with power struggles. MFO did collaborate across sectors and manage relationships, but their approach was different. They ruffled feathers among local authorities, not least by their insistence that long-term unemployed residents, including some with criminal records, were capable of doing regeneration work themselves. MFO members were not only organizers; they were activists, and unapologetically so. MFO's approaches sought ownership of the regeneration process for the marginalized. They were sometimes confrontational, but also diffused conflict; they made enemies in high places, and also engaged the disengaged. When they lacked the approval of state actors, they continued without it.

In this chapter, we tell the story of the origins of Marsh Farm Outreach, their success in hosting the Organization Workshop (OW), and the events leading to it. This is significant because the OW represents a concrete and replicable application of the emancipatory "done-by" community regeneration process that MFO fought for. Since its inception, the OW method has been utilized in many poor and oppressed communities in the Global South (Carmen and Sobrado 2013). MFO implemented it in the UK for the first time, leading to a wave of self-organizing, including the creation of social enterprises and meaningful re-employment. We believe the OW method may be of significant interest to community organizers, but there has been little written in, or translated into, English about it. For these reasons, we are focusing here on describing the OW method itself and the obstacles MFO encountered when staging it.

The story told here is based on the accounts of members of MFO and its precursor, Exodus Collective, and participants in the OW. Glenn Jenkins was involved in all three settings. We also draw from local newspapers, archival material, correspondence, and legal proceedings to corroborate events.

What Is the Organization Workshop?

The OW is a large-scale community capacity-building process, "community capacitation," devised in the 1960s by Clodomir Santos de Morais, a Brazilian sociologist and a comrade of Paulo Freire, the critical pedagogue (Carmen and Sobrado 2013). The OW served the Brazilian Peasants League, helping them to resist the economic domination of the *latifundia* — an exploitative agricultural system established during Brazil's colonial period — and the military police that enforced it.

The OW can appear strange to community organizers in the Global North, who tend to work with relatively small neighbourhood or community groups. The OW brings groups together to achieve an objective without external leadership. In the process, they learn to self-organize. The objective may be to transform a neglected space, create something new, generate income, harness means of production, or organize community governance. It is important for the OW to be of a large scale because of the holistic and relational nature of community capacity-building. Gavin Andersson (2004) explains how "Moraisian" approaches to capacity-building differ from Western ones: Western approaches involve breaking organizational capacity down into component parts and focusing on each part separately. Such approaches are individualistic and assume that competition is the goal. By contrast, Moraisian capacity-building — capacitation — builds the capacity of the community as a whole. Relationships are important, and cooperation is the goal.

Capacitation grows through shared learning experiences, not applications of theory. It is learning by doing. That is not to say there's no theory involved. The OW includes lectures and seminars, but these are about the history of human organization and the philosophy of the movement. They are for inspiration, not instruction. It is important that participants share a sense of the values and purpose of the movement, and a common language to speak about it, with opportunities for dialogue beyond practical activities.

The OW requires four elements: a venue; a large group, ideally over 200; an objective; and the tools required to achieve that objective. If funds are available, often from NGOs, they are used to pay participants' wages. The OW provides everything needed to achieve the objective, apart from one thing: instructions. The OW has no leader, no hierarchy, and no one to tell participants what to do. However, experts can be on hand to advise when asked. For example, engineers or accountants may provide information relevant to their expertise.

Invariably, there will be an initial period of chaos. This is when the group realizes the need to self-organize in order to navigate the challenges of planning, coordination, decision-making, division of labour, and leadership selection. The essence of the OW is the shift from chaos to self-organized, purposeful activity. This is capacitation. In this environment, a group can learn to self-organize, creating projects and enterprises that meet local needs and for which the group remains wholly responsible.

Many community organizers have experienced an impasse. Simple ideas encounter multiple challenges, especially in poor places. Resource shortfalls and interference from self-defined or externally imposed community leaders, some of whom are often difficult characters, can lead to chaos. Community organization is difficult under such circumstances, but the OW holds the promise of achieving it. Capacitation must be learned, and the OW can teach it.

Another obstacle the OW addresses is the scale of the issues faced by communities. Unemployment, environmental degradation, widespread mental health problems, and economic decline are systemic issues, and they are interconnected. As such, they cannot be solved by individuals or small groups in isolation (Stott et al. 2022). This dilemma is sometimes referred to as "the paradox of embedded agency" (Seo and

Creed 2002, 223), meaning the apparent futility of individual actions against an institutionalized system. Lone activists often feel they are swimming against the flow, and that is not sustainable. Systemic issues can only be tackled by grassroots action at scale, such as is facilitated in the OW. To understand what motivated MFO's vision to host the OW, we first establish the context of the Marsh Farm housing estate, the origins of MFO in the early 1990s.

Marsh Farm: The Lived Experience

The housing estate at Marsh Farm was built as part of the post-war expansion of Luton in the 1950s and 1960s. It was largely owned by Luton Borough Council, with three tower blocks providing affordable homes for poor people. Luton was a satellite of London with growing primary industries. At the heart of Luton's economy was Vauxhall automotive manufacturing, which employed thousands. There was close to full employment, and many people moved to Luton for work.

Glenn's childhood memories of Luton are fond ones. His dad worked for Whitbreads, delivering beer to pubs, and his mum worked in the Electrolux factory nearby making electrical goods like vacuum cleaners and fridges. Both jobs meant steady, long-term, and fairly well-paid employment. It was a working-class lifestyle, and with that goes camaraderie. Work and social clubs were at the heart of the community. Trade unions were strong and provided mutual support. For Glenn, although the 1970s had been a decade of industrial conflict, this was also a time of solidarity and belonging. You knew your neighbours, and everyone was connected.

In 1979, Glenn started working for British Rail as a train driver. The same year, Margaret Thatcher became prime minister, and throughout the 1980s industrial conflict was heightened as national economic restructuring brought the closure of many large industrial employers and trade unions fought to protect jobs. This drove people like Glenn to become active in trade unions, and that involved learning how to organize.

During the Thatcher era (1979–1990), industries dropped away.

Many residents left Luton, seeking work elsewhere. Others became long-term unemployed or found only precarious jobs. UK unemployment rose sharply in the early 1980s, reaching a peak of 12 per cent in 1984, its highest rate since the 1930s (Office for National Statistics 2021). That unemployment was concentrated in areas like Luton that had relied on manufacturing. Many people felt derelict: shut down like the buildings in which they had worked. Glenn became part of the unemployed masses of his generation, who had been used to working in and were reliant on Luton's industries. By the early 1990s Luton had become a desert of abandoned warehouses and factories, and Marsh Farm was one of its most deprived neighbourhoods.

Community disruption like this is common in post-industrial places. Frey, Winter, and Julian (2019, 6) characterize it as a trauma. Rather like a blow to the head, it "disrupts connections and undermines complexity," diminishing the community's ability to cope. However, although Marsh Farm was shaken, its community ties, class consciousness, and capacity to organize had not disappeared. Out of necessity, people began to self-organize. The following sections detail the key moments represented in Figure 9.1, from the context of growing unemployment in the early 1980s to the realization of the OW in 2015.

Figure 9.1. Milestones in the evolution of MFO.

The Exodus Collective

In 1992, Glenn became a founding member of a group called the Exodus Collective. The Collective formed a housing co-operative, using its members' benefit money for tools and building materials, and renovated a derelict farm and former hospice. This work was done by and for the people who then lived at Marsh Farm. The Collective was about excluded people reclaiming their place, and its first dance event promoted that stance: they called it "Dance with a Stance." The approach became popular because it was needed, and soon people were dancing in disused quarries, farms, and factories.

With the restoration of the buildings came a restoration of dignity and community feeling. However, these efforts also created tensions. The dances diverted revenue from pubs, and the housing co-op diverted profit from landlords. Police and local authorities were often unimpressed by what they perceived as anti-social behaviour. Tension was inevitable. But having a "collective" structure with no hierarchy helped to diffuse conflict, or at least to confound it. If someone asked to speak to whoever was in charge, that would be everyone. The collective structure drew on organizing principles from anarchism, Gandhian civil disobedience, and Freirean philosophy. As such, it was alien to the organizing norms of local authority structures. After eight years of non-violent direct action, Exodus Collective won the right to access some disused land for non-commercial use.

The group became aware of other communities who were self-organizing, while a copy of Freire's (1970) *Pedagogy of the Oppressed* found its way around the Collective. In the book, Freire argues that the excluded can be co-creators, and that this leads to more sustainable regeneration. The group realized that they were not acting alone. Their approach had a strong heritage.

A significant moment arrived in the story of the Collective when members acted to bring an end to escalating riots. During the 1990s, there was growing social unrest in Marsh Farm, including riots that involved heavy policing (Brace 1995). The relationship between the police and the young people at that time was volatile. Police drove around at night following kids on the streets. A 16-year-old was arrested, and rumours circulated that the police had broken his arm. After ongoing friction, some teenagers made a protest, burning a car. The police responded in large numbers and the conflict escalated into riots. At that time, the UK was on the cusp of a change in policing methods. Police began marching through the streets with shields in paramilitary blocks. Helicopters flew overhead, and community members felt like they were being invaded.

There was a dance scheduled for what would have been the third day of rioting in 1995. The Collective debated whether it would be right to go ahead with the dance, as it would draw people away from the riot. Martin Luther King said, "a riot is the language of the unheard," (1968, n.p.), but some believed that this riot had been provoked. Collective members agreed that the riot would endanger local people, and so they went ahead with the dance, announcing that the riot was a trap.

The morning after the dance, the Collective received a call from Radio Bedfordshire, saying that Marsh Farm had been empty. Police were just sitting on park benches in their riot gear, while everyone who might have been rioting was at the dance. Police denied Exodus's role in stopping the riot (McKay 1998, 199), but the *Luton News* called the Collective the "Pied Pipers of Hamelin" (Wainwright 2003, 113). Years later, local young people devised a play called *Riots to Revoluton* ("Delivering Creativity" 2017, 110), which celebrated the moment when a rave stopped the riot. Stopping the riot became emblematic of the community's capacity to self-organize, and from there the vision expanded.

Marsh Farm Development Trust

In 1999, the Collective joined forces with over 30 other residents' groups and partner organizations, establishing the Marsh Farm Community Development Trust (the Trust). Together, they won £48 million in regeneration funding, for a 10-year period, from the Labour government's New Deal for Communities (NDC) program. The scheme promised to give "some of our poorest communities the resources to tackle their problems in an intensive and co-ordinated way" (Department for Communities and Local Government 2005, n.p.). The NDC's community participation strategy also had an economic rationale, promoting "opportunities for making the delivery of local services more cost effective within neighbourhoods" (Lawless and Pearson 2012, 511). In other words, community groups were expected to do more with less. NDC money was usually channelled through local authorities as "accountable bodies," who sought partnerships with local organizations like the Trust, to ensure that change was "community-led." For Marsh Farm residents, this promise was a beacon of hope.

The Collective's involvement in the bid for NDC funding is detailed in Hilary Wainwright's (2003) *Reclaim the State: Experiments in Popular Democracy*, which describes how the community collectively challenged the government's commitment to community-led development. Wainwright (2003, 122) notes how "community representatives competed with the council, notably council officers, for control." The Trust realized that compromise was necessary. They needed to conform to the required governance arrangements to secure funding. However, the compromise did not sit well with the Collective, and the seeds of further conflict had been sown.

Later evaluations of the NDC reflected on the tensions between internal and external stakeholders, exacerbated by ambiguity over the meaning of community participation (Lawless and Pearson 2012). There were those in the Council who simply expected efforts to be "interpreted by citizens as improvements in transparency and accountability" (Yetano, Royo, and Acerete 2010, 786), those who doubted the authenticity of citizen empowerment (Taylor 2007), those who recognized that lack of engagement was a barrier to the NDC's success (Lawless and Pearson 2012), and those who saw the need for "major cultural shifts" to close the power gap (Taylor 2007, 314).

The reality for organizations who won NDC funding was that responsibilities would be "pushed down to communities and individuals at the same time that control is retained at the centre, through the imposition and internalisation of performance cultures that require 'appropriate' behaviour" (Taylor 2007, 314). As the Trust developed its strategy for community outreach, community members hotly contested the meaning of "appropriate behaviour" and who was permitted to decide it.

Marsh Farm Outreach

Between 2001 and 2003, the Trust established its vision. The Trust would use its funding to help the excluded transform their own future. This involved a community empowerment strategy with an outreach team composed of members of Exodus Collective and other residents' groups. This team became Marsh Farm Outreach (MFO). MFO was allocated six paid positions and stretched the allotted funds by combining part-time posts with voluntary work. Members maintained a flat structure within the group, regardless of who was paid. Combining children's activities, arts, and music with community consultations, MFO quickly engaged large numbers. Marsh Farm residents participated in designing green spaces and other improvements, which helped to restore community bonds and a sense of ownership over place.

However, all was not well. Tensions between the Trust and the Luton Council remained. The Council installed a councillor on the Trust's board and commissioned an audit, invoking concerns about accountability. The audit report noted a lack of documentation: outreach workers "had no training in casework" and "were not able to demonstrate that they had carried out an evaluation of the potential for intervention and developed an action plan" (Ecotec 2003, 37). The report framed this as a "lack of management oversight" (Ecotec 2003, 38).

The Council understandably wished to fulfill its role as the accountable body, but if community development work was really to be done by and for the excluded, it was unlikely they would have the necessary experience or desire to adopt the cumbersome bureaucratic performance cultures and protocols that the report assumed were appropriate. The concept of management oversight was incompatible with MFO's flat organizational structure, on which they refused to compromise. The report provided the grounds for the Luton Borough Council to restructure the Trust's board and budget, ending many of its early initiatives, including funding for MFO.

As many MFO members had previously been unemployed, they did not see this loss as a significant obstacle. They were used to operating on very little and continued their outreach work on a voluntary basis. This removed the pressure to conform to the performance cultures of the Council, which they saw as unhelpful. After all, the Council's formal evaluations had anticipated low community engagement, but MFO's engagement efforts had nonetheless been successful. These experiences renewed MFO members' belief in their ability to take grassroots action effectively, inspiring them to tackle bigger challenges.

Plugging the Leaks: Solving Joblessness Bottom-up

MFO took on the challenge of addressing long-term unemployment. Solving this problem bottom-up is made harder by the stigma attached to joblessness. In addition, winning funding is harder for the poor because of their lack of experience with managing money and their inability to underwrite funding. This was the challenge that eventually led MFO to the OW method, via the more modest Plugging the Leaks initiative that launched their economic development strategy in 2005. This project helped extend their assessment of local capacity and the potential for community-led economic regeneration.

The Plugging the Leaks project spanned two years. It was based on a model created by Bernie Ward and Julie Lewis (2002), which sees the local economy as a "leaky bucket." In other words, most of the money that comes into poor areas from benefits and the like tends to be spent elsewhere. To "plug the leaks," MFO encouraged the community to imagine locally owned enterprises that captured and recirculated money. The first step was to map the community's cash flow. They distributed a survey, asking for a rough breakdown of each household's income and expenses. Initially, the survey response was too low for a meaningful analysis. MFO's solution was to go door-to-door around the neighbourhood, explaining the purpose of the project and asking people to complete the survey on the spot. This achieved a better response rate, with 625 households from a possible 3200 completing the survey.

The survey revealed that most of the community's money was spent on three things: housing, which was mainly rented from private landlords, and often substandard; food, which came from outside-owned retailers and was often unhealthy; and socializing, often in pubs owned by large breweries. In all three cases, money was passing through the hands of residents and into the buckets of private businesses and individuals outside of the community. Analyzing the results, the group identified the potential for 80 to 100 local jobs, which could boost regeneration.

Plugging the Leaks offered insights into the economy, but this clarity also brought the next obstacle into focus: bottom-up job creation is about more than opportunities; for MFO it was also about empowerment. They understood from experience the "numbness" that comes with long-term unemployment. They saw how people who have been jobless for a long time can become unaccustomed to routine and often lose self-belief. Loss of a career can also mean loss of identity and purpose. This is not helped by the types of jobs that come to post-industrial places when big businesses move in: they are often low-skilled, low-paid, and precarious. MFO saw potential for more meaningful income generation that would benefit the community. Their vision was for unemployed people to create local enterprises and help regenerate the economy. This strategy would require capacity-building, and the OW offered that promise.

The Marsh Farm Organization Workshop

When you see the benefits of a positive change you have made yourself, that inspires you to continue. This was the basis of MFO's strategy, but the team lacked a means of making it happen at scale. In the early 2000s, a community development officer named Marrek Lubelski invited an OW scholar, Gavin Andersson, to Luton to meet MFO and the Trust. Andersson talked about his PhD research and the work he had been doing in southern Africa. He explained Moraisian principles and the format of the

OW, which he had been delivering with Chilean social psychologist Ivan Labra and his wife, Isabel "Mama Isa" Labra. The OW empowers communities to self-organize and represented a concrete way for MFO and the Trust to transform job creation in Marsh Farm. Andersson and the Labras had been working with the same values of bottom-up development for the excluded. Learning from these outsiders, a new vision was born: the OW could happen in Marsh Farm.

The PLACE Framework highlights the role an outsider can play when the outsider's divergent perspectives are linked with those of the local place. In this case, the outsiders provided a set of ideas and practices — the OW — which resonated with MFO's values and provided legitimacy through the evidence of its past success.

The Battle for the OW

In 2002, the Trust funded feasibility work, as part of which the Labras visited Marsh Farm. They offered technical advice, project planning, and activity analysis, and they told stories of their past projects. Their presence brought hope. Marsh Farm would be the first community in the UK to host an OW. With help from Andersson and the Labras, MFO wrote a bid for funding from the NDC to host the OW with 100 people over eight weeks, with follow-up support. What they did not realize was that the visit marked the start of a 10-year struggle for MFO to make the vision a reality.

Significant tension arose from the need to seek government funding for the OW. OWs in the Global South are generally funded by grants from NGOs, which are often specifically earmarked for OWs (Imagine 2016, 50), but that funding pathway was not available for Marsh Farm Outreach. At first sight, the NDC seemed the perfect match. One of its stated keys to change was "increasing community capacity (i.e., enabling people to do more for themselves)" (Department for Communities and Local Government 2005, n.p.). However, the NDC carried a significant requirement for impact assessment, and with that came risk-aversion. This is understandable, as public expenditure must be accountable, but the wish to empower communities conflicted with bureaucratic structures that retain control from above. This tension manifested itself in successive challenges to MFO's bid.

The NDC was intended to be community-driven, but its appraisal process was not. The OW was radical, while government administrators were cautious. Over the years, MFO's unconventional track record had made some councillors apprehensive, to say the least. The appraisal process was intended to mitigate risk, but it also allowed opportunities for vested interests to interfere. The process spanned many administrative levels. As the budget-holders, the Trust had to allocate budget and forward the proposal to the local Council, which acted as the accountable body. From there, a regional government agency needed to approve the proposal before it could be submitted to the appropriate department in London. All this needed to be done before 2011, when the scheme ended. Despite lingering animosity from past events, the Trust's board was supportive once the feasibility work was approved, but the proposal was to be declined at every subsequent stage.

It is understandable why funders were apprehensive of the OW. It was expensive, large, unprecedented in the UK, and it had been proposed by a group with a track record of civil disobedience. Moreover, its bottom-up approach was counter to the familiar top-down logic of local government. The OW represented a paradigm shift: its success depended entirely on participation from the community, many of whom were long-term unemployed.

In 2008, the Trust budgeted £1.14 million for the OW, with £130,000 match funding offered by the Learning and Skills Council, a publicly funded quasi-NGO, sponsored by the Department for Business, Innovation and Skills and the Department for Children, Schools and Families, that supported continuing education initiatives in England from 2001 to 2010. However, the regional agency labelled the proposal "novel and contentious," because there was no precedent for the OW in Europe. This label effectively increased the amount of paperwork, requiring additional approvals.

A reworked proposal reached the regional agency in 2009 but was refused. The agency was unconvinced about the scale of the OW. In addition, despite the success of the OW in South America and Africa, the agency expressed concerns it would not have "cultural legs," meaning that the model would not transfer well to the UK. The agency also called for detailed business plans for the potential enterprises, for reassurance of the ventures' sustainability and projected returns on investment. This was a confounding obstacle, because the intention was for OW participants to devise the business plans themselves, within the workshop.

Another confounding concern was that the group did not have experience managing such a large budget. But this was intentional: MFO wanted to give people this experience through the OW. Finally, the agency expressed reservations over the impact new local enterprises would have on larger, established businesses in the area. Again, this impact was deliberate: MFO wanted to build community businesses and "plug the leaks."

"Carry On Camping"

Rather than view this knock-back as a defeat, MFO found humour and motivation in it. If they could overcome this obstacle, it would create a precedent of government support for authentic grassroots participation. This attitude is what Bob Jessop describes as "self-reflexive irony," that is, when "participants recognise the likelihood of failure but proceed as if success were possible" (Jessop 2003, 110), finding creative solutions at the limits of possibility.

In this spirit, the Trust worked with MFO to address the regional agency's concerns, submitting a third, more detailed application in December of 2009, making the OW a priority project for 2010–11, the final year of the NDC, subject to approval. The Trust also drew up a contingency plan for reallocating the funds in case the OW fell through. Time was running short. It was August when ministerial rejection arrived, citing the same reasons as before. The letter was signed by Andrew Stunell, the MP for Hazel Grove, 150 miles north of Luton. Stunell was also a lay minister of his local church in Romiley, Manchester. Suspecting Stunell had not fully read the proposal, signing off the rejection only on the request of civil servants, MFO's solution was for a group to travel with tents to camp in Romiley Churchyard and speak with Stunell directly. Stunell was out of the country for several days on business, so they waited.

The wait built suspense, and the local community in Romiley was supportive. The congregation brought cakes and the local pub offered food. One local also posted an encouraging blog entry entitled "Carry on Camping" (Dobson 2010). The activity attracted the attention of another church minister, who agreed to chair a meeting with Stunell. At this meeting, MFO requested a formal review of the decision to decline the OW proposal, which Stunell carried out within two weeks. MFO and the Trust then received ministerial approval and the project had the green light from the government.

Successive U-Turns

As the group celebrated, another obstacle appeared. A representative from the regional agency who was seconded to the Trust visited MFO, informing members that Companies House[1] listed MFO as being in liquidation. It was true: MFO was due to attend court the next day to contest the liquidation order, which resulted from an unreasonable fine from a hire purchase company concerning a broken photocopier. The liquidation order was rescinded. However, at that point, around £22,000 was also claimed by a subcommittee of the Trust for back rent on MFO's premises. This claim was publicized in the local newspaper, which depicted MFO as financially precarious and announced that they were to be taken to court over it (Johnson 2010). The claim was overturned in court, because the agreement with the Trust had been that only funded groups paid rent. Nonetheless, the damage to MFO's reputation had been done. The Trust cancelled the contract to deliver the OW, considering MFO's marginal financial status too great a risk for the allotment of public funds.

MFO initiated a second wave of lobbying, and Stunell suggested a solution: another organization could formally manage the OW. MFO approached the Development Trust Association — the national membership body for local development trusts — which agreed to act as a guarantor. This would mean the project could go ahead. However, in the interim, the Marsh Farm Development Trust had already reallocated much of the funding under its contingency plan, to compensate for overspending on another project. Stunell remained supportive but was unable to provide further funding. Furthermore, there was not enough time remaining under the NDC scheme to deliver the OW as proposed, nor to resubmit a revised proposal to make use of the time and money remaining.

The successive U-turns were chronicled in the local press (Johnson 2010, 1), which highlighted the tension between local and Council control and the rift that had grown between MFO and the Trust. For some, the events had become a farce. But for MFO, their success in navigating the bureaucratic structures this far had been significant. They would not give up.

Partnering with Other Agencies

In the following period, from 2013 to 2014, MFO took a new approach. They devised Bottom-up Development (BUD), an adult learning program funded by North Luton Community Learning College, which was based in Marsh Farm. This was a five-day course that demonstrated bottom-up community economic development principles. The college asked MFO to deliver BUD as part of its broader employability initiative. This modest success earned MFO renewed legitimacy, and they used the resulting revenue to partially fund further efforts towards the OW.

They also engaged with the public employment service, which had originally posed a significant obstacle: if job-seekers were paid to participate in the OW, they would lose their unemployment benefits. Conversely, if they were not paid, they would be forced to cut their participation short if the service found them temporary work. Collaborating with the employment service allowed job-seekers to participate in the OW without compromising their benefits. In addition, the employment service had a new scheme: the New Enterprise Allowance program, which was designed to financially support the unemployed through the early stages of venture creation. They agreed that OW participants could be part of the program, allowing them to both retain their benefits and also access seed-funding for any new enterprises created during the OW. The college then also agreed to offer training in accounting, health and safety, customer services, and finance as part of the OW. It was a promising partnership.

MFO proposed a reduced budget of £90,000 to the new Cabinet Office Social Action Fund (COSAF). Combined with the organization's own contributions, this was enough to run a smaller OW. With the Development Trust Association as guarantor, the funding was granted, and the Marsh Farm OW was finally realized in 2015, with 45 people taking part over eight weeks.

Organization Workshop in Practice

The Marsh Farm Organization Workshop (MFOW) transformed two acres of derelict land that had become an unofficial rubbish tip (i.e., dump) into a community garden with raised vegetable beds, polytunnels, a wooden roundhouse, beehives, and over 100 fruit trees. MFOW participants organized to create support functions, including a catering team, IT support, a health and safety team, a group to manage and allocate resources, a budgeting group with an accountant, and a contract manager.

There were moments of confusion, arguments, and setbacks, but these discomforts are a necessary part of the OW. Working together to overcome them is the key. Participants described their experiences with surprise:

> We were thrown in at the deep end. But, even though it sometimes felt like none of us knew what we were doing, it still worked. I was dumbstruck, seeing all these people working together to achieve the same thing. (MFOW participant, 60 years old)

> I felt physically better, I had a feeling of freedom and my spirits lifted. I didn't realize I had so much stamina! (MFOW participant, 40 years old)

> The Organization Workshop has made a huge difference to me — without it, I think I would probably be in jail by now. The OW has been a lifeline. (MFOW participant, 25 years old)

In the second phase, 13 participants created social enterprises that survived beyond the OW. 20 others successfully found employment during the OW or soon after. There were also significant health and well-being outcomes (Imagine 2016, 41, 44). It was a transformative experience for people, reigniting their desire to participate.

MFO now offers support to other communities in the UK wishing to run their own OWs, including the town of Hastings, whose OW had 61 participants, supported by Ivan Labra.[2] Labra noted:

> If you go to any rural area, in countries like Angola, Mozambique or Zimbabwe, you'll get people joining in the OW by the hundreds. [In the UK] there are many restrictions and regulations

Figure 9.2. Participation in the Marsh Farm Organization Workshop, 2015. Pictured: members gather in the iron-age-style round-house, under construction, in Marsh Farm. They cleared derelict land and built this structure for community use in the first phase of the OW. (Photo credit: Imagine, 2016)

and it's not so easy to organise. [Also] the level of social participation of people (in the UK) is sometimes very low — people
here often have little experience in getting together and working
together toward a common goal. . . . We sometimes miss this as
individuals and are affected by life and stress — getting people
to work together in itself, and feeling like they belong is a heal-
ing experience. (Quoted in Gerve 2018, 1–2)

MFO has now established itself as a Community Interest Company
(CIC). The organization has renovated the original farmhouse of Marsh
Farm, turning it into a community hub, now home to other CICs and
social enterprises, including some created in the OW: Fidel Gastro's social club; a music recording studio; Sauce of the Lea Cafe; Revoluton Arts;
and Luton Urban Radio.

Reflections

This case contributes to the PLACE Framework as an example of *linking
divergent perspectives*. The clash between top-down and bottom-up logics
appeared to be irreconcilable. While this story is unique, such struggles
between public agencies and community groups are common. In the UK,
numerous regeneration schemes have aimed at the poorest communities, with mixed results. Such schemes often temporarily paper over
cracks, rather than bringing about lasting change. It is something of a
puzzle why well-meaning actors from the public, social, and community
sectors engage in self-defeating power struggles, despite appearing to
share the same goal of regenerating poor places. The case of MFO demonstrates the obstacles that arise when a community group refuses to compromise their commitment to genuinely community-led regeneration.

MFO successfully *amplified the local capacity and assets* for community-
led regeneration, and they understood that the community development
practices promoted by public agencies would not address local problems

at a structural level. That required a more radical "done-by" solution. Although public agencies "talked the talk" of promoting community leaders, the actual transfer of decision-making involved a power struggle.

The clash was partly due to how the problem was framed. For policy-makers, the problem of worklessness was economic, but for the community it was personal. Local and regional agencies found themselves lodged between these two competing perspectives. Giving up control was hard for them, particularly when they lacked trust in community groups, and especially as they remained fully accountable to national departments for spending. When the government announced that communities would lead their own regeneration processes, the wheels of top-down administration remained in motion when it came to funding. Truly shifting to "bottom-up" models of regeneration would require a systemic change.

Community groups are often disheartened by such obstacles. But those involved with MFO were aware of the need for deeper change and remained determined. From decades of community action, its members had developed a clear philosophy and strong values that sustained them through challenging times. The OW offered a model that met their community's needs and represented their values. Its successes in far more authoritarian political climates suggested that success must also be possible under the UK's Labour government in the 1990s.

Rather than accepting the hierarchies and performance cultures of government agencies, MFO attempted to control its own destiny. With little to lose, the organization was willing to take risks. Its members' resilience and creativity contributed to their success, but that creativity required knowledge of the system. While their approach was grassroots, members well understood the top-down structures of municipal and national politics. Camping in the churchyard was a way of bypassing the local Council to reach the signatory of their funding rejection. They knew he would not have read the proposal in full, and their public display meant that he could not ignore it. Understanding their own community was also essential, which is why a rave was able to stop the rioting when the police could not.

Doing bottom-up development is hard, but it is made harder when projects must compete with the contrasting logic of top-down development administration. Celebrating obstacles as loci for change created a compelling narrative that helped to motivate MFO members through successive setbacks. From the early days of civil disobedience in Marsh Farm to its role in supporting other communities to host the OW, MFO's approach has not compromised on its key principle of involving the most marginalized community members in transforming their own future, even when that seemed impossible.

As such, their story is valuable to all communities, even if their approach is not for everyone. Their pioneering work has extended the realm of possibility for community participation in the UK. It is likely that competing definitions of engagement will continue to raise issues for community organizations and the public bodies that work with them. But, while government schemes wax and wane, community organizers remain, and we have yet to see the full extent of what is possible for the role of communities in the economic regeneration of post-industrial towns.

We believe that the OW is a viable local solution for poor and post-industrial communities in the Global North. However, communities wishing to do it are likely to encounter similar challenges for funding and legitimacy, as long as existing channels of regeneration funding are bound to top-down bureaucratic structures. The OW challenges current Western notions of capacity-building because its effects are relational rather than individual, holistic rather than targeted, and long- rather than short-term, and ultimately because its beneficiaries are in the driving seat. We hope that initiatives like the OW will become better understood and valued by authorities at a municipal level, and that MFO's resilience and creativity can inspire other community groups.

Notes

1. Companies House is the United Kingdom's registrar of companies and is an executive agency and trading fund of the UK government, falling under the remit of the Department for Business, Energy and Industrial Strategy.
2. Isabel Labra died in her sleep on March 27, 2009. She did not get to see the Marsh Farm OW realized, but her contribution to it, and to community development in southern Africa, will be remembered.

Acknowledgements

We would like to extend heartfelt thanks to Marsh Farm community members for their ongoing work. Without their inspirational efforts to regenerate their community, this story could not be told. This chapter is dedicated to the memory of Matthew Mark Chance, Melanie Watt Roy, Tony Jules, and Glenn Lawson. The achievements described here are theirs. They did not live to see this book published, but their tireless work for Marsh Farm will not be forgotten.

References

Andersson, Gavin. 2004. "Unbound Governance: A Study of Popular Demand Organization." PhD diss., Open University.

Brace, Matthew. 1995. "Extra Police Sent to Riot-Hit Estate: Violence in Luton: 'Outsiders' Blamed as Mob Attacks Officers." *The Independent* (London), July 7, 1995.

Carmen, Raff, and Miguel Sobrado, eds. 2013. *A Future for the Excluded: Job Creation and Income Generation by the Poor: Clodomir Santos de Morais and the Organization Workshop.* London: Zed Books.

"Delivering Creativity in the Heart of Communities." 2017. *Riots to Revoluton Case Study.* Revoluton Arts. https://www.revolutonarts.com/about-us/case-studies/phase-1/riots-to-revoluton.

Department for Communities and Local Government. 2005. "New Deal for Communities." https://web.archive.org/web/20070607005116/http://www.neighbourhood.gov.uk/page.asp?id=617.

Dobson, Julian. 2010. "Carry on Camping." *Living with Rats: Exploring Better Ways to Live, and How to Make Better Places to Live In.* October 7, 2010. http://livingwithrats.blogspot.com/2010/10/carry-on-camping.html.

Ecotec. 2003. *Review of Marsh Farm NDC.* Luton, UK: Luton Borough Council and Government Office East.

Freire, Paulo. 1970. *Pedagogy of the Oppressed.* New York: Herder and Herder.

Freire, Paulo. 2005. *Education for Critical Consciousness.* New York: Continuum International Publishing Group.

Frey, Ronald, Rosmarie Winter, and Roberta Julian. 2019. "Neoliberalism as Trauma: Intergenerational Disadvantage in an Australian Community." Paper presented at the 11th International Social Innovation Research Conference, Glasgow, September 2019.

Gerve, Lukas. 2018. "Working Together." *Organisation Workshop Hastings* 1: 1–2.

Imagine. 2016. *Marsh Farm Organisational Workshop: Final Evaluation Report.* March 2016. https://coanalysis.blog.gov.uk/wp-content/uploads/sites/115/2016/07/Final-Evaluation-Document_Summary.pdf.

Jessop, Bob. 2003. "Governance and Metagovernance: On Reflexivity, Requisite Variety, and Requisite Irony." In *Governance as Social and Political Communication,* edited by Henrik P. Bang, 101–16. Manchester: Manchester University Press.

Johnson, Christina. 2010. "It's Another U-turn in Whitehall Farce." *Luton on Sunday* (Luton, UK), October 24, 2010.

King, Martin Luther, Jr. 1968. "The Other America." Transcript of speech delivered at Grosse Pointe High School, Grosse Pointe, MI, March 14, 1968. *Grosse Pointe Historical Society.* http://www.gphistorical.org/mlk/mlkspeech/.

Lawless, Paul, and Sarah Pearson. 2012. "Outcomes from Community Engagement in Urban Regeneration: Evidence from England's New Deal for Communities Programme." *Planning Theory & Practice* 13, no. 4: 509–27.

McKay, George, ed. 1998. *DiY Culture: Party and Protest in Nineties Britain.* London: Verso.

Office for National Statistics. n.d. "Unemployment Rate (Aged 16 and Over, Seasonally Adjusted)." *Labour Market Statistics Time Series* (LMS). https://www.ons.gov.uk/employmentandlabourmarket/peoplenotinwork/unemployment/timeseries/mgsx/lms.

Seo, Myeung-Gu, and W.E. Douglas Creed. 2002. "Institutional Contradictions,

Praxis, and Institutional Change: A Dialectical Perspective." *Academy of Management Review* 27, no. 2: 222–47.

Stott, Neil, Michelle Fava, Jennifer Brenton, and Natalie Slawinski. 2022. "Partnerships and Place: The Role of Community Enterprise in Cross-Sector Work for Sustainability." In *Handbook on the Business of Sustainability: The Organization, Implementation, and Practice of Sustainable Growth*, edited by Gerard George, Martine R. Haas, Havovi Joshi, Anita M. McGahan, and Paul Tracey, 118–36. Cheltenham, UK: Edward Elgar.

Stott, Neil, Michelle Fava, Paul Tracey, and Laura Claus. 2018. "Playing Well with Others? Community Cross-Sector Work in Poor Places." Paper presented at the Re-thinking Cross-Sector Social Innovation Conference, Harvard Kennedy School, Cambridge, MA, April 6-7, 2018.

Taylor, Marilyn. 2007. "Community Participation in the Real World: Opportunities and Pitfalls in New Governance Spaces." *Urban Studies* 44, no. 2: 297–317.

Wainwright, Hilary. 2003. *Reclaim the State: Experiments in Popular Democracy*. London: Verso.

Ward, Bernie, and Julie Lewis. 2002. *Plugging the Leaks: Making the Most of Every Pound That Enters Your Local Economy*. London: New Economics Foundation.

Yetano, Ana, Sonia Royo, and Basilio Acerete. 2010. "What Is Driving the Increasing Presence of Citizen Participation Initiatives?" *Environment and Planning C: Government and Policy* 28, no. 5: 783–802.

CHAPTER 10

Stories of an Evolving Social Enterprise Ecosystem: The Experience of Waterford, Ireland

Felicity Kelliher, Senan Cooke, Sinead O'Higgins,
Nicola Kent, and Liz Riches

Introduction

In Ireland, social enterprise (SE) is regarded as a business model with a small but increasing contribution to national, regional, and local social and economic development (European Commission 2020, 10). It is defined as "an enterprise whose objective is to achieve a social, societal or environmental impact, rather than maximising profit for its owners or shareholders" (Department of Rural and Community Development 2019b, 8).

This multi-faceted definition meets the core criteria of the European Commission operational definition in relation to economic activity, the social dimension, and profit/asset distribution and governance (European Commission 2020) and echoes Clarke and Eustace (2009), Forfás (2013), and the Waterford Social Enterprise Network Report (Cooke, Goggin, and Riches 2019), as well as insights from SE research (Jones and Keogh 2006). Those at the heart of the SE sector speak of "an enterprise that trades with a social purpose. It's different from the market-based capitalist model. It's about the benefit of more rather than the benefit of the few" (Nicola Kent).[1] This suggests an overriding emphasis on social contribution by those at the grassroots.

On paper, SEs and the entrepreneurs who start them are supported by a tapestry of national and local SE networks, advocacy groups, and organizations. Stakeholder contributions to the SE ecosystem at the regional and local levels are underpinned by the Social Enterprise Policy for Ireland (Department of Rural and Community Development 2019b) and the allocation of dedicated government funding, training, and mentoring for SE growth and sustainability. The sector also benefits from a range of fiscal and taxation arrangements, including tax relief, the Seed Capital Scheme, the Employment Investment Incentive, and Start-up Refunds for Entrepreneurs. However, while the sector is seen as "a flexible and effective model which has delivered a positive response to social and societal issues" (Department of Rural and Community Development 2019a), there are significant challenges in securing further growth. At a 2021 national social enterprise symposium, expert panel members highlighted that:

> There is a disconnect between policy, research and the realities of practice at grassroots level around the inequalities of access and opportunity, intersectional pay gaps, limitations to finance in terms of access and permissions to open a bank account based on [the] status of migrant entrepreneurs. (Kelliher, Hynes, and Mottiar 2021)

The same symposium panel called for the need to "maintain individual and collaborative networks with a variety of stakeholders . . . so we have better access to different types and levels of resources."

Propelled by this call for action, this chapter seeks to understand grassroots stakeholders' perspectives to bridge the potential gaps between policy-makers, researchers, and those at the grassroots of social enterprise. It does so by documenting the reflections of the five authors as embedded members of the Waterford (population: 116,175) SE ecosystem in the Republic of Ireland. It begins with an overview of social enterprise in Ireland before focusing on a single case study: Waterford

Social Enterprise Network, which is based in the southeast corner of Ireland and seen by many as "the capital of social enterprise in Ireland" (Cooke 2018). The authors represent three of the four main categories in the Irish SE ecosystem referred to in Table 10.1: policy and statutory institutions; research and education; and networks, support, and advocacy (European Commission 2020). The perspectives of the fourth category — financial intermediaries — are drawn from literature (Doyle and Lalor 2012).

The discussion draws on the PLACE Framework (Slawinski and Smith 2019), with particular focus on the "A" principle: *amplify local capacities and assets*. While the listed support agencies and organizations are specific to the Waterford/Irish experience, the insights gleaned from their interrelationships are hopefully transferable to other countries and contexts.

Social Enterprise in Ireland

There is a long history of social enterprise activity in the Republic of Ireland, reaching back to at least the eighteenth century (Bolger 1977). Established in January 1994 and dissolved on August 1, 2014, Forfás was the national policy advisory board for enterprise, trade, science, technology, and innovation in Ireland. According to Forfás (2013), there are four main types of SE in Ireland, based on their objectives and activities: (1) commercial opportunities with a social dividend, (2) economic and community development, (3) public service delivery, and (4) employment opportunities for the marginalized, commonly known as work integration social enterprises (WISEs). WISEs are typically not-for-profit, community-based SEs that mobilize diverse resources from the market, state funding, and public and philanthropic donations (O'Shaughnessy and O'Hara 2016), although relatively little is known about their suitability as a bedrock for a sustainable SE sector (Doyle and Lalor 2012). The four types are not mutually exclusive, and in practice there is overlap among them (O'Shaughnessy and O'Hara 2016).

In recent years, successive Programmes for Government[2] have considered the important role of social enterprise, and the sector has been enriched by the emergence of national support networks, advocacy groups, and increased access to social and micro-financial support mechanisms (European Commission 2020). Today, the four categories of stakeholders within the ecosystem engage the four main types of enterprise shown in the inner circle of Figure 10.1. The outer circle exhibits some of the tangible artifacts in the ecosystem, including local and regional support agencies with SE responsibility and various training and support schemes.

Ireland is also an active participant in the European Social Enterprise Regions pilot program launched in 2018, offering the Irish SE community access to an extensive SE network at the European level through the Europe Direct Network. Of particular importance is the Social Enterprise Policy for Ireland 2019–2022, the first of its kind, which has been cautiously welcomed by the sector, with regional SE stakeholders acknowledging its value in promoting awareness: "As small as it might be, it has made some inroads in terms of increasing awareness around the SE

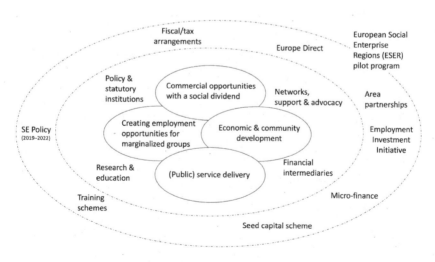

Figure 10.1. The social enterprise ecosystem in Ireland.

model" (Liz Riches). However, there is less surety of the policy's value in growing and strengthening social enterprise at the grassroots level, and a need remains for a model of how the SE ecosystem ethos can work in practice.

Grassroots SE Ecosystem Development: The Waterford Way

> The enterprising community is not just about business and eco-
> nomics. It involves the viability of a social, economic and cultural
> ecosystem that sustains the Irish economy . . . and improves all
> aspects of community life. (Cooke 2018, 10)

County Waterford is one of the Republic of Ireland's 26 counties, resting at the heart of the country's southeast region and named after the city of Waterford, which accounts for nearly half of the county's population. Chapter contributors are based in Waterford City and embedded in Dun-hill Rural Enterprises (Company Limited by Guarantee) Ireland and the Copper Coast European Geopark, circled in Figure 10.2.

The county has a population of 116,175 (Central Statistics Office 2016), representing approximately 2.5 per cent of Ireland's population and 4.4 per cent of its social enterprises. Waterford has a lower proportion of professional and managerial/technical workers than Ireland as a whole (Oireachtas Library & Research Service 2020), and the regional gross domestic product is just 70 per cent of the national average. The economic crisis of 2008–11 had a particularly negative impact on Waterford's economy, compounded by the closures of the local operations of several multinational companies and leading to persistently high rates of unemployment.

Social enterprise is an important and growing sector within Waterford, as reported by the Waterford Social Enterprise Network in 2019; of the estimated 7,400 social enterprises operating countrywide, some 325 exist in Waterford. Research findings reported in the Waterford Social

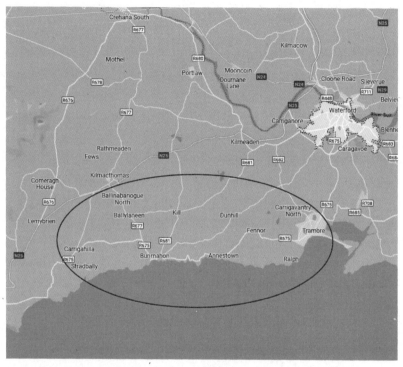

Figure 10.2. County Waterford and Copper Coast European Geopark, Ireland. (Map data from Google, 2023)

Enterprise Network study indicate that 24.4 per cent of existing SEs were established as far back as the 1970s, 58 per cent are independent, and 98 per cent rely on the local market for the provision of their goods and services, suggesting a deep SE embeddedness in the wider community. However, to understand another's journey, one must first walk in their shoes. Grassroots practice is best articulated by key stakeholders within the Waterford SE ecosystem itself, as are the five co-authors of this chapter (Table 10.1).

At the core of this story is Waterford's multi-award-winning international SE centre of excellence — Dunhill, Fenor, Boatstrand, and Annestown (DFBA) Community Enterprises, established in 1993 — and the UNESCO-accredited Copper Coast Global Geopark, established in the early 2000s. The Copper Coast area includes seven villages: the original DFBA plus Bunmahon, Stradbally, and Kill. Outward-looking since its inception, DFBA works to "develop our community, socially, economically and culturally by harnessing the talents of our people and the resources available." In 2020, the European Union RUBIZMO Project,[3] an 11-country consortium including Irish Rural Links,[4] nominated DFBA as the social enterprise "hot spot" in Ireland. By 2022, there were 25 registered SEs in the DFBA/Copper Coast area involved in enterprise, education, social programs, environment, tourism, arts, recreation, and childcare.

Initiated and supported by DFBA, the Copper Coast Global Geopark is the only geopark in Europe run as a social enterprise, and the only volunteer-run, UNESCO-accredited global geopark in the world (Dunhill Rural Enterprises Ltd, n.d.). Its future goals include a modern climate-action-oriented project embedded in the park. In addition to Senan

Table 10.1. Authors' roles in Waterford social enterprise ecosystem.

Name	Category	Role
Senan Cooke	SE director/community leader	Secretary/Director of Dunhill Rural Enterprises CLG Ireland; founding member of the Dunhill, Fenor, Boatstrand and Annestown (DFBA) community enterprises, established in 1993; author of The Enterprising Community (2018); founding member of Copper Coast Global Geopark
Nicola Kent	SE trainer and advocate	Power of You, Waterford, Ireland; SE mentor, Waterford Area Partnership CLG
Sinead O'Higgins	Policy & statutory institution	Waterford Libraries, Waterford City and County Council; Europe Direct Waterford
Felicity Kelliher	Research & education	SE researcher and advocate, South East Technological University; member of the Social Enterprise Research Network Ireland
Liz Riches	Networks, support & advocacy	SICAP (Social Inclusion & Community Activation Programme); Education, Employment and Enterprise Manager, Waterford Area Partnership CLG; Waterford Social Enterprise Network Ireland

Cooke's pivotal role in DFBA, Dunhill Rural Enterprises CLG, and Copper Coast Global Geopark, the remaining four authors are members of diverse local support agencies and institutes (Table 10.1). Each of these entities has a distinct purpose, although some overlap. Table 10.2 provides a partial list of additional relevant support agencies, limited to those discussed in this chapter.

As noted previously, many of these enterprises and those who support them overlap and therefore can be conceived of as an interconnected web. The local ecosystem has both national and European Union connections, as shown in the outer circle of Figure 10.1, with a broken line indicating the fluid nature of these stakeholder interactions. Waterford Integration Services is a humanitarian non-governmental organization (NGO) that has supported over 5,000 refugees, asylum seekers, and other migrants in Ireland's southeast since 2006. Waterford Area Partnership is one of 49 local development companies operating throughout Ireland, governed by partnerships between the state and the community and voluntary sectors.

The Waterford Area Partnership can refer social enterprises to those equipped to support commercial opportunities with a social dividend. Not solely restricted to social enterprise but with a dedicated SE development officer, Waterford Local Enterprise Office is one of 31 dedicated teams across the country's local authority network and the first stop for anyone seeking information and support on starting or growing a business in Waterford. Depending on their trajectories, businesses may also find support in regional and national business development support agencies, including the South East Business Incubation Centre, the New Frontiers Programme housed at the South East Technological University, Enterprise Ireland, and the Irish Development Authority. Established SEs also have access to a growing range of advocacy and sector organizations, including Social Enterprise Republic of Ireland and the Irish Social Enterprise Network (Table 10.2).

Enterprises with an economic and community development or public service delivery focus may find Waterford City & County Council

Table 10.2. The main actors in the Waterford SE ecosystem.

Type of Institution/ Organization	Actor	Purpose/Overview
Social enterprise (representative sub-set only)	Dunhill Rural Enterprises CLG Ireland	Registered not-for-profit and limited liability company, with charitable status
	Copper Coast European Geopark	Designated UNESCO Global Geopark
	Power of You	Start-up and enterprise mentor consultancy
	Shona Project	Supports young and adolescent women; offers the Survival Kit for Girls program
Policy and statutory institutions	Waterford City & County Council, including Waterford Libraries	Authority responsible for local government
	Waterford Area Partnership	One of 49 local development companies governed by partnerships between the state and community and voluntary sector
	Waterford Local Enterprise Offices (LEO), Social Enterprise division	Provides advice, information, and support for starting up or growing a business
	Department of Rural & Community Development	Responsible for the Social Enterprise Policy (2019–2022)
	Pobal	Agency working on behalf of government to support communities and local agencies towards achieving social inclusion and development
	European Union LEADER Programme for Rural Development	Helps rural communities across the European Union to engage with and lead or direct local development

Type of Institution/ Organization	Actor	Purpose/Overview
Networks, supports, and advocacy	Waterford Social Enterprise Network	Local network of Waterford social enterprises focusing on training, development, collaboration, and grassroots representation in the sector
	Europe Direct Waterford	One of a network of local contact points serving as the direct link between Waterford residents and European Union institutions; housed in Waterford City's Central Library
	Waterford Integration Services	Humanitarian non-governmental organization providing services including advocacy, integration, and language classes and outreach programs to refugees, asylum seekers, and migrants
	The Wheel	Ireland's national association of community and voluntary organizations, charities, and SEs
	Irish Social Enterprise Network	National representative network of SEs in Ireland
	Social Enterprise Republic of Ireland	Network of social enterprise practitioners and supporters
	Social Economy Europe	The social enterprise reference point at the European level, SEE represents the voices of 2.8 million enterprises in Europe
Research and education	South East Technological University	Established in May 2022; an amalgamation of Waterford and Carlow Institutes of Technology
	SE Research Network Ireland	Research network of established higher education institutions, individual academics, and graduate students researching the social economy
Financial intermediaries	Rethink Ireland (previously Social Innovation Fund Ireland)	Rupports non-project organizations working in communities across the country
	Traditional banks/credit unions	Credit unions are financial co-operatives whose members save and lend to each other at fair rates

Source: Adapted from European Commission (2020, 42, Table 6), and supplemented by local knowledge.

(WCC) their optimal first port of call. WCC is responsible for local government and acts as a gateway to national government departments, including the Department of Rural and Community Development, which has responsibility for the national Social Enterprise Policy (2019–2022). Via Europe Direct, the WCC Central Library is an active European Social Economy Region partner and offers access to Social Economy Europe's network of 2.8 million social economy enterprises and organizations.

In the wider ecosystem, the European Union LEADER program for rural development accepts applications based on projects that improve, among other things, enterprise development and basic services targeting hard-to-reach communities and rural youth. Separately, Pobal is an intermediary body established by the Irish government and European Union in 1992 to manage a European Union grant for local development. It provides management and support services to around 31 programs in Ireland in the areas of Social Inclusion and Equality, Inclusive

Figure 10.3. Members of Barefoot Farm with examples of their produce, which includes (left to right) mixed salad leaves, German sauerkraut, and water kefir. See further at www.dunhillecopark.com/barefoot-farm.html. (Photo credit: Felicity Kelliher, 2022)

Employment and Enterprise, and Early Years and Young People, allocating approximately €717 million in 2020 alone.

The SE sector is also supported by the adoption of the European Commission's Social Economy Action Plan of December 2021, following extensive dialogue with citizens and stakeholders. However, as anticipated in the PLACE Framework (Slawinski and Smith 2019), stakeholder knowledge of this plan and enterprise engagement with plan resources will both be essential to ensure that the measures and supports within the action plan actually reach the ecosystem grassroots.

South East Technical University engages in SE education, community support, and research, and partners with WCC and Waterford Area Partnership on European Social Enterprise Regions and Europe Direct projects. South East Technological University researchers are active members of the social economy research network of Ireland, and the university offers a part-time Certificate in Social Enterprise Management program. Collectively, these activities provide access to national and international research and practice, affording the ecosystem capacity to both gain from and contribute to better, research-informed practice.

Stories from the Field

Each author points to the long tradition of social enterprise in Waterford and highlights the need for SE leaders as a first step: "those leaders and those businesses and enterprises with a conscience, something that has that potential to deliver a little bit more for society" (Sinead O'Higgins). Sinead O'Higgins highlights the value of visible leaders in building a strong SE community:

> In Waterford, a lot of the social enterprises that have been here for a while seem to have that rural, grassroots community kind of feel. There are visible leaders in this space; Senan has personally contributed so much to the national picture and the national policy and bringing different communities together.

All chapter authors point to Waterford's multi-award winning enterprises and in particular, the DFBA Community as an international SE centre of excellence. Senan Cooke was a founding member and secretary of DFBA from its establishment in 1993 until 2021, when he formally retired. He is also a founding member of Dunhill Rural Enterprises CLG and author of *The Enterprising Community* (Cooke 2018). Contemplating the foundations of the SE ecosystem in Waterford, Cooke emphasizes the value of being embedded in the community, and tells the story of his own early life experience, which has influenced his contributions as an SE pioneer:

> I started off with *Muintir na Tire*[5] in my home parish of Kilmacow in County Kilkenny. I was also a member of the Gaelic Athletic Association and very involved in the local club from fourteen years of age when growing up. At the time both organizations were rooted in the community and attracted a huge number of volunteers. *Muintir* was very strong on the development of people and place. It held weekly education classes, public speaking, and competitive question times against other branches and organized and implemented a range of local improvement projects that benefited the community. The [Gaelic Athletic Association] identified strongly with place, as the local club teams represented the parish in competition against neighbouring and county-wide parish teams. Both organizations strongly identified with people and place, each in its own way, and their activities became a hotbed for the development of social enterprises.

Drawing on his early life experience, Cooke sought to immerse himself in Dunhill's local rural community when he moved there in the mid-1970s by getting involved in the Gaelic Athletic Association and rural regeneration. Since then, he has been involved in setting up and managing numerous social enterprises in Waterford, and he has been instrumental in the significant growth of SE development in the DFBA and Copper Coast Global Geopark area over the past 30 years. Cooke contemplates the success of DFBA, the Copper Coast Global Geopark, and his role as secretary/director of DFBA and Dunhill Rural Enterprises CLG, which manages the Ecopark:

> The ecosystem created is very important. It is made up of a whole range of organizations, activities, and concepts that integrate and interact with each other and add value to each other. The socio-economic, cultural ecosystem is very strong in Dunhill. There is an unusual level of collaborative entrepreneurial spirit at play in a rare cluster: there are 108 commercial farmers and 154 small businesses in the DFBA, among which 28 small businesses and 70 jobs are located in the Dunhill Ecopark. So the local ecosystem is seriously important; if you were to look inside it, you'd be able to see many interdependent stakeholders adding value to each other's activities. I'm talking about the school, church, Gaelic Athletic Association, Ecopark, constructed wetlands, global geopark, pub, squash club, parish hall, heritage village, Anne Valley Walkway & Wildlife Sanctuary, Dunhill Castle, and other social and private enterprise and heritage projects. It's the identification with place that Irish people have: that this is our place and we're going to look after our place. We are determined to leave the community in a better condition than what was inherited. This is driving the community agenda. This is the strived-for legacy.

These stories bring light to the ecosystem (Figure 10.1), underpinned by the spirit and commitment within the community. Over 200 volunteers are involved in DFBA/Copper Coast related social enterprises across all age groups, including young people and retirees, united in their desire to contribute to current and future generations. Encouraged from the beginning to offer exemplar insights to others in terms of social enterprise development, DFBA and the geopark organize an annual program to engage visiting parties, schools, and students, retirement and specialist education groups, and community development groups from around the area. While Dunhill is an international exemplar, it also gains from the county-wide SE ecosystem, which includes actors from the core areas highlighted by the European Union report 2020 (Table 10.2).

Waterford city is really strong on social enterprise. The city has historically suffered areas of disadvantage. There are lots of voluntary organizations working in childcare, elder care, health care, enterprise, education, environment, social housing, and a vast range of social inclusion projects. In rural Waterford, social enterprise development is equally vibrant and growing, despite the twin challenges of the COVID-19 pandemic and Brexit, which are disrupting the socio-economic status quo. Many new opportunities are appearing, some of which are very suited to social entrepreneurs and social enterprise development. The state agencies working in the field are slowly adjusting to the dramatic changes taking place throughout the country and within every community. (Senan Cooke)

Acknowledging Waterford's noted excellence as a "hot spot" in Europe, Sinead O'Higgins reflects on the city's qualities:

Almost like a big town, a lot of people know each other. So there's a lot of links and a lot of both formal and informal networks that exist already, which makes it easier for this kind of thing. It really seems to have become a buzzword, but I think the ecosystem is getting all the parts of your community together. It's an inviting space where people can share and pursue common goals. At its heart is the promotion of, first of all, the person and the social enterprise that that person is in, and then maybe those social enterprises come together for a social enterprise network to be part of something bigger and to have that voice in shaping policy at the national level, and maybe at the European Union level, so that makes it an ecosystem.

She goes on to discuss what happens at Waterford Library as an example of what can be achieved when communities come together for the common good:

> Often what happens in the library is we maybe start off as a venue for something and then we are completely drawn into that ecosystem. That's how the Shakti program happened. It's about 15 women, all of whom are migrants, most in direct provision[6] who wanted to find a safe space, which ended up being the library. We were just the venue for three mornings a week where they did the usual classes — computers and English and literacy — but on the third day, they studied social enterprise and how they could potentially set up some small businesses. They made this absolutely fantastic intercultural quilt. We made a little video about it last week, and it has been on display for the last month in Central Library. So I think even seeing the potential of social enterprise on a micro scale for migrant women gives us the catalyst. We hope to do a lot more work with migrants, in particular female migrants. It's an area I'm particularly interested in, and we've made great friendships and connections there, so that's how it happens.

Drawing on her experience of local networks, Liz Riches offers insight into her role as Education, Employment and Enterprise Manager with Waterford Area Partnership:

> When I took up a role within Waterford Area Partnership in 2010, it involved supporting both micro businesses and social

enterprise. Under that program, Senan and I looked at how we could bring people together around the social enterprise area in Waterford, and together we established the Waterford Social Enterprise Network. As a network we were involved in the Social Finance Foundation/University College Cork pilot study of three areas in Ireland to identify and map social enterprise activity. This study informed the development of the National Social Enterprise Policy in 2019. Our local snowball research approach led to the identification of over 300 existing or potential social enterprises in Waterford, and we (Waterford Social Enterprise Network) produced the *Social Enterprise in Waterford: Mapping Survey & Case Studies* report in 2019. That was quite a steep learning curve for me as to what's out there in terms of community, enterprise, or small elements of trading that local sporting, youth, education, arts, and heritage organizations are doing in the SE space. Being involved in that study meant that in Waterford, we were quite tied in and connected and became known as being engaged, which led to wider awareness and publicity around the sector here.

However, networks alone do not amount to an SE ecosystem, and in the case of Waterford, their activities need to be supplemented by the ecosystem actors and supports highlighted in the European Union 2020 report on Ireland. Liz Riches points to the challenges of connecting individual networks to the wider ecosystem to ensure greater potential for sustainable activity in the sector:

> I think networks have a function as part of the social enterprise ecosystem, but they need a large amount of support to be able to achieve their objectives. I also recognize that they can be transient. There are now multiple social enterprise networks in Ireland, but there need to be structured links between the local,

regional, and national networks and policy implementation bodies. The local networks need to be properly resourced to enable equality within the ecosystem.

Embedded in the social enterprise community as founder and CEO of Power of You, Nicola Kent offers an insider view:

> For me, social enterprise is solving a social issue, whether that is cultural or it's environmental, or it's a social problem. And what it is doing is giving people hope and leaving no one behind, and maybe improving their lives. I see the ecosystem like nature; I see it like a web. I think if the web works, aid really helps. When a person has a social enterprise idea and they want to go further, then that support helps. For example, in my business, it's about the individual: empowering people, empowering women I suppose. When I meet someone new, I just want to know more about them and their idea, and how we could support them. If the individual is strong in themselves and their idea, the rest is easy. I look at who they are, their values, their vision: it's all about the foundation. Once that's there, the trunk of the tree grows, the branches grow, and the rest happens. And so that ecosystem is really important. I think my part in that ecosystem is the foundation, is people. That's what I'm interested in. And we've created a little community together as well, that, you know, we're there for each other if we need each other. So that individual support in an idea that is not really supported in the wider ecosystem of enterprise is important; our goal is to give those people strength in what they're doing.

While grassroots SE activity has been evident since the 1970s, Liz Riches believes SE awareness is only now growing among some of the key actors that can influence the sector's ecosystem:

Organizations that might have considered themselves as a community development or social economy organization now have a greater understanding of the benefits of taking a business approach to achieving their social objective. Some of those organizations have started to explore the concept of a social enterprise ecosystem, supported by engagement with the European Research Council and their mapping tool.

Senan Cooke reinforces this view, and believes that the two most important initiatives from Department of Rural and Community Development following its launch of a Social Enterprise Policy in 2019 are its awareness campaign and the completion of a national census (currently being carried out, 2022–23):

> It is only when the census is completed that social enterprise will be seen for what it is. It will be a growing area of enterprise, job creation, and social inclusion in the difficult times facing the country. With state agency support we will be able to create networks and collaborative initiatives that will further drive social enterprise expansion. Social enterprise is set to become a powerful economic driver that will embrace social inclusion, widespread participation of the many human assets, and the resources they can attract to critical projects. The projects focus on providing a range of new services, facilities, education, and employment opportunities, all of which are so badly needed in the country at this time.

Research and education have a significant role to play in the ecosystem as one of the four categories (Figure 10.1), upholding an ethos that requires thought to ensure knowledge transfer and the realization of value in practice. Felicity Kelliher, who specializes in small firm management capability development at South East Technological University, has a particular interest in social enterprise:

I'm an academic, so there are two parts to this for me: one is my personal desire to contribute to the community I live and work in, and the other is to contribute to the research community. It's unquestionable that the Waterford Social Enterprise community has a vibrancy that holds it up as an exemplar in Ireland and beyond. A bit like Sinead, my colleagues and I seek to offer maybe one little thing more to this community through our contributions as a university. Community contributions include offering research-informed advice; co-hosting events; working with agencies, government departments, and Europe Direct representatives; and helping with practice-led research studies. In many ways, these are our visible contributions to the community. However, it's worth noting that much of this work is voluntary and it's difficult to stitch this activity into our professional roles. In other countries, the state has created programs to support academics' involvement in grassroots activities. The challenge is that this is a nascent research area without significant research to build on and without a history of research funding, so you have to be brave to risk your reputation on it. It's maybe easier for me to be brave, as I'm further on in my career, but we also need early career researchers and doctoral candidates to engage with SE research to build a sustainable research community in Ireland. There is a real risk here — you are asking professional researchers to invest time and energy in the potential to contribute to this emerging body of knowledge — so we need collegial, institutional, and government support and access to funding streams to ensure this happens. The value of Social Enterprise Research Network Ireland is unquestionable, as it brings together SE research groups and individuals from across the higher education and wider community ecosystem. We're working together to help build bedrock on which to stand while both tracking and contributing to social enterprise and the wider social economy in Ireland. The recent social enterprise symposium and discourse events in 2020 and 2021 and the forthcoming special issue of the *Irish Journal of Management* (2022) are working towards solidifying cross-institutional research engagement and sharing academic contributions from the Irish research community. These first steps ultimately aim to provide a platform for sustainable research in the area.

Bringing in a wider European perspective through the Europe Direct Centre has also had a powerful effect in terms of enabling Waterford to link local, national, and European action on SE policy and practice. Sinead O'Higgins is a librarian at Waterford's Central Library and also runs the Waterford Europe Direct Centre:

> When Europe Direct got involved, we were conscious not to do anything to infringe on what is a strong established network. We could offer one little thing more, that link to the European Commission, along with other practical help we could give in terms of access to our buildings or events.

O'Higgins highlights the value of existing networks when it comes to embedding Europe Direct in Waterford and growing relationships within and between the various stakeholders in the ecosystem:

> When we were doing our first big event as a European Social Enterprise Regions partner, the Citizens Dialogue[7] in Dunhill, I remember going to the Dunhill Board as Senan's guest. It was really inspiring to see how much the social enterprises mean to people who are in the middle of them. They asked me to explain why we would want to be involved and what we had to contribute. So the ecosystem was very much there already, built by the DFBA social enterprises and community leaders and activists who are very open to working with other agencies and individuals, which I think is very refreshing.

Waterford Europe Direct's role in terms of the ecosystem would be keeping the link to the European Commission and making sure that the absolutely amazing work that's been done on the ground, both in Waterford and in the southeast, is showcased in Europe. I make those links, which we hope will be useful in some way, whether that means linking with the Head of Sector for the Social Economy at the Commission or taking any opportunity that there is to promote Waterford Social Enterprises at the European Union level, like the events we've run together with Dunhill and South East Technological University and Waterford Area Partnership and others. We have run three events in partnership to showcase what we do here in Waterford and what Europe does. I am always amazed that at our Europe Direct annual meeting we get notice of training on European Union policies and priorities. The Commission lines up all these amazing speakers for us and someone says that the European Green Deal and Digital Transition are going to be the big things for the next couple of years. Then you hear the Irish government talking about the same things. Many of our policies and funding streams come from Europe, so it's an important link: sometimes we're not as aware as we could be about the support that we gain from being European Union citizens.

Stakeholders believe that communities are more aware of the Waterford SE ecosystem now and that the Social Enterprise Policy (2019–2022) has had an impact on that awareness. Individuals and groups are starting to look at the ecosystem in a more serious way in terms of determining how they can increase income in their local SE-related projects. However, Liz Riches highlights that elements within the ecosystem require greater support and engagement to ensure ecosystem sustainability in the longer term:

I would like to see increased enggement from the local authority in a strategic way. I think one of the big things that we are missing is connection with commercial markets and the enterprise sector. We need action on the third objective of the national policy, which is around policy alignment and joined-up thinking around social enterprise practice. It needs to be structured strategically: social and community enterprises need personnel in order to grow and build their social enterprises. They need managers that have business training. Boards need to be trained in terms of those business skills and how they can be utilized to achieve the social objective. I think we need to have those conversations about national networks as well and where we're connected, and some mechanism to feed up and down from the local level to the national can be embedded in the wider ecosystem. Yes, there is an ecosystem, but I don't think it's a strong ecosystem that is fully supported and integrated and interconnected. I'm not sure that we're at that yet.

Contemplating the future of the social enterprise ecosystem, each author has unique perspectives. Nicola Kent points to the potential for "students to do research. Get them when they're young" and for "partnerships with industry." Felicity Kelliher reinforces this view, highlighting the need for government support to help enhance SE research activity. While the proposed country-wide sectoral census is welcome, Felicity advocates a "hub-and-spoke census proposal led by a cross-institutional team" to truly capture SE community insights across the country and to embed collaborative action at the heart of the SE research community:

It's through these collaborations that we'll build a community of researchers, and in time a body of research that can be drawn on to inform the evolution of the ecosystem. As they say, many hands make light work.

Sinead O'Higgins believes that WCC and Waterford Europe Direct's future role is going to be "a combination of community-building and information-providing: trying to help people join the dots, making those connections, and linking in to what is happening at European Union level." Ultimately, the dream is that SEs are "invited to the table and 100 per cent keep knocking on the door" (Nicola Kent). The need for "joined-up thinking" (Liz Riches) and "dedicated research and intellectual resources" (Felicity Kelliher) should ideally be underpinned by "an IT platform to promote a shared learning culture among social enterprises and community groups' country-wide to help sustain and grow the local national ecosystem" (Senan Cooke).

Senan Cooke concludes with the view that Ireland's sense of place offers bedrock for sustainable action: "The identification with place that Irish people have, that this is our place and we're going to look after our place . . . that's the legacy in this."

Establishing a Sense of Place within an SE Ecosystem

This chapter has examined a single ecosystem: that of Waterford in the southeast of Ireland. It considered the disconnection between the resources and capacities that ecosystem stakeholders can provide to SEs in theory (Kelliher, Hynes, and Mottiar 2021; Slawinski and Smith 2019) and the difficulties SEs have in accessing these resources and capacities in practice. Underpinned by the principles of the PLACE Framework for community development, with particular reference to the "A" principle of *amplifying local capacities and assets* (Slawinski and Smith 2019), Figure 10.1 illustrates the optimal means of communicating and engaging the resources and supports available to different types of social enterprises within the local and wider SE ecosystem. This visualization tool offers guidance to SEs within or entering the local ecosystem and offers a reminder to support agencies and/or new agents of the various other national and international supports and agencies available to both SEs and to themselves, which facilitates interplay between network stakeholders in the ecosystem.

Figure 10.1 can help other places develop similar maps of their own SE ecosystems to identify resources and capacities and to establish a means to increase their visibility and accessibility to social entrepreneurs. In theory, social entrepreneurs have access to all SE stakeholder organizations and to each other, but they can have difficulty locating those responsible for social enterprise activities in each organization or community. This challenge is compounded by the fact that stakeholders often provide supports beyond those directly related to social enterprise, and the uninitiated can find it difficult to identify relevant personnel and departments. Developing a visual representation of the local SE ecosystem is a formidable task, as "there are different kind of models — the social entrepreneur model is different from the social enterprise and the community enterprise model" (Nicola Kent), and these differences have created some confusion as to what is or is not a social enterprise. Figure 10.1 and Table 10.2 move some way towards a greater understanding of which support agencies and stake-holders are most valuable to particular types of enterprise by facilitating the matching of enterprises with specific agencies' core purposes.

As the study of SE ecosystems develops as a research area, there may be opportunities to draw on ecosystem research in the entrepreneurship literature for insight, while the potential for progress in practice is in-finite, as articulated in the DFBA motto: There is no limit to what can be achieved by a community working together.

Notes

1. Direct quotations from specific contributing authors to this chapter are identified by the author's name.
2. Programme for Government documents what a government hopes to achieve over its time in power. It includes policies for areas such as health care, the economy, transport, climate change, housing, immigration etc., and also outlines how the government will function.
3. See https://rubizmo.eu/project.
4. Irish Rural Link, formed in 1991, is a national network of organizations

and individuals campaigning for sustainable rural development in Ireland and Europe.

5. Established in 1937, *Muintir na Tíre ("people of the country")* is a national voluntary organization in Ireland dedicated to promoting the process of community development.

6. When individuals request international protection (e.g., claims asylum), they are entitled to direction provision (e.g., accommodation, meals, a small weekly payment, a medical card) while the International Protection Office processes the application. While asylum seekers do not have to accept direct provision, they are not entitled to any other help from the state if refused.

7. Citizens Dialogues are public debates with European Commissioners and other European Union decision-makers, such as members of the European Parliament and national, regional, and local politicians.

Acknowledgements

We sincerely thank The Waterford Social Enterprise Community for its valuable input and support for the research discussed in this chapter.

References

Bolger, Patrick. 1977. *The Irish Co-Operative Movement, Its History and Development*. Dublin: Institute of Public Administration.

Central Statistics Office. 2016. *Census 2016 Results*. http://www.cso.ie.

Clarke, Ann, and Anne Eustace. 2009. *Exploring Social Enterprise in Nine Areas in Ireland*. Enniscorthy, Ireland: Dublin Employment Pact, Clann Credo, Ulster Investment Trust, and PLANET.

Cooke, Senan. 2018. *The Enterprising Community: A Bottom Up Perspective on the Capacity within Communities to Regenerate*. Dublin: Dublin City University Centre for Evaluation, Quality & Inspection.

Cooke, Senan, Seamus Goggin, and Liz Riches. 2019. *Social Enterprise in Waterford: Mapping Survey & Case Studies 2019*. Waterford: Waterford Social Enterprise Network.

Department of Rural and Community Development. 2019a. "Minister Ring Publishes First-ever Social Enterprise Policy for Ireland, Department of Rural and Community Development." Press release, July 17, 2019.

Department of Rural and Community Development. 2019b. *National Social Enterprise Policy for Ireland 2019–2022.* Dublin: Government of Ireland.

Doyle, Gerard, and Tanya Lalor. 2012. *Social Enterprise in Ireland: A People's Economy?* Cork: Oak Tree Press.

Dunhill Rural Enterprises Ltd. n.d. Dunhill Ecopark (website). Accessed July 28, 2023. http://www.dunhillecopark.com

European Commission. 2020. *Social Enterprises and Their Ecosystems in Europe: Country Report Ireland.* Luxembourg: Publications Office of the European Union.

European Commission. 2021. *Social Economy Action Plan.* December 9, 2021. https://ec.europa.eu/social/main.jsp?catld=1537&langld=en&.

Forfás. 2013. *Social Enterprise in Ireland: Sectoral Opportunities and Policy Issues.* Dublin: Government of Ireland.

Jones, Declan, and William Keogh. 2006. "Social Enterprise: A Case of Terminological Ambiguity and Complexity." *Social Enterprise Journal* 2, no. 1: 11–26.

Kelliher, Felicity, Briga Hynes, and Ziene Mottiar. 2021. "Bridging the Disconnect between Policy, Practice and Research in Social Enterprise." Plenary session at the IAM-SERNI Social Enterprise Symposium & Interactive Discourse, Irish Academy of Management Conference, Waterford, August 2021.

Oireachtas Library & Research Service. 2020. *Dáil Eireann Constituency Profile: Waterford.* Dublin: Houses of the Oireachtas.

O'Shaughnessy, Mary, and Patricia O'Hara. 2016. "Social Enterprise in Ireland: Why Work Integration Social Enterprises (WISEs) Dominate the Discourse." *Nonprofit Policy Forum* 7, no. 4: 461–85.

Slawinski, Natalie, and Wendy K. Smith. 2019. "Rebuilding Community through Social Innovation: A PLACE Model." *Cambridge Social Innovation Blog.* February 6, 2019. https://socialinnovation.blog.jbs.cam.ac.uk/2019/02/06/rebuilding-community-through-social-innovation-a-place-model/.

EPILOGUE

Natalie Slawinski, Ario Seto, Mark C.J. Stoddart,
Brennan Lowery, and Kelly Vodden

This volume answers calls for more community-engaged research to address the complex societal problems facing communities (Bammer 2019) and to better understand the potential for place-based social enterprise (PBSE) to offer solutions (Lumpkin and Bacq 2019). It showcases the crucial role of community in binding people together, providing identity and a sense of belonging in an increasingly placeless world (Relph 1976), while also offering a meaningful arena for local action towards sustainable development (UN 2015). By focusing particularly on PBSE as a vehicle for local innovation towards more sustainable communities (Lumpkin, Bacq, and Pidduck 2018), this volume offers novel insights into the potential of these initiatives through rich accounts and in-depth engagement with community partners. Most chapters in this volume are the product of academic–practitioner relationships that have been developing for years. By following a collaborative co-authorship approach to integrating academic and practitioner knowledge, this volume draws on the lived experiences of social entrepreneurs and community leaders, filling a gap in existing research by showing practices and processes used by social enterprises and community leaders to build community resilience and sustainability.

The chapters presented in this volume employ a wide range of methods and approaches to offer their unique accounts of PBSE. Drawing on methods including participant observation, participatory action research (McIntyre 2008), social network analysis (Prell 2012), longitudinal research, in-depth interviews, and focus group discussions, the case studies offer diverse accounts that reflect the heterogeneous nature of PBSEs and the tools they use to revitalize their communities. They capture rich descriptions of the strategies applied within PBSEs to drive cultural, environmental, social, and economic development, thus providing more fully developed perspectives on community revitalization, resilience, and renewal. This volume situates these locally rooted strategies in academic literature emanating from a variety of disciplines, including organization studies (Peredo and Chrisman 2006; Shrivastava and Kennelly 2013), entrepreneurship literature (Hertel, Bacq, and Belz 2019; Welter et al. 2017), cultural and economic geography (Beer et al. 2020; Cresswell 2015; Relph 1976), and sociology (Baldacchino 2010), tying various perspectives together through the overarching PLACE Framework to provide holistic insights into how to navigate the many challenges and tensions found in community development work. The findings advance our understanding of the importance of citizen participation, agency, empowerment, distributed leadership, community entrepreneurial ecosystems, and the roles of PBSEs in community development and regeneration.

Some key challenges and themes emerged across the different chapters and contexts of this volume, reflecting the numerous tensions and competing demands that arise when doing community development work and when launching and operating a PBSE. Community development work requires addressing the often competing goals of stakeholders, including funders, NGOs, local businesses, civic groups, and others (Chapter 2; Lumpkin and Bacq 2019). Similarly, social enterprises often face tensions between their commercial goals and their social goals (Chapter 6) or between their short-term goals and long-term goals (Chapter 1). These tensions are often well described by a broader overarching theme of two dual imperatives: economic sustainability (e.g., ensuring a PBSE can persist and thrive as an economic entity) and social sustainability (e.g., ensuring long-term positive community impacts and social buy-in). A PBSE may also inadvertently create conflict if community opinion is divided on how its work and vision may affect the community's identity and built environment.

As the studies in this volume demonstrate, these competing goals can be addressed by community members and/or social entrepreneurs who engage in both/and thinking (i.e., the "E" in the PLACE Framework; see Chapter 6 and elsewhere in this volume). However, this does not mean that tensions will automatically disappear. As research on paradoxes in community development shows, tensions between community goals and the goals of the social enterprise are often contradictory, interrelated, and persistent, and new tensions may emerge even as others are addressed (Slawinski et al. 2021). This insight points to the challenging nature of PBSE work and may also explain why these enterprises often struggle (Lyon and Sepulveda 2009; Sheppard 2018). Like entrepreneurial ventures, social ventures are precarious after they are launched, yet unlike for-profit businesses whose main focus is financial sustainability, hybrid organizations such as PBSEs additionally struggle to achieve the dual goal of achieving both social and financial aims.

Depending on their mission, some PBSEs need to have longer-term goals because they deal with more protracted social and environmental issues such as job creation, community livability, advancing respectful relations between Indigenous and settler communities, and climate change. Ensuring long-term growth for a social enterprise requires a balance between achieving the social mission and maintaining financial sustainability. The Placentia West Development Association (PWDA) and the Bonavista Historic Townscape Foundation (BHTF), two of the PBSEs featured in this volume (Chapter 4), each have more than 20 years of experience. Their strategies are complex, but both have carefully considered how to focus on customer needs by developing establishments that can deliver goods and services that are in demand. For example, BHTF opened a restaurant and cultural centre, built alliances with local governments, community members, government agencies, other non-profit organizations, and other businesses, and developed a long-term, evolving Townscape Plan through which they can envision pathways to their futures. As a result, they are able to offer more activities to the community, and in turn these activities attract more initiatives and entrepreneurial ventures.

Tensions and challenges also arise when writing a volume of chapters co-created between practitioners and academics. Collaboration between academic researchers and community practitioners implies a set of power relations, particularly in settings where extractivist research practices have taken knowledge from communities and regarded community members' knowledge as secondary to that of academic researchers (Post and Ruelle 2021). In general, community practitioners risk giving more to researchers than they get back, with researchers "taking data" and failing to honour the community's needs by, for example, acknowledging and honouring community members' contributions, ensuring research has practical benefits, and sharing research results with community members in appropriate ways. Different temporalities of work can mean different expectations and consequent frustration, such as the seasonality of life in many rural communities that often clashes with academic calendars (Halseth et al. 2016). Additional challenges include the cycles of academic grants and application processes, publication demands, and promotion and tenure expectations for academics that can push researchers to rush community relationships to meet university-based metrics.

There are also tensions for academic researchers who conduct community-engaged scholarship. The relational nature of collaboration presents risks such as the possibility that community partners may become unable to continue dedicating their time to participate in the research and writing process, as they already have to juggle their community engagement and business activities. Another challenge lies in the limits to academic independence, such as the need for researchers to share findings with the academic community in ways that are honest but also do not compromise relationships with community partners. This situation can be particularly challenging when researchers identify limitations to an organization's ability to deliver on their mission, such as conflicts with other local actors. As such, researchers are advised to tread carefully with airing the "dirty laundry" of partner organizations or risk harming vital community relationships. Increasingly, researchers must agree not to publish work considered harmful to community, which is particularly important in working with Indigenous Peoples but is also a general tenet of community-based research (First Nations Information Governance Centre 2022). Finally, interdisciplinary work presents its own challenges as disciplines often exist in silos with their own language, paradigms, tools, conventions, and expectations, and these divisions have proven difficult to overcome (Ison 2008).

Limitations and Opportunities for Future Research

This volume includes some key limitations that present opportunities for future research. First, the chapters come from a narrow geographic and cultural scope, that is, mostly from the Anglo-American Global North, leaving much room for further inquiry into how PBSE manifests in a broader range of social, political, and economic contexts. For example, we might ask how different PBSEs look in the Global South, where institutional and historical (e.g., Idris and Hati 2013) or socio-economic and cultural realities create different challenges (Bidet and Defourny 2019; Galeano 1997; Lashitew, Branzei, and van Tulder 2023; Littlewood and Holt 2018). In Latin America, for instance, some work has been done on social enterprise in the context of emancipatory social movements (Marti, Courpasson, and Dubard Barbosa 2013). The complementary notion of *buen vivir* draws on Latin American Indigenous traditions to promote community development that prioritizes social and ecological well-being and offers an alternative to dominant forms of development (de Sousa Santos 2018; Gudynas 2011). Similarly, our volume offers only limited coverage of PBSEs in Indigenous community contexts, suggesting that possibilities for the integration of social enterprise with Indigenous knowledge systems and values require further examination, and that this effort should be co-led by Indigenous and settler scholars working together. Furthermore, research could examine how different PBSEs look in the more corporatist and social democratic political cultures of northern Europe, where close communication and collaboration among state, business, and labour interests are more common than in North America (Hall and Soskice 2001; Lijphart 2012).

This volume also raises some additional themes that could be explored in future research. For example, research could examine more closely the role of leadership in supporting PBSEs and communities, such as which types of leadership are most effective in different contexts, and whether bottom-up solutions or top-down approaches, or both together, work best and under what conditions. In Chapter 1, Shorefast took a top-down approach to get to a bottom-up solution by starting with a vision and resources and then building capacity to generate more participation in decision-making within Shorefast and the community. Chapter 2 offers a more diffuse version of leadership by showing the broad range of roles that community members have played in the revitalization of the Old Cottage Hospital, rather than only focusing on one heroic leader as prior research and political discourse in NL has tended to do (Vodden 2010). Another area that is ripe for future research is leadership succession planning. Many of the case studies in this volume do not discuss the continuity of the PBSE, the role of succession planning in that continuity, or the implications of leaders retiring or leaving the organization.

Gender is another theme that warrants future research. Because PBSEs address social issues, they engage with and often seek support from various members of the communities and may offer more opportunities for women to be involved, compared with other entrepreneurial contexts (Welter et al. 2017). In Chapter 2, many of the community leaders who have led the effort to revitalize the Old Cottage Hospital are women. Chapter 4 explores the monetization of domestic skills, Chapter 6 touches on Girls Who Fish, and Chapter 7 discusses women's reflections on the Toquaht principle of *heshook-ish tsawalk* (interconnectedness) to redefine economic development. Management research has examined the impact on companies of women leaders. For example, studies have found that companies with more women in leadership positions tend to be more profitable and productive than those with fewer women leaders (e.g., Smith, Smith, and Verner 2006), and women-led businesses are more likely to focus on products and services that meet the needs of women and other under-served groups, which can lead to the development of new markets (e.g., Rosca, Agarwal, and Brem 2020). Thus, it would be interesting to assess if women-led PBSEs would also have different strategies in community development. This question is particularly important in communities where men are seasonal workers or need to work outside their communities, such as those in Newfoundland and Labrador. More broadly, none of the chapters engage with questions of the role of LGBTQIA+ practitioners and leaders in such enterprises, or the current and potential role of PBSEs in advancing rights and/or well-being in these communities.

The PLACE Framework highlights potential tensions and opportunities relating to PBSEs linking insiders and outsiders. In Chapter 1, we saw that Shorefast actively leveraged this dynamic, by bringing outsiders such as artists, designers, and academics into the community, and attempted to mediate a respectful relationship with the local community by emphasizing the strengths of Fogo Island. In addition, Zita Cobb was both an insider and an outsider, having lived away for decades before returning home to launch Shorefast. In Chapter 2, some of the key individuals who led the charge to save the Old Cottage Hospital straddled insider–outsider roles, such as Joan Cranston, who is originally from Ontario but had embedded herself in the community for decades and had become accepted as a local leader. Finally, Chapter 3 revealed the ties that SABRI had with both local partners on the Great Northern Peninsula and external agencies like the provincial and federal governments. Affirming previous social network analyses in the region, some key collaboration gaps were identified. National and international partners are few, although one business partnership established with an Icelandic shipping firm is explored. These examples also raise the question of how to bring together local (including Indigenous) knowledge and scientific expertise in ways that acknowledge the validity of both and promote positive outcomes.

Future research could examine these tensions and opportunities in more depth.

PBSE–government relations is another theme. PBSEs are businesses that focus on addressing specific social and environment issues within a particular community or geographic area. They often work closely with government agencies and local officials to address community needs that overlap with related areas of government responsibility and jurisdiction, frequently by implementing policies and programs and by securing funding for initiatives. Government support for social enterprises can come in the form of grants, tax incentives, and other forms of financial assistance. Additionally, government agencies may also partner with social enterprises to provide services or implement programs. As a result, PBSEs frequently find themselves in both partnerships and lobbying activities, reaching out to their elected officials or other government offices to secure funding or negotiate partnerships, or to advocate for support and/or policy change in their areas of interest. This process can cause tensions, particularly when the agency or governing party of the day has different viewpoints and approaches than the PBSE and its leadership. Changes of government may also disrupt established working relationships and create unexpected challenges.

Examples of these tensions can be seen in Chapter 2, where the nature of government funding programs often leaves the BBHCCH struggling to support its holistic activities in the Old Cottage Hospital while depending on narrowly defined funding programs that address specific community well-being issues (e.g., daycare, healthy food) in departmental silos. The various levels and layers of government are also often bewildering, as in the case of the EU-based Waterford in Chapter 10. PBSE success may depend on knowing how to pull strings or how and when to apply pressure to bring about key decisions (like the sit-in outside Stunell's residence in Chapter 8). It may also depend on knowing how to dance to the different tunes of different funding agencies, including assuring PBSE donors or funders that an organization carries out its due diligence and would stand up to an audit of how funds are used.

Several chapters caution that PBSEs are not a replacement for government services, but complements that can help communities enhance their local assets (see also Steiner, Farmer, and Bosworth 2020). As experience has already shown in other parts of the world (e.g., the UK), state actors seeking to withdraw services from certain areas, such as rural communities, often tout social enterprise as an alternative to public services (Steiner and Teasdale 2019). This dynamic can co-opt asset-based rhetoric to laud community resilience as a justification for austerity measures (Daly and Westwood 2018). The experiences shared in this volume underline that PBSEs can only succeed at enhancing community well-being when the essential foundation of public services and infrastructure is provided. Given their differing roles, we should not see PBSEs as an alternative or replacement for government involvement in community development, but should devote greater attention to examining the dynamics of PBSE–government relationships and how they may facilitate or impede community development in specific contexts. Such further research would provide insight into factors that optimize PBSE–government relationships for maximum contributions to community well-being.

Finally, PBSEs and their community development work can bring about unintended consequences. For example, making a place more attractive can paradoxically make it more expensive to live in as housing prices go up, which can create difficulties for local residents to access the market, as hinted in Chapter 4 (see also *CBC News* 2023). This dynamic has been explored in sustainable tourism studies, for example, where successful tourism development has raised the profile of communities and contributed to "rural gentrification" through in-migration or converting housing to short-term vacation rentals (e.g., Villa 2019). A potential unintended consequence is when PBSEs do a really good job of advocating for their community and improving local conditions, governments may come to see that community as no longer requiring support and decide to reduce investments in the community and/or the PBSEs themselves.

Lessons for Practitioners

The PLACE Framework provides a set of general principles that community leaders and social entrepreneurs can apply to overcome their communities' unique challenges and leverage place-based assets in their communities or regions. These principles are best understood through dialogue with different stakeholders and by engaging with various perspectives. They offer a possible starting point for conversations among a variety of actors, including policy-makers and community leaders looking to revitalize their communities. The case studies shared in this volume seek to show the diverse range of approaches that communities can take to implement the principles of the PLACE Framework in ways that make sense for their local contexts.

For social entrepreneurs seeking to demonstrate their value propositions to investors, incubators and accelerator programs, or government funding agencies, this volume offers tangible evidence of the outcomes of social enterprise across a wide variety of sectors, such as tourism, fisheries, health and wellness, real estate, and agriculture. It also recognizes social entrepreneurs' key role as boundary-spanners who can navigate multiple sectors and domains of community life, while providing them with the PLACE Framework as a complementary approach emphasizing a holistic vision of community development and diverse forms of value.

This volume also contributes to an emerging community of place-based social enterprises in Newfoundland and Labrador and beyond. Place-based social entrepreneurship can be a very isolating experience and field of endeavour. It can be difficult for social entrepreneurs to find others in their community who share their mindset, and when engaging with bureaucratic institutions like universities or government, one often finds more roadblocks than supports. The case studies presented here shed light on a community of practice to reassure place-based social entrepreneurs that they are not alone in their work and that they can leverage a network of peers, mentors, and support services in order to find the resources they need to overcome challenges and create value in their communities.

These case studies also offer practical lessons and policy recommendations for stakeholders who are in positions to support PBSEs. Local governments can support initiatives led by social enterprises as a delegated approach to project development or they can partner with social enterprises directly to tap into new sources of funding that may not be available to municipalities. For upper-level government agencies, a key message from this volume is that each community and region has its own unique set of assets and challenges, requiring place-based policies and programs. Rather than prioritizing particular sectors or activities, funding programs should take approaches that allow local actors to identify economic development opportunities that make sense for their contexts. However, while social enterprise is a promising avenue for community economic development, it is not a panacea, nor is it a replacement for basic services like health care and high-speed Internet. Communities still need this essential infrastructure, and only when these services are provided can social entrepreneurs design innovative solutions to enhance community well-being even further.

Conclusion

Communities everywhere are grappling with how to prepare for and respond to mounting social, economic, geopolitical, and environmental disruptions that often feel beyond their control. One strategy for navigating the rough waters of globalization is to re-localize economic relationships, assets, and practices through place-based social enterprise. This volume offers examples of how such enterprises are finding ways to reimagine and reshape futures for the communities within which they are embedded. We hope that other community leaders will draw inspiration and new tools from these examples and that future research will continue to explore the unique and important roles that PBSEs play in building more resilient communities.

References

Baldacchino, Godfrey. 2010. *Island Enclaves: Offshoring Strategies, Creative Governance, and Subnational Island Jurisdictions.* Montreal and Kingston: McGill-Queen's University Press.

Bammer, Gabriele. 2019. "Key Issues in Co-creation with Stakeholders when Research Problems Are Complex." *Evidence & Policy* 15, no. 3: 423–35. https://doi.org/10.1332/174426419X15532579188099.

Beer, Andrew, Fiona McKenzie, Jiří Blažek, Markku Sotarauta, and Sarah Ayres. 2020. *Every Place Matters: Towards Effective Place-based Policy.* Abingdon, Oxon, UK: Regional Studies Association.

Bidet, Eric, and Jacques Defourny. 2019. "Introduction: The Rising Interest for Social Enterprise in Asia." In *Social Enterprise in Asia*, edited by Eric Bidet and Jacques Defourny, 1–14. New York: Routledge.

CBC News. 2023. "Bonavista Is Looking to Shut out Airbnb as Long-Term Housing Gets Swallowed up by Investors." February 6, 2023. https://www.cbc.ca/news/canada/newfoundland-labrador/bonavista-housing-market-1.6736419.

Cresswell, Tim. 2015. *Place: An Introduction*, 2nd ed. New York: Wiley.

Daly, Mary, and Sue Westwood. 2018. "Asset-based Approaches, Older People and Social Care: An Analysis and Critique." *Ageing and Society* 386: 1087–99. https://doi.org/10.1017/S0144686X17000071.

de Sousa Santos, Boaventura. 2018. *The End of Cognitive Empire: The Coming of Age of Epistemologies of the South.* Durham, NC: Duke University Press.

First Nations Information Governance Centre. 2022. *The First Nations Principles of OCAP.* Akwesasne: First Nations Information Governance Centre. https://fnigc.ca/wp-content/uploads/2022/10/OCAP_Brochure_20220927_web.pdf.

Galeano, Eduardo. 1997 [1973]. *Open Veins of Latin America: Five Centuries of the Pillage of a Continent*, 25th anniversary edition. Translated by Cedric Belfrage. New York: Monthly Review Press.

Gudynas, Eduardo. 2011. "Buen Vivir: Today's Tomorrow." *Development* 54, no. 4: 441–47.

Hall, Peter A., and David Soskice, eds. 2001. *Varieties of Capitalism: The Institutional Foundations of Comparative Advantage.* Oxford: Oxford University Press.

Halseth, Greg, Sean Markey, Laura Ryser, and Don Manson, eds. 2016. *Doing Community-Based Research: Perspectives from the Field*. Montreal and Kingston: McGill-Queen's University Press.

Hertel, Christina, Sophie Bacq, and Frank-Martin Belz. 2019. "It Takes a Village to Sustain a Village: A Social Identity Perspective on Successful Community-Based Enterprise Creation." *Academy of Management Discoveries* 54: 438–64.

Idris, Aida, and Rahayu H. Hati. 2013. "Social Entrepreneurship in Indonesia: Lessons from the Past." *Journal of Social Entrepreneurship* 4, no. 3: 277–301. https://doi.org/10.1080/19420676.2013.820778.

Ison, Ray. 2008. "Methodological Challenges of Trans-disciplinary Research: Some Systemic Reflections." *Natures Sciences Sociétés* 16: 241–51. https://doi.org/10.1051/nss:2008052.

Lijphart, Arend. 2012. *Patterns of Democracy: Government Forms and Performance in Thirty-Six Countries*, 2nd ed. New Haven, CT: Yale University Press.

Littlewood, David, and Diane Holt. 2018. "Social Entrepreneurship in South Africa: Exploring the Influence of Environment." *Business & Society* 573: 525–61

Lumpkin, G.T., and Sophie Bacq. 2019. "Civic Wealth Creation: A New View of Stakeholder Engagement and Societal Impact." *Academy of Management Perspectives* 33, no. 4: 383–404. https://doi.org/10.5465/amp.2017.0060.

Lumpkin, G.T., Sophie Bacq, and Robert J. Pidduck. 2018. "Where Change Happens: Community-level Phenomena in Social Entrepreneurship Research." *Journal of Small Business Management* 56, no. 1: 24–50.

Lyon, Fergus, and Leandro Sepulveda. 2009. "Mapping Social Enterprises: Past Approaches, Challenges and Future Directions." *Social Enterprise Journal* 5, no. 1: 83–94. https://doi.org/10.1108/17508610910956426.

Marti, Ignasi, David Courpasson, and Saulo Dubard Barbosa. 2013. "'Living in the Fishbowl': Generating an Entrepreneurial Culture in a Local Community in Argentina." *Journal of Business Venturing* 28, no. 1: 10–29. https://doi.org/10.1016/j.jbusvent.2011.09.001.

McIntyre, Alice. 2008. *Participatory Action Research*. London: Sage.

Peredo, Ana Maria, and James J. Chrisman. 2006. "Toward a Theory of Community-based Enterprise." *Academy of Management Review* 31: 309–28.

Post, Margaret, and Morgan Ruelle. 2021. "Power in Engaged Scholarship: Dimensions and Dynamics of Knowledge Co-Creation." *Gateways:*

International Journal of Community Research & Engagement 14, no. 2: 1–9. https://doi.org/10.5130/ijcre.v14i2.8009.

Prell, Christina. 2012. *Social Network Analysis: History, Theory & Methodology.* London: Sage.

Relph, E. 1976. *Place and Placelessness.* London: Pion.

Rosca, Eugenia, Nivedita Agarwal, and Alexander Brem. 2020. "Women Entrepreneurs as Agents of Change: A Comparative Analysis of Social Entrepreneurship Processes in Emerging Markets." *Technological Forecasting and Social Change* 157. https://doi.org/10.1016/j.techfore.2020.120067.

Sheppard, Emma. 2018. "'Social Enterprises Go Bust All the Time': How the Sector Is Tackling Its Image Problem." *Guardian*, March 12, 2018. https://www.theguardian.com/small-business-network/2018/mar/12/social-enterprises-go-bust-all-the-time-how-the-sector-is-tackling-its-image-problem.

Shrivastava, Paul, and James J. Kennelly. 2013. "Sustainability and Place-Based Enterprise." *Organization and Environment* 26: 83–101.

Slawinski, Natalie, Blair Winsor, Daina Mazutis, John W. Schouten, and Wendy K. Smith. 2021. "Managing the Paradoxes of Place to Foster Regeneration." *Organization and Environment* 34, no. 4: 595–618.

Smith, Nina, Valdemar Smith, and Mette Verner. 2006. "Do Women in Top Management Affect Firm Performance? A Panel Study of 2,500 Danish Firms." *International Journal of Productivity and Performance Management* 55, no. 7: 569–93. https://doi.org/10.1108/17410400610702160.

Steiner, Artur, Jane Farmer, and Gary Bosworth. 2020. "Rural Social Enterprise: Evidence to Date, and a Research Agenda." *Journal of Rural Studies* 70: 139–43. https://doi.org/10.1016/j.jrurstud.2019.08.008.

Steiner, Artur, and Simon Teasdale. 2019. "Unlocking the Potential of Rural Social Enterprise." *Journal of Rural Studies* 70: 144–54.

United Nations. 2015. *Transforming Our World: The 2030 Agenda for Sustainable Development.* New York: United Nations. https://sustainabledevelopment.un.org/content/documents/21252030%20Agenda%20for%20Sustainable%20Development%20web.pdf.

Villa, Mariann. 2019. "Local Ambivalence to Diverse Mobilities: The Case of a Norwegian Rural Village." *Sociologia Ruralis* 59, no. 4: 701–17.

Vodden, Kelly. 2010. "Heroes, Hope, and Resource Development in Canada's

Periphery: Lessons from Newfoundland and Labrador." In *The Next Rural Economies: Constructing Rural Place in Global Economies*, edited by Greg Halseth, Sean Markey, and David Bruce, 223–38. Oxfordshire, UK: CABI International.

Welter, Friederike, Ted Baker, David B. Audretsch, and William B. Gartner. 2017. "Everyday Entrepreneurship: A Call for Entrepreneurship Research to Embrace Entrepreneurial Diversity." *Entrepreneurship Theory and Practice* 41, no. 3: 311–21. https://doi.org/10.1111/etap.12258.

CONTRIBUTORS

Jennifer Brenton is a post-doctoral research fellow with the Erb Institute for Global Sustainable Enterprise at the University of Michigan. She earned her PhD from Memorial University and was an External PhD Scholar at the University of Cambridge Judge Business School. Her research interests include place, social enterprise, community-based enterprise, and cross-sector work. Her research explores the role of place in shaping social enterprises and cross-sector partnerships and how place-based organizations can drive community regeneration and development. In addition to her research, Brenton has worked as a social enterprise consultant on topics of governance, business plan development, and marketing.

Jennifer Charles boasts a diverse background in Newfoundland's startup, social enterprise, and academic realms. A graduate of Memorial University, Charles holds an MSc in Business, Bachelor of Commerce (co-op, hons.), and Bachelor of Arts (English). Since 2015, she has continued her connection to Memorial University's Faculty of Business and Centre for Social Enterprise as a part-time research assistant in the fields of social enterprise and rural resilience. In this role, she is authoring a mini-case series highlighting social enterprise success stories around the province through the lens of the PLACE Framework. She was a co-founder and inaugural executive director of Newfoundland's first co-working space and founding co-creator and program director of TEDxStJohn's. As a certified yoga instructor, Charles is the sole proprietor of Wild Cove Wellness, a health and fitness business dedicated to enhancing the physical, mental, and emotional wellness of residents and visitors on Fogo Island. She and her family live on Fogo Island year-round and are working to establish a mid-size, regenerative farm in the coming years.

Alan Cobb is co-founder and chair of the Board of Directors for Shorefast. He enjoyed a long career in the senior ranks of the Canadian federal public service and the private sector and has worked in policy and operations for the Industry, Science and Technology, Treasury Board, and Employment and Immigration federal ministries. He also headed the initial federal offshore oil and gas regulatory agency, based in St. John's. After retiring from the federal government, Alan provided management consulting services to the public and private sectors, and worked with a leading technology firm as advisor to the CEO. Since Shorefast's inception in the early 2000s, he has volunteered his time in a variety of roles in service of Shorefast's economic development and charitable work.

Zita Cobb is co-founder and CEO of Shorefast, and innkeeper of Fogo Island Inn. Growing up on Fogo Island, she developed a deep belief in the inherent value of place and profound respect for the human ways of knowing that emerge from respectful relationships with nature, culture, and community. She held senior financial roles in the high-tech industry, notably with JDS Fitel, subsequently JDS Uniphase, where she contributed to building the company into one of the most successful high-tech innovators in history. She returned home to Fogo Island in the early 2000s and, along with her brothers Anthony and Alan, founded Shorefast. In 2016, Cobb was awarded the Order of Canada. She volunteers her time and energies to the active direction and management of Shorefast's projects and community enterprises on Fogo Island.

Senan Cooke is secretary and director of Dunhill Rural Enterprises CLG Ireland, a founding member of Copper Coast Global Geopark, and director of Social Enterprise Republic of Ireland (SERI), formed by some of Ireland's leading SE practitioners and supporters to champion for the sector. Widely considered a pioneer of the social enterprise community in Ireland, Cooke was involved as a founding member of seven social entreprise start-ups and has authored three books, each drawn from his community experience. *The Enterprising Community* (2018) focuses on a bottom-up perspective on the capacity within communities to regenerate; two other volumes focus on the history of the Gaelic Athletic Association in the country. Cooke was previously employed by Waterford Crystal Ltd as master craftsman/training and communications manager before becoming a lecturer at Dublin City University (2006–14).

Joan Cranston was born in Toronto, grew up in Ottawa, and attended university in Montreal, where she obtained a degree in physiotherapy. She moved to Grand Falls, Newfoundland, in 1983 and "the Rock" has been her home ever since. She has lived and worked in Norris Point since 1988, for many of those years at the old Bonne Bay Cottage Hospital, both in its former life as a cottage hospital and in its current incarnation as a social enterprise incubation centre. She volunteers as the coordinator for the Bonne Bay Cottage Hospital Heritage Corporation, which has owned and operated the centre since 2001. She has provided physiotherapy services to the communities on the coast of the Great Northern Peninsula for over 30 years. Currently, she is a member of the NLSUPPORT Patient Advisory Council as well as the Pan Canadian Patient Council. These councils are both part of the Strategy for Patient Oriented Research of the Canadian Institutes of Health Research.

Susan Cull is executive vice president, for Shorefast and executive chair of the Fogo Island Economic Development Partnership. After receiving her Master's in project management from York University, Susan spent eight years in project development and management with the Newfoundland and Labrador Economics and Statistics Agency. But the pull of home never faded, so in 2014 she and her family moved back to Fogo Island. Passionate about community development, Cull is involved with several local Fogo Island organizations in the economic, social, recreation, and education sectors.

Michelle Darlington is head of Knowledge Transfer at the Cambridge Centre for Social Innovation. She holds a PhD in drawing from Loughborough University. Her specialty is in visual and creative methods for teaching and research. She has published in the areas of social innovation and arts education, and has been researching community economic development since 2017.

Sam Elliot has an extensive background in business, education, and industry. He holds a Bachelor of Vocational Education degree (business major) and a Certificate in Business Administration through Memorial University. For 17 years, he was the executive director of St. Anthony Basin Resources Inc. (SABRI), a social enterprise with an annual operations budget of approximately $1.5 million. Prior to joining SABRI, Elliot was employed as a personnel officer, a human resources/costing coordinator, an instructor, an interviewer, and assistant manager with a finance company. He was also the director on the board of St. Anthony Seafood Limited (17 years), finance chair on the Port Authority of St. Anthony, and treasurer for St. Mary's Anglican Church. He previously served as a director with the Nortip Development Cooperation, a director with the Nordic Economic Development Corporation, finance chair of the Grenfell Historical Society, chair of the St. Anthony Library Board, and member of Labrador-Grenfell Health's Board of Trustees.

Rebecca Franklin, an associate professor of management at New Mexico State University and adjunct professor at Memorial University, received her PhD in business administration with a specialization in entrepreneurship from Oklahoma State University in 2013 and was a visiting assistant professor at Tulane University. She later moved to Newfoundland for a tenure-track position at Memorial University. She has published papers in *Journal of Management*, *Entrepreneurship Theory and Practice*, *International Small Business Journal*, and *Journal of Developmental Entrepreneurship*. Prior to pursuing her PhD, she founded and established two businesses. During her time as an entrepreneur, she was honoured in

Oklahoma Magazine's Top 40 Under 40, The *Journal Record*'s Achievers Under 40, and Urban Tulsa's Top Movers and Shakers. She served as a board member of various organizations, including six years as a mayoral appointee to the City of Tulsa's Economic Development Commission, founding member of Young Professionals of Tulsa, president of Tulsa-Now, and advisory board member for the OSU Culinary School.

Hadley Friedland is an associate professor in the Faculty of Law at the University of Alberta. Her research focuses on Indigenous law, Aboriginal law, family law, child welfare law, criminal justice, and therapeutic jurisprudence. She has published numerous articles and collaborated to produce accessible Indigenous legal resources for Indigenous communities, legal professionals, and the general public. She is co-founder of the Wahkohtowin Indigenous Law and Governance Lodge, an interdisciplinary initiative developed to uphold Indigenous law and governance through supporting community-led research.

Diane Hodgins is executive vice president of Shorefast, where she focuses on place-based community economic development activities to help communities thrive in the global economy. She serves as a "numeric linguist": a translator for the complex and often ambiguous language of business and finance. Diane works to create modern tools like Economic Nutrition^{CM} which answers the all-important question: "Where does the money go?" Using a whole-thinking approach that puts people and place at the centre of every decision, she and her team create systems that invest in culture and ensure knowledge and financial capital strengthen communities. Diane is passionate about sharing Fogo Island's alternative community business model, in which social and economic value are achieved in tandem.

Jamie Jamieson moved around a lot as a child and at 18 became a Londoner. He earned a degree in philosophy and literature from Warwick University, worked a variety of jobs (carpenter, bookseller, labourer, roofer, brick mason, tutor, truck driver, milkman, English teacher, shop-floor supervisor), lived in Italy and Switzerland, and eventually made a career in marketing. He met his wife, an Oklahoma native, in Italy and later moved to Tulsa. He started a development company and won the right to turn a 10-acre tract of downtown Tulsa into new housing. He co-founded a neighbourhood revitalization effort alongside residents, business owners, and city planners. That formative experience led to other roles centring on urban life, including transportation infrastructure design, food security, housing, Main Street revitalization, parks and trails design and funding, land-use policy, flood mitigation, and the arts. Jamieson's efforts helped lead to Tulsa's "form-based" zoning policy, its "Complete Streets" policy, its semi-permanent funding for mass transit, and to much greater investment in bike lanes.

Glenn Jenkins is a community organization facilitator based in the Marsh Farm estate, Luton, UK. He is a founding member of Marsh Farm Outreach CIC and has been working in bottom-up community development for more than 30 years, specializing in design and facilitation of self-help projects in housing, employment, arts, entertainment, social enterprise, and neighbourhood regeneration by and for long-term unemployed and socially excluded people.

Felicity Kelliher is professor of management practice and chair of RIKON (www.rikon.ie) at the School of Business, South East Technological University (SETU), Ireland. A Fulbright Scholar, she has published widely in management and development journals and has co-authored three books. Her research focuses on small and micro firm management capability development, cooperative and community of practice activities, and rural network engagement. She works closely with social enterprise stakeholders and policy-makers in Ireland, including Waterford Europe Direct and the Department of Rural and Community Development. Felicity is past-chair of the Irish Academy of Management and a member of the Social Enterprise Research Network Ireland (SERNI).

Nicola Kent is fascinated with human-centred tools to navigate change, looking at real social problems in Ireland's society and developing solutions through creative tools with the people who know the problems. She works as an entrepreneurial tutor and mentor with enterprise support agencies, engaging in the design and delivery of enterprise and social enterprise workshops. She works with those from migrant and traveller communities, people in recovery from substance abuse, people with criminal records, people with disabilities, and long-term unemployed. She is the founder and owner of Power of You (https://powerofyou.ie), an organization that encourages the most vulnerable in Ireland's society to change by embracing fear, insecurity, and uncertainty as a doorway to opportunity and encourages people to build a strong framework around their social enterprise.

Sara Langer is a PhD student in transdisciplinary sustainability at Grenfell Campus, Memorial University. She obtained her bachelor's degree in sustainable research management from Grenfell and completed her master's degree at Queen's University in global development studies with a focus on Indigenous ecology, conflict resolution, and peacemaking. Langer has presented research at international conferences, and her current PhD research is on alternative models of economic development in small, outport fishing communities in Newfoundland. She is especially interested in various modes of knowledge mobilization and translation such as podcasting with Coastal Routes Radio, social media communications with Rural Resilience Research Group, graphic recording/visual notetaking, and participatory art installations.

Brennan Lowery is a transdisciplinary researcher and passionate supporter of entrepreneurial endeavours to build more sustainable communities. With both academic and practical experience in community-based entrepreneurship and innovation, Brennan is developing an emerging research agenda on how rural and resource-based communities can craft self-determined sustainability narratives and how these can include entrepreneurial strategies to advance sustainability goals. Brennan completed his doctorate in 2020 through Memorial University's Interdisciplinary PhD program, and has held postdoctoral fellowships in the Future Ocean and Coastal Infrastructures project (based at the Memorial Faculty of Business Administration) and the Marine Biomass Innovation project (based at Grenfell Campus, Memorial). Brennan is manager of Navigate Entrepreneurship Centre, which seeks to transform and grow communities in western Newfoundland by supporting aspiring entrepreneurs. He has also been involved in economic development initiatives in western Newfoundland, such as the development of the recently opened Centre for Research and Innovation, and is an adjunct professor with the Environmental Policy Institute at Grenfell Campus, Memorial University.

Johnny Mack is from the Toquaht Nation (Nuu-chah-nulth) and is an assistant professor jointly appointed to the Peter A. Allard School of Law and to the First Nations and Indigenous Studies program at the University of British Columbia. He has an LLB and an LLM and is a PhD candidate at the University of Victoria. His PhD research has earned a CGS scholarship from SSHRC and the Trudeau Foundation (2011). Mack's research investigates the legal relationship between Indigenous and settler peoples in contemporary settler states, particularly Canada. He has published in the *Review of Education, Pedagogy and Cultural Studies,* and in the edited volume, *Storied Communities: Narratives of Contact and Arrival in the Constitution of Political Community* (UBC Press, 2010). He is grateful for the opportunity to reside and work on the ancestral, traditional, and unceded lands of the Musqueam people.

Lorenzo Magzul received his PhD from the University of British Columbia in 2013. His thesis, focused on the experience of two Indigenous communities, the Blood Tribe in Canada and the Mayan town of Patzún in Guatemala, investigated the importance of social capital in adaptation to impacts of climate change. From 2014 to 2016, he worked as a post-doctoral fellow at the University of Victoria's Gustavson School of Business on the project "The Search for Sustainable Development in the Toquaht Nation."

Matthew Murphy is an associate professor in the Gustavson School of Business at the University of Victoria where he teaches and carries out research related to sustainability and social entrepreneurship. His current research focuses on Indigenous self-determination, sustainable community development, and interactions between Indigenous communities and extractive-industry firms. Murphy's earlier research examines interactions between businesses and civil society organizations, issues of trade justice, and social entrepreneurship.

Elizabeth Murphy (MEd, MBA in social enterprise and entrepreneurship) is currently the chair of the Placentia West Development Association, vice chair of the Placentia West Regional Heritage Committee, and a board member of the Heritage Foundation of Newfoundland and Labrador. She has been a part of the Heritage Committee since it was established in 1983 and led the development of a heritage-based social enterprise that includes the Paddle House Museum, the Tea Rose Restaurant, and the Livyer's Lot Economuseum. Elizabeth taught for more than 30 years and was a member of the Newfoundland and Labrador Teaching Association's provincial council for eight years. She received the Centennial Study Award for the use of technology in remote education in 1998, the Newfoundland and Labrador Prime Minister's Award for Teaching Excellence in 2004, and the Provincial Award for Community Service in 2008. She is an avid crafter.

Sinead O'Higgins is an acting senior executive librarian based in the southeast of Ireland, managing seven library branches in Waterford and Europe Direct Waterford. She has over 20 years of library experience, with 12 of these years also managing the day-to-day running of Europe Direct Waterford. She is interested in developing local social and social economy networks and working with stakeholders to organize a wide range of events, conferences, exhibitions, Citizens' Dialogues, lectures, and cultural events to best meet the information needs of the communities served (www.waterfordlibraries.ie).

Kimberly Orren is the founder of Fishing for Success in Petty Harbour, Newfoundland, a non-profit with a mission to transmit traditional fishing knowledge and skills. The organization also promotes the use of local fish as a culturally significant and sustainable food. A former high school science teacher turned fish harvester, Orren was raised in Newfoundland and moved to Florida in 1977 as a teenager with her family. On her visits home to Petty Harbour, she witnessed the ongoing effect of fishery closures and decided that she wanted to teach kids to fish. She volunteers for the Social Justice Cooperative NL, is the lead facilitator for Project WET Canada in Newfoundland and Labrador, and serves on advisory committees for Food First NL, Ocean Frontier Institute/Governance Research, Too Big To Ignore, and the Canadian Ocean Literacy Coalition. In 2018, Orren was honoured as St. John's YWCA Woman of Distinction. Currently, she is working on a project with Memorial University to facilitate a network of people and resources called Outdoor Learning NL and as a research partner in the Ocean Frontier Institute's PLACE Framework project.

Astrid V. Pérez Piñán is assistant professor at the School of Public Administration, University of Victoria, where she teaches graduate courses in the Community Development and Public Administration programs. Her current research engages with the measurement turn in global and community development and the processes that lead to the (re)articulation of alternatives to the mainstream economic paradigm for well-being. She also conducts research on the politics and policies of colonization and decolonization.

Liz Riches has worked in the community development and community networks sector in Ireland for over 30 years. She is currently the Education, Employment and Enterprise Manager at Waterford Area Partnership CLG (WAP), where she also established Waterford Social Enterprise Network as a communication and peer support space for social enterprises in Waterford. Prior to her employment in WAP she managed Ballybeg Community Development Project in Waterford, establishing a horticulture training project and the social enterprise Ballybeg Greens. She is particularly interested in the role of digital marketing in the promotion of social economy services and products, building awareness of the sector, and positively impacting on customer engagement with enterprises that promote greater social and economic equality.

Amy Rowsell is director of special projects and impact for Shorefast based on Fogo Island, NL. She contributes to strategic planning and impact evaluation as well as program development across various areas of focus, including community engagement, environmental stewardship, and Shorefast's Punt Premises: an interactive cultural interpretation centre dedicated to carrying forward the history of the inshore fishery. Amy holds an Honours Bachelor of Arts in history and gender studies from the University of Ottawa, and a Master of Arts in the history of medicine from McGill University. Though born and raised in Ottawa, Amy's paternal ancestry is entirely from Newfoundland and she permanently relocated to Fogo Island in 2017.

Cloy-e-iis Judith Sayers is president of the Nuu-chah-nulth Tribal Council (NTC) and chancellor of Vancouver Island University in British Columbia, Canada. The role of the NTC is to represent 14 First Nations in three regions stretching along 300 kilometres of the Pacific coast of Vancouver Island. Dr. Sayers is also an adjunct professor of law and business and teaches Aboriginal economic development and Indigenous law at the University of Victoria. She was the elected chief of the Hupacasath First Nation for 14 years, and held the National Aboriginal Economic Development (NAED) chair at the University of Victoria, a joint appointment of the Faculties of Law and Business. She was awarded an honorary Doctor of Laws from Queen's University, was admitted to the Aboriginal Business Hall of Fame in 2009 by the Canadian Council of Aboriginal Business, and has received numerous other awards for her work. Most recently, she was named to the Order of Canada.

Ario Seto is a post-doctoral researcher at the Ocean Frontier Institute, Memorial University. An anthropologist, his current research focuses on the intersectionality of mediatized practices, community-building, and values, particularly in terms of the emerging public morality, democratic resilience, grassroots economic solidarity, and marketization of digital living. His recent book, *Netizenship: Activism and Online Community Transformation* (Palgrave Macmillan, 2017), details the disciplining practices and ethics in shaping militant netizens in online forums.

Gordon Slade is Shorefast's director and served as deputy minister of fisheries for Newfoundland and Labrador and as vice-president of the Atlantic Canada Opportunities Agency (1987–95). In 1996, he became an independent consultant in the fields of heritage, cultural tourism, and community development. He was CEO of One Ocean, an organization that encourages dialogue between the fishing and petroleum industries, and is the former chair and managing director of Battle Harbour Historic Trust. In 2005 Slade was appointed a member of the Order of Canada, and in 2020 he was invested into the Order of Newfoundland and Labrador.

Natalie Slawinski is professor of sustainability and strategy and director of the Centre for Social and Sustainable Innovation at the Gustavson School of Business, University of Victoria, and an adjunct professor at Memorial University. She earned her PhD from the Ivey Business School at the University of Western Ontario. Her research focuses on understanding sustainability, temporality, place-based organizing, and paradoxes in organizations, and has been published in such journals as *Organization Science, Strategic Management Journal,* and *Organization Studies.* Her most recent research examines these themes in the context of social enterprise and community entrepreneurship. Slawinski serves as an advisor to Memorial University's Centre for Social Enterprise and is a research fellow at the Cambridge University Judge Business School's Centre for Social Innovation. She is a member of the editorial review board at *Organization & Environment.*

Wendy K. Smith is the Emma Smith Morris Professor of Management at the Lerner School of Business and Economics and the faculty director of the Women's Leadership Initiative at the University of Delaware. She studies how leaders and organizations navigate organizational paradoxes such as tensions between today and tomorrow, stability and change, collaboration and competition, and social missions and financial demands. She describes these ideas in her TedxTalk, "The Power of Paradox." Smith has been named as highly cited — one of the top 0.1 per cent of cited researchers in the field of business — in 2019, 2020, and 2021, with publications in top journals such as *Administrative Science Quarterly, Academy of Management Journal, Academy of Management Review,* and *Harvard Business Review.* Her recent book, co-authored with Marianne Lewis, is *Both/And Thinking: Embracing Creative Tensions to Solve Your Toughest Problems* (Harvard Business School Press, 2022).

Mark C.J. Stoddart is a professor in the Department of Sociology at Memorial University, with research interests in environmental sociology, social movements, and communications and culture. He is the author, with Alice Mattoni and John McLevey, of *Industrial Development and Eco-Tourisms: Can Oil Extraction and Nature Conservation Co-Exist?* (Palgrave Macmillan, 2020). His work appears in a range of international journals, including *Global Environmental Change, Energy Research & Social Science, Organization & Environment, Environmental Politics, Journal of Sustainable Tourism, Environmental Communication, Mobilities,* and *Social Movement Studies.*

Neil Stott is a management practice professor of social innovation, co-director of the Cambridge Centre for Social Innovation, Judge Business School, and Fellow of Lucy Cavendish College, University of Cambridge. He is also a Fellow of the Royal Society of Arts, Fellow of the Inter University Seminar on Armed Forces and Society, a Fellow in Clayton State University's Center for Social Innovation & Sustainable Entrepreneurship, and an adjunct professor in the Faculty of Business Administration at

Memorial University. He was chief executive of Keystone Development Trust until April 2015. Keystone is one of the largest development trusts in the UK delivering community development, social enterprises, and property development. Previously, Stott was head of Community Development at Canterbury City Council, principal officer (Community) at Cambridge City Council, and a youth and community worker for several children's charities.

Kelly Vodden is a research professor with the Environmental Policy Institute at the Grenfell Campus of Memorial University. She has been engaged in rural community and regional development research, policy, and practice across the country, particularly in Newfoundland and Labrador, for more than 25 years. She has published and led projects on topics ranging from rural regional governance and development models to climate change adaptation, rural drinking water systems, and labour force mobility, and has written and presented widely on these topics.

Blair Winsor is an associate professor at Memorial University, where his research efforts focus on entrepreneurship in the province. He joined Memorial University's Faculty of Business Administration in August 2013, having previously taught entrepreneurship, innovation management, and small business management at Edinburgh Napier University in the United Kingdom. He completed his doctorate at the University of Warwick's Business School in 2010. He also has a Bachelor of Arts in political science from Memorial University, a Bachelor of Laws from the University of Ottawa, and an MBA from Italy's Luigi Bocconi Commercial University. In addition to his academic pursuits, over the last 40 years Winsor has been an entrepreneur, angel investor, and consultant in the UK, the US, and Canada.

INDEX

accessibility, 137, 149, 151, 153–54, 167, 169–71, 219, 239, 259, 278; of healthcare, 94, 96, 127; of housing, 4, 94; of information, 38, 40, 45, 143, 166, 176; of networks, 57, 87, 95, 166, 265, 268–69; of resources, 65, 78, 81, 85, 94–95, 117, 147, 172, 176, 249–50, 261, 277, 281–82

accountability, 46, 68, 241–42, 245–46, 253

adaptability, 177, 198, 202–03; adaptive reuse, 61, 143, 170

advocacy and lobbying, 12, 29, 63, 69, 78, 82, 170–72, 209, 213, 216–25, 228–29, 242, 259–67, 276, 282n, 292

agencies: business development, 55, 84, 265, 282; government, 7, 28, 59, 79, 82, 85–89, 92–93, 97–100, 233, 253, 272, 276, 287, 289, 292–95; local and regional, 223–24, 246–48, 252–53, 255n, 261–65, 277–78

agency, 15, 60, 118, 128, 130, 236, 286

agriculture, 4, 60, 62, 117, 124, 235,

250, 268, 271, 294, 300; aquaculture, 97

ambiguity, 163–64, 176, 178, 232, 241

Analytic Hierarchy Process (AHP), 199

Andersson, Gavin, 235, 244–45

Anne Valley Walkway & Wildlife Sanctuary, Waterford, 271

approaches, 11, 28–29, 40, 45, 52, 59, 110, 162, 169, 189–90, 203, 227, 234, 239, 254, 274, 276, 285; "as-is," 64, 66; bottom-up, 2, 7, 246, 249, 252–54, 290; deficiency-based, 81, 102, 111; "done-by," 216, 233; "done-for," 233; either/or, 163, 177; form-based, 221–22, 224, 227; holistic, xiv–xv, 5–6, 8, 36, 56, 85, 160, 165, 175, 177, 196, 201, 204, 254, 286, 292–94; inclusive, 52; Moraisian, 235, 244; place-based, 4–5, 9, 13, 29, 31, 36, 63, 67, 109, 118, 160; "plug the leaks," 243, 247; top-down, 59–60, 252, 290; Western, 194, 200, 235, 254

arts, 13, 30–31, 33, 61, 120, 221, 242, 252, 264, 274, 306; arts communities, 212, 219, 226; crafts, 61,

64, 115–17, 123–24, 127, 129, 174;
fibre arts, 9, 31, 35, 43, 60,
115–16, 124, 273; furniture and
woodworking, 9, 31–32, 35, 42;
music, 61, 64, 126–27, 216, 220,
242, 252; painting, 116; studios,
32–33, 43, 252
Asset-Based Community Development (ABCD), 13, 32, 43, 110–11,
126, 129; Asset-Based Community Engagement (ABCE), 11
assets, xiv, 5–6, 11, 13–14, 27, 42–43,
52, 56, 59, 70–72, 79, 85–86, 93,
102, 109–12, 121–22, 125–30,
176, 215, 252, 276, 281, 292,
294–95
Association for New Canadians, 174
associations, 85, 99–100, 114, 219
Atlantic Canada Opportunities Agency
(ACOA), 82, 92, 95, 99, 130
authenticity, 14, 116, 144, 151, 153–54,
241, 247; performative, 143
authorities, local, 55, 102, 111, 232–34,
239, 241, 254, 265, 279–80
awards, 9, 38, 152, 263, 270
Baine, Johnston and Company, 139
balance, 5, 16, 85, 137, 161, 164–65,
170–72, 201, 287; iisaak, 192–93
barriers, 9, 52, 57, 68, 209, 241
Basque fishers, 137, 143
Bass brothers, 225–26
Battle Harbour, 135–54
Battle Harbour Historic Trust
(BHHT), 136, 139–54
Battle Island, 135, 138, 152

belonging, 1, 3–4, 8, 9, 41, 119, 167,
215, 237, 281
Big Brook, 83
Black community, 208–09
boards, 64, 66, 68, 71, 112, 121–22,
141, 151–52, 215, 217–19, 242–43;
structure, 83, 212–14; training,
280
Boat Harbour, 60, 113
Bonavista Peninsula, 60, 113
Bonavista, 13, 44, 60, 109–10, 112–14,
117–30; Alexander Bridge House,
119; the Big Store at Mockbeggar,
119; Garrick Theatre, 119–20,
123–26; Historic Church Street
Revitalization Project, 120–21;
Historic Property Investment
Program, 120; Historic Society
(BHS), 118–19, 123; Historic
Townscape Foundation (BHTF),
113, 117–30, 287; Keough
Building, 119; Memorial United
Church, 119; Orange Hall, 119;
Ryan Premises, 119
Bonne Bay Cottage Hospital Heritage
Corporation, 11, 44, 52–54,
61–72; New Rural Story Forum,
54; Old Cottage Hospital, 53–54,
60–72, 290–92; Old Cottage
Hospital Museum, 62, 64
bottom-up. See approaches
boundary spanners, 6, 12, 55, 57–58,
65, 69, 78, 100, 294
Bradley, John, 120
Brazilian Peasants League, 235

Brexit, 272

brokers, 12, 42, 53, 55–59, 64, 86

budgets, 37, 62, 88, 243, 246–48, 250

Building a Better Block, 211

Bunmahon, 264

business models, 87, 95, 172, 220, 258

businesses, 2, 7, 37–38, 55, 66–68, 87,
    121, 161, 194–96, 200–01, 244,
    247, 265; local, 28, 42, 56, 70,
    79, 113, 115, 127, 174, 271–73, 280,
    286–87; tourism, 35, 38, 118, 120,
    122–23, 149

buy-in, 119, 137, 147–48, 286

Cambridge Centre for Social
    Innovation, 233

capacities, xiv, 5, 7, 13–14, 38, 42–43,
    87, 102, 115, 128–29, 142, 148,
    216, 238, 240, 269; building, 112,
    235–36, 244–45, 254, 290;
    inventories, 110–11, 114

capital, xvi, 28, 33, 168, 259; bonding,
    85, 93, 99–100; community, 5,
    12, 56, 68, 70, 79, 92–99, 112,
    154; types, 56, 85–87, 100–01, 164

capitalism, xvi, 203, 258

Centre for Addiction and Mental
    Health (CAMH), 174

chambers of commerce, 83, 93, 99, 224

Charles Curtis Memorial Hospital,
    94, 97

churches, 119, 210, 271; Memorial
    United, Bonavista, 119; Romiley
    Methodist, 247–48, 253; of St.
    James the Apostle, Battle
    Harbour, 139, 143, 145

Citizens Dialogue, Dunhill, 278, 283n

Clarenville Farm and Market, 60

Clearwater Seafoods, 83, 92, 94–96

climate change, 1, 4, 16, 147, 160,
    282, 287; adaptation, 1, 307

Coaker, William Ford, 59–60

Cobb brothers, 30

collaboration, 3, 55, 87, 102, 121, 147,
    188, 259, 271, 276, 280, 285. See
    also partnerships

common goals, 56, 59, 116, 174,
    212–13, 217, 233, 252, 272–73

community: definition, 3; empower-
    ment, 8, 232, 234, 241–42, 244,
    286; engagement, 54–55, 69, 111,
    113, 124, 130, 187, 191, 196, 201,
    217, 285, 288; hubs, 60, 64, 70,
    123–25, 252; kitchens, 62, 124;
    meetings, 32, 162, 210, 213–14,
    218–24; pride, 11, 13–14, 42,
    109–10, 126–27, 144–45, 208,
    217, 229

Community Business Development
    Corporation (CBDC), 44

Conche, 60

conservation: environmental, 80, 152,
    173; fisheries, 15, 95, 98; heritage,
    118–20

Copper Coast European Geopark,
    262–66, 271–72

COVID-19, 34, 272

crises, 29, 47, 137; cultural, 159;
    economic, 262; environmental,
    4, 56

culture, 3, 8–9, 16, 31, 35, 43, 53, 61,

63, 109–10, 121, 145, 147, 150, 152, 159, 166–67, 168–69, 171, 173–74, 186–88, 191, 194–96, 218; counterfeiting, 148; intangible, 114–15, 136, 143–45; material, 129, 136, 143, 145, 152

Daniel's Harbour Hatchery, 64

data, 40, 101, 151, 190–91; collection, 37, 39, 88–89; databases, 196; extraction, 288

de Morais, Clodomir Santos, 15, 235, 244

decision-making, 2, 12, 28, 42, 83, 87, 102, 111, 121, 123, 128, 151, 173, 189, 197–98, 232–33, 290, 292

donations, 96, 120, 140–41, 147, 214, 260

downtowns, 13–14, 208–10, 216, 218–22, 226–27

Dunhill Castle, 271

Dunhill Rural Enterprises CLG, 262, 264–66, 270–71; Ecopark, 271

Dunhill, Fenor, Boatstrand, and Annestown (DFBA) Community Enterprises, Ltd., 263–65, 270–72, 278, 282

Economic Nutrition Certification Mark (ENCM), 35

Eimskip, 92, 94, 97

elders, 65, 69, 94, 98, 100, 117, 124, 171, 194, 272

entrepreneurship, 52–53, 55–56, 66–68, 123, 228, 294. See also social entrepreneurship

environment, 16, 34, 46, 56, 70, 81,

98, 137, 147, 152, 159–60, 170, 175, 193, 196–98

ethics, 38, 187, 189–90

European Commission, 258, 260–61, 267, 279; Europe Direct, 261, 264, 267–69, 277–79; European Social Enterprise Region Programme (ESER), 261, 268–69, 278; Fisheries Areas Network (FARNET), 44; Green Deal, 279; Social Economy Action Plan, 269

European Union, 265, 272–74, 279, 281, 283n; LEADER Programme for Rural Development, 266–68; RUBIZMO, 264, 282n

Exodus Collective, 235, 239–40, 242

families, 55, 100, 117, 123, 139, 146, 166–68, 194

Feild, Bishop Edward, 139

Fidel Gastro's Social Club, 252

finances, 15–16, 58, 98, 102, 114, 160–65, 172–73, 188, 198, 223, 248, 287; benefits, 35, 151

Fisheries and Oceans Canada (DFO), 82, 93, 95, 99

fisheries, 15–16, 27–31, 43, 79–83, 93–95, 98, 110, 117–19, 137–38, 159–60, 165–78, 294; boats, 32, 84, 139, 171; by-products, 98; groundfish moratorium, 8, 29–31, 79, 81–82, 109, 113–14, 117, 120, 135, 141, 148, 152, 159, 166–68, 172; Labrador fishery, 135, 138–46, 152–54; processing, 31, 83, 94,

97–98, 117–18, 169–70; quotas,
79–80, 82–83, 102; salt fish, 140,
143, 145–46; trawlers, 29, 167

Fishing for Success, 43–44, 159–60,
165, 168–78; Girls Who Fish, 15,
165, 168–69, 173, 290; Women
Sharing Heritage (WiSH), 165, 174

Fogo Island, 8–11, 13, 27–44, 147, 153,
291; Arts, 30; Co-operative
Society, 8, 31; Inn, 9, 27–28,
31–34, 38–39, 43; Workshops, 9,
32–33, 42

Fogo Process, 8, 30–31

food security, 1, 199, 244, 292

Forfás, 258, 260

Fort Worth, Texas, 225–26

Freire, Paulo, 233, 235, 239

French Shore Tapestry, 60

funding, 34–35, 68, 85, 87, 92–93,
95–97, 99, 114, 118–20, 130, 161,
176, 210, 221–23, 234, 240–46,
249–50, 253–54, 259–60, 277,
292, 294–95

Gaelic Athletic Association, 270–71

gender, 187, 201–02, 290–91;
LGBTQIA+, 171, 291; men, 115,
168, 291; women, 55, 115, 159,
165, 174, 187, 195, 203, 266, 273,
275, 290–91

gentrification, 293

Global North, 235, 254, 289

Global South, 55, 234, 245, 289

globalization, 1, 4, 9, 28–29, 33,
35–36, 46, 164, 169–70, 188,
203–04, 295

Goose Cove, 83

governments, role of, xvi, 6–7, 28, 78,
93, 287, 293–95

grassroots movements, 53, 60, 65, 70,
114, 212, 215, 219, 237, 243, 247,
259, 262–63, 269, 275, 277

Great Northern Peninsula (GNP), 53,
60–66, 79–82, 88–93, 100–02,
139, 291; Community Place, 65;
Crafts, 64; Development
Corporation (GNPDC), 63

Grenfell Foundation, 94

Grenfell Historic Properties, 152

Grenfell, Wilfred, 59–60, 139–40

Gros Morne region, 92; Cooperating
Association, 63; National Park, 53

grounded normativity, 188–89, 200

Hancock, Gordon, 141

Happy Valley-Goose Bay, 140, 144

Harris, Leslie, 141

healthcare, 37, 53, 61–65, 70, 96–97,
139–40, 174, 236, 272, 282, 295

Hearn, Leo, 159, 166–68, 176

heritage, 13, 15, 41, 58, 70, 79, 98, 112,
122, 129, 136–37, 143–45, 152–53,
167, 186, 194, 271, 274; artifacts,
137, 143–47, 151; buildings, 70,
112, 114, 118–20, 129, 137, 143–47,
176, 208, 221; fishing, 43–44,
159, 166–71, 176–77; oral
histories, 61, 69, 93–94, 98, 126,
191; traditions, 9, 16, 27, 31–32,
141, 153, 167, 173, 176, 186, 224

historic sites, 136, 143–44, 154;
Historic Sites Association of

Newfoundland and Labrador, 152; Historic Sites and Monuments of Canada, 141, 152

housing, 4, 8, 92, 94, 98, 127, 216, 222–23, 226, 237, 239, 244, 272, 282n, 293

identity, 1, 13–14, 59, 78, 110, 126–27, 213–15, 217, 244, 285, 287; cultural, 5, 70, 80, 159, 168, 186, 198

immigrants, 128, 159, 166, 168–69, 174, 265, 267, 273, 282n; refugees, 174, 265, 267

inclusivity, 3, 11, 35, 53–54, 57–62, 111, 170–71, 225, 266, 272, 276; in entrepreneurship, 52, 56, 68–70, 72, 123

income, 197, 245; generation, 16, 114, 172, 178, 235, 244, 279

Indian Act, 185

Indigenous communities, 16, 29, 55, 171, 187–91, 195–98, 200, 287, 289

industry, 4, 31, 55, 58, 62, 67, 87, 92–93, 110, 113, 115, 117–18, 127, 138–39, 203–04, 224, 237–38; industrialization, 166, 170; post-industrialism, 56, 70, 232, 238, 244, 254

inequalities, 1, 16, 55, 259

information technology (IT), 92, 162, 250, 273, 281

infrastructure, 87, 97, 101, 117, 124, 147, 149, 151, 170, 197–98, 208, 293; communication, 41, 93, 95–99, 101, 295; transportation, 84, 97, 151

insiders and outsiders, 52, 123, 213, 233, 291; knowledge, 16, 42, 275; linking, 31, 42, 61, 65, 71, 100, 102; tensions, 164, 169, 173–74

interdependencies, 80, 101, 161, 169, 172, 176, 271

International Grenfell Association (IGA), 139–40

internationality, 35, 79, 89, 93, 97, 99–101, 139, 263, 269, 281, 291

investment, 13–14, 87, 92, 94–96, 99–102, 120, 139, 142, 147, 208, 221, 223–26, 293

Ireland, 2, 12, 29, 258, 260–62, 274–78, 281; Department of Rural and Community Development, 258–59, 268, 276; Early Years and Young People, 269; Employment Investment Incentive, 259; Enterprise Ireland, 265; Irish Development Authority, 265; Irish Rural Link, 264, 282n; Irish Social Enterprise Network, 265, 267; *Muintir na Tíre* (People of the Country) 270, 283n; Pobal, 266, 268; Programmes for Government, 261, 282n; Social Enterprise Policy, 268, 276, 279–80; Social Enterprise Republic of Ireland (SERI), 265, 267; Social Inclusion and Community Activation Programme (SICAP), 264; the Wheel, 267

Island Rooms, 168, 170

jobs, 4, 70, 81, 167, 188, 202, 212, 229, 234, 237, 251, 260, 271; creation, 32, 35, 94–95, 97, 110, 115, 194, 198, 200, 202, 244–45, 276, 287; training, 30, 56, 124, 136, 148, 150, 280; unemployment, 110, 113–14, 237–38, 244, 246, 249

Joe Batt's Arm, 41

Kennedy, Colleen, 63

Kent, Michaela J., 63

Kill, 264

knowledge, 12, 42, 44, 58–59, 144, 169, 253, 277, 285; Indigenous, 16, 187–89, 198–201, 289; local, 16, 31–32, 54, 65, 69, 122, 129, 159, 197, 288, 291; sharing, 38–40, 122, 269, 276

L'Anse aux Meadows, 94, 98; National Historic Site, 152

labour force, 81, 113, 118, 121, 128; laws, 32; organization and unions, 60, 121, 237, 290

Labra, Ivan and Isabel, 245, 251–52, 255n

land, 62, 168, 250–51; connection to, 167–68, 171, 174, 186, 193–94, 198, 201, 275; landscapes, 27, 118, 127, 145–46, 175, 198; land use planning, 1, 210–11, 215–16, 221–25

leadership, 11–12, 40, 42, 55, 67–69, 72, 86, 154, 162, 212–13, 290; consensus, 233; distributed, 286; inclusive, 11, 52, 53, 57–60; top-down, 60

Leif Eriksen Foundation, 94, 98

Liberalism, 188–89; neoliberalism, 102, 189

libraries: Fogo Island Inn library, 33; Norris Point Public Library, 62, 64; Tulsa Central Library, 222; Waterford City Central Library, 267–68, 273, 278

livability, 13–14, 97, 109, 113, 119, 124, 126–27, 214, 287

Livyer's Lot Économusée, 60, 114, 117, 124–25

local scale, 5–6, 44, 102, 128–30, 160, 243, 259, 280, 295; economies, 4, 28, 43, 109, 243; governments, 15, 55, 78, 246, 268; ownership, 68; resources, 2, 6, 28, 85; solutions, 28, 46, 254

long term, 34, 36, 64, 70, 72, 97, 102, 128, 151, 200, 234, 286–87

Low, Colin, 30

Lubelski, Marrek, 244

Luton, 232, 237–52; Borough Council, 237, 243; *Luton News*, 240; North Luton Community Learning College, 249; RevoLuton Arts, 240, 252; Sauce of the Lea Cafe, 252

Maa-nulth First Nations Final Agreement, 185–86, 188

Mack, Anne, Wii-tsuts-koom, 188

Mack, Chief Burt, 187

Macoah, 198

manufacturing, 237–38

Māori, 198

mapping, 32, 80–81, 89, 101, 113, 126, 243, 274, 276

markets, 1, 5, 24, 127, 173, 258, 260, 287; farmers', 60, 117, 124; global, 9, 188, 203; local, 115–17, 263, 293

Marsh Farm, 11, 232–35, 237–55; Development Trust, 240–50; Outreach (MFO), 11, 13, 15, 232–38, 242–54

Mary's Harbour, 135, 140, 149, 152

Mauri Model Decision Making Framework (MMDMF), 198–99

mayors, 209–11, 216, 220–25, 227

Memorial University xiii–xiv, 95, 98–99, 141–42, 151; Extension Service, xiii, 30; Institute of Social and Economic Research (ISER), xiii

Morais, Clodomir Santos de, 15, 235

Morgan, Kepa, 198, 200

municipalities, 79, 92, 99–100, 123, 254; councils, 121, 128, 211, 218, 237, 241–43, 246, 249, 253, 264–66

nature. See land

neighbourhoods, 4, 208–12, 217, 219, 221, 225, 238, 241

networks, 11, 14, 52, 65, 86–87, 122, 165, 219, 259–61, 272–76, 280; academic, 39; entrepreneurial, 57, 67–68, 122, 259; social, 40, 55, 80, 88–89, 100, 176

new urbanism, 209–10, 226; Popsicle Test, 211, 221, 223

Newfoundland and Labrador (NL), 8, 40–41, 54, 59–61, 63, 109, 113–14, 135–40, 159, 172, 291, 294; English School District, 94; provincial government, 30–31, 33–34, 44, 59, 63, 89–93, 95, 98–100, 102, 109, 113, 136, 291

newspapers: New York Times, 140; Tulsa World, 210

non-governmental organizations (NGOs), xvi, 6, 34, 246, 265, 267; non-profits, 9, 45, 55, 79, 101, 119, 159, 165, 210, 219, 287

Norris Point, 11, 44, 53, 63–64, 70–72; Trails Tales Tunes, 64

Norstead Viking Village, 94, 98

North Atlantic, 29, 38, 97, 117; Forum, 37

NunatuKavut, 137

Nuu-chah-nulth, 185, 187, 192–99; Ha'hoolthii (Chiefly territories), 198; Ha'wiih (Chiefs), 192, 194; language, 192, 196–97, 199; Tribal Council (NTC), 187

O'Dea, Shane, 141

Oklahoma City, 210, 221; bombing, 210, 221

Organization Workshop (OW), 235–37, 253–54; Marsh Farm OW, 244–54

Otaru, 153

outmigration, 4, 8, 27, 30, 110, 113, 130, 148, 160

ownership, 6, 68, 83, 130, 190, 234, 242

partnerships, 78–80, 92–93, 98–102, 121, 148, 171, 174, 234, 241, 250, 279, 292; academic-community,

30, 36–37, 40, 97–99, 102, 136–37, 152; business, 83, 92, 97, 280, 291

passion, 53, 57, 62–63, 65, 67–68, 70, 162, 166, 168, 226

Petty Harbour, 14, 16, 43–44, 159, 165, 167–74, 178n

place: attachment to (see belonging); embeddedness, 69, 103, 128, 148, 160, 164–65, 175–77, 236, 263, 270, 280, 291, 295; history in place, 136–37, 142, 145–47, 152; rootedness, 2, 6, 59, 114, 164, 169, 175, 270, 286

PLACE Framework, 2, 8–17, 29, 40–45, 53, 62, 66, 70–72, 80, 102–03, 154, 188, 202–03, 212, 233, 245, 252, 269, 281, 286, 291, 294; history, 29, 40–44; promoting community leaders, 11–12, 42, 62–65, 70–72, 188, 202, 212–14, 233, 253; linking divergent perspectives, 12, 14, 42, 63–64, 71, 78–80, 86, 102–03, 154, 188, 214–15, 233, 252; amplifying local capacities and assets, 13–15, 42–43, 71, 80, 102, 110, 113, 118, 121, 128–30, 154, 188, 202–03, 215–17, 252–53, 260, 281; conveying compelling narratives, 14–15, 43, 58, 65, 71–72, 135, 141–42, 152–54; engaging both/and thinking, 14–16, 43, 64, 71–72, 154, 160, 162–63, 165, 169, 173, 175–78, 189, 203, 217, 225, 287

place-based development, 4–5, 9, 63, 153–54, 164–65, 175–77, 189, 203–204, 294–95; organizations, 219, 226

placelessness, 28–29, 46, 164, 285

Placentia West, 109–10, 112–13, 115, 124, 126, 129; Development Association (PWDA), 13, 44, 60, 112–17, 121–30

policies, 40–41, 44, 85, 93, 102, 128, 215, 225, 232, 259, 269, 273, 278, 280, 292, 295; policy-makers, 5, 59, 67–69, 71, 259, 275, 294

politics, 1, 59, 87, 113, 120, 142, 154, 188, 196, 203, 215–17, 229, 232–33, 253, 283n, 289–90

populations: decline, 9, 27, 30, 56, 70, 79, 81, 118, 121; growth, 127, 139; retention, 13, 102

Port au Choix, 65

potlatching, 193

poverty, 160, 234, 236–37, 243, 252–54

problem solving, 7–8, 60, 113–14, 121–22, 130, 160, 175, 199, 240, 243, 275

Quin-Sea Fisheries Ltd., 83, 94

radio, 223; KWGS, Tulsa, 221; Luton Urban Radio, 252; National Public Radio, US, 221; Radio Bedfordshire, 240; Voice of Bonne Bay (VOBB), 62, 64–65

reciprocity, 188, 193–95, 198, 229

regulations, 32, 185, 191, 196, 203, 208, 223–25, 251

relationality, 112, 122, 129, 147, 235,

254, 288; *heshook-ish tsawalk*, 192, 195–96, 290

relationships, 37, 46, 66, 85, 88–89, 109, 147, 163–64, 186–87, 233–34, 239–40, 278, 285, 288–89, 291, 295; academic-community, 29, 36, 71, 186–87, 285, 288–89 (*see also* community-engaged research); between actors, 37, 66, 85, 88–89, 109, 126, 143, 161–64, 233–34, 239; economic, 46; organizational, 92, 99, 278; to/ with place, 136, 147, 186–88

remoteness, 12, 31, 37–38, 78, 135, 142, 146

research: community-engaged, 7, 28–29, 36–40, 45–47, 54, 285; fieldwork, 136, 145–46, 148–49, 152–53, 165; interviews, 88, 101, 112, 136, 148–49, 165, 191–92, 194, 201, 286; methods, 16, 187–91, 285–86; Participatory Action Research (PAR), 190; Social Network Analysis (SNA), 88–89; surveys, 118, 136, 145, 149–53, 243–44, 274

resistance, 30, 60, 235; institutional, 217, 224–25

resources, 2, 6–7, 12–13, 57–58, 60, 69, 78, 85–86, 102, 109–10, 121–22, 151, 154, 160, 163, 226, 240, 250, 259–60, 264, 276, 281, 290, 294; distribution, 68, 79, 111, 258; human, 114, 281;

natural, 1, 29, 98, 101, 137–38, 153, 195

restoration, 13, 98, 117–20, 136, 139, 141–44, 151, 219, 239

revenue, 7, 15, 64–65, 79, 83, 92, 95, 97, 116, 130, 147, 169, 173, 177, 239, 249

risk, 66, 111, 163, 192, 198, 215, 233, 245–46, 248, 253, 277, 288–89

Rockefeller Foundation, 211

rurality, 2, 4–5, 12, 38, 40–41, 44, 54–57, 59–60, 66–67, 70–71, 78–79, 81, 85, 87, 100–03, 112, 127–29, 141–42, 148, 176, 251, 268, 269–72, 293

Sager, Michael, 226

Sanger, Ches, 141, 143

Save Our Char Action Committee, 95, 98

schools, 98, 117, 119, 124, 126, 139, 166, 271

selfhood, 212, 244, 247; self-defeat, 14, 43, 252; self-determination, 8, 14, 185, 191, 200–02, 212; self-organization, 114, 168, 232, 234–38, 240, 245; self-reliance, 14, 16, 66, 110, 129, 186

services: provided by social enterprises, 61, 110, 116–17, 121, 126, 267–68, 292–93; public, 31, 102, 130, 136, 142, 202, 232, 241, 260, 265, 276, 287, 291–95

settlers, 27, 29, 202, 204, 287, 289

Sexton, Marina, 63

Shorefast Foundation, 1–2, 9–13,

27–44, 290–91

Simms, David, 63–64

skepticism, 122, 148

skills, 13, 57–59, 67, 70, 72, 110–11, 142, 162–63, 212, 216; domestic, 114–15, 122, 129, 290; fishing, 168–69, 259; traditional, 9, 12, 15, 42, 173, 176

Social Economy Europe, 267

social enterprise: defined, 1, 258–59, 275; hybridity, 5, 12, 87, 161–62, 287; models, 6, 12, 54, 87, 95, 147–48, 243, 258–61, 282; place-based (PBSEs), 1–2, 6–8, 17, 28, 44, 46, 59, 78–79, 100, 128–29

social entrepreneurship, 6–7, 11–12, 14, 28, 46, 110, 114–15, 122–23, 162, 165, 175–76, 282, 294–95

social media, 39, 217; Internet trolls, 218

South East Technological University, 264–5, 267, 269; New Frontiers Programme, 265

spirals, 4, 70, 229

St. Anthony Basin Resources Inc. (SABRI), 12, 44, 78–85, 87–103, 152

St. Anthony, 81–83, 97; Port Authority, 84, 93; Rising Sun Developers, 83; St. Anthony Seafoods Ltd., 84, 92, 94, 97

St. Lewis and St. Lewis Inlet, 135, 139, 146, 148–49

stakeholders, 2, 12, 15, 37, 55, 69, 78–80, 87–88, 100–02, 161, 234, 241, 259, 269, 281–82, 294–95

Stradbally, 264

strategies, 6, 13, 15, 35, 55, 69, 127–29, 162, 174, 177, 212–13, 216, 241–44, 279, 286–87, 295

students, 34, 37, 54, 81, 124, 166, 186, 267, 272, 280; student jobs, 97

Stunell, Andrew, 247–49

sustainability, 1, 54, 71, 72, 79–81, 86–87, 100–01, 162, 164, 175, 194, 196, 200–01, 259, 279–80, 286; economic, 16, 59, 101, 173, 247, 287; environmental, 32, 167; sustainable development, 85, 185, 188, 200, 210; Sustainable Development Goals (SDGs), 3–5, 285

taxes, 197, 214, 259, 292

temporalities, 145, 288; seasonality, 97, 117, 137, 149, 153, 168, 288, 291

tensions, 15–16, 66, 87, 153, 160–65, 169–178, 232, 239, 245–46, 286–87, 291–92; between values, 153, 164, 172; paradoxes, 127, 153, 161–64, 236; selective coupling, 162

Toquaht Nation, 14, 16, 185–204; constitution, 185–86, 193–94; economic development plan, 199–200; Environmental Protection Act, 193–94; government, 185–86, 188, 191, 193–97, 200–01, 204; Hahoulthee (traditional territory), 185,

193–194; Project Assessment System (TPAS), 16, 186–92, 199–204

tourism, 14–15, 31–39, 60, 80, 92, 94, 97, 115–16, 118, 120, 127, 135–37, 143–54, 169, 172–73, 194, 197, 293

trails, 64, 92, 117; Iceberg Trail, 85, 95, 98; snowmobile, 97

transformative change, 2, 56, 59, 65, 69–70, 154, 246, 251

transportation, 38, 142, 227; ferries, 32, 38, 41, 146, 149; mass transit, 210–11, 228, 305; roads, 120–22, 151, 209, 211, 227; transit-oriented development, 211, 227

Tribal Resource Investment Corporation (TRICORP), 190

Tulsa, 13, 208–10, 214–15, 223–29; 6th Street Task Force, 212, 223; Alliance for an Accessible City, 219; Arts and Humanities Council, 212, 221; Brookside Neighbourhood Association, 212; Centennial Walk, 222; City-County Vision 2025, 220; Comprehensive Plans, 222–23, 227, 229; County Fairgrounds, 220; Economic Development Commission, 227; Home Owners for Fair Zoning, 223; Infill Taskforce, 209; Inner Dispersal Loop, 209; Leadership Tulsa, 212; Mid-town Coalition of Neighborhoods, 212, 223; Move That Bridge, 223; North Tulsa County Neighborhood Association, 223; Opera, 220; Planning Commission, 216, 224, 227; Sustainable Tulsa, 221, 223; University of Tulsa, 220; Urban League, 223; Village at Central Park, 226; Young Professionals (YPTulsa), 212, 215, 219

TulsaNow, 11, 13–14, 210–29; Blue Dot Meeting, 221; and the Performing Arts Centre (PAC), 220, 222; Streetlife Project, 221–22; Time to Twilight Zoning?, 222

Umeek (Richard Atleo), 192–93

unintended consequences, 111, 293

uniqueness, 5, 13, 58, 78, 127, 163–64, 172, 252, 280, 294–95

United Kingdom (UK), 2, 15, 29, 232–34, 238, 240, 246–47, 251–52, 254, 255n; Cabinet Office Social Action Fund (COSAF), 250; Labour Party, UK, 240, 253; New Deal for Communities (NDC), 240–42, 245–47, 249; New Enterprise Allowance, 249

urban renewal 3, 208–10, 214, 217, 225, 227–28

urbanization, 4, 16, 160

values, 87, 100, 126, 161, 214, 218, 228, 233, 236, 245, 253, 275–78, 289, 294; creation, 5–7, 56, 59, 58, 88, 100, 150, 160–61, 165, 167, 172, 212; local and place-based, 5, 67, 110, 204, 270–71; recognition, 13, 27, 33, 42, 58,

109, 119, 121–22, 129, 145, 151, 163, 173, 177, 254, 261; Toquaht, 16, 186, 188–89, 191–94, 199

ventures, 65, 67–68, 83, 115, 167, 249

vertical collaboration, 85, 100; gaps, 92

visions, xiii, xv, 36, 53–54, 57, 59–60, 64, 66, 69, 72, 87, 118, 153, 185, 188–89, 191, 196, 203–04, 212–13, 217, 219–21, 225–26, 228, 233–34, 240, 242, 244–45, 275, 287, 290, 294

volunteers, 38, 62, 83, 112, 121, 127–28, 165, 213–15, 224, 264, 270–71

Walsh, Sheila, 63

Waterford, 12, 258–60, 262–74, 278–81; City and County Council (WCC), 265–69, 280–81; County Waterford, 262–63; Integration Services, 265–66; Local Enterprise Office (LEO), 265–66; Power of You, 264, 266, 275; Shakti Program, 273; Shona Project, 266;

Social Enterprise Network (WSEN), 262–64, 274, 277–78; South East Business Incubation Centre, 265; Waterford Area Partnership CLG (WAP), 264–66, 269, 273–74, 279

well-being, 1–5, 16, 22, 34, 60, 83, 97, 121, 126–27, 137, 164, 174, 188–89, 194, 196–99, 201, 214, 251, 289, 291–93; indicators, 196–202

Wilton, Gary, 63–64

work integration social enterprises (WISEs), 162, 260

workshops, 29, 38, 40–45, 117, 174. *See also* Organization Workshop

world views, 16, 55, 187, 192–94, 199

Yates, Joyce, 141

youth, 13, 93, 97, 102, 120, 127–28, 159, 166–69, 171, 212, 240, 266, 268, 271, 274, 280; young leaders, 34, 56, 70, 219